Writer's Guide to 2012

Writer's Institute
Publications ™

www.WritersInstitutePublications.com

Editor in Chief: Susan M. Tierney

Contributing Writers:

Judy Bradbury
Meredith DeSousa
Lynda Durrant
Chris Eboch
Sue Bradford Edwards
S. M. Ford
Barbara Kramer
Christina Hamlett
Mark Haverstock

Casie Hermansson
Veda Boyd Jones
Judith Logan Lehne
Sharelle Byars Moranville
Darcy Pattison
Patricia Curtis Pfitsch
Katherine Swarts
Peggy Thomas
Leslie J. Wyatt

Copy Editor: Susan Tarrant

Production Editor: Joanna Horvath

Publisher: Prescott V. Kelly

Editorial Director: Pam Kelly

Cover image supplied by iStockphoto.

International Standard Book Number: 978-1-889715-64-3

1-800-443-6078. www.writersbookstore.com
email: services@writersbookstore.com

Contents

Business

Research

Ideas

Contests

Index

MARKETS

New Starts & New Technology Fuel Optimism

The Year in Magazines

By Mark Haverstock

T he magazine market continues to march ahead, but it has never really matched the sales and revenue numbers it enjoyed prior to the ongoing economic crunch. As 2012 progresses, publications likely to prosper at the newsstand will be the ones willing to evolve and adapt to the ever-changing market conditions.

Consolidation continues. The six major newsstand publishers (Time Inc., American Media, Bauer, Hearst, Wenner, Conde Nast) control 78 percent of consumer title unit sales, up from 71 percent a year ago, according to AudienceDevelopment.com. The good news is that Hearst and American Media have made major newsstand commitments in these uncertain times and may be in a position to do some of the heavy lifting when it comes to effecting some much needed reform in the market.

Some of the big names that have been around for a while—*Rolling Stone, Vanity Fair, Wired, Esquire*—have been operating on their highest levels ever, according to Rob Hill, Editor of *Treats!* In an interview with MrMagazine.com, Hill said, "It's obvious that Jann Wenner [of *Rolling Stone*] has counterintuitively invested heavily when everyone else was battening down the hatches and they are thriving. And to see what Bloomberg has done with *Businessweek* is very inspiring. It's a vital, exciting, and poignant product. Very impressive. The competition and fear that the last few years have produced was maybe the best thing that ever happened to magazines—it's forced them to hustle, rethink their medium and their place in the media landscape." (www.mrmagazine.com/interviews/April28-2011.html)

The number of new magazine starts last year was encouraging, and is likely to continue when all the titles are fully counted.

The number of new starts last year was encouraging, and is likely to continue when 2011 titles are fully counted. A total of 438 new consumer magazines were introduced into the marketplace in the first half of 2011, according to Samir Husni, aka Mr. Magazine. The number includes a mix of special issues, annuals, and those with a publication frequency of four or more times a year.

Business-to-business titles are still struggling, however, according to the audit agency BPA Worldwide. Its US Consumer Trac Data report for the six-month period ending June 30, 2011 indicated *Billboard* saw a remarkable 100 percent decrease in newsstand sales. The report indicated only two magazines in the gain column: *American Woodworker,* up 34 percent and *Marin,* up 22 percent.

Weekly celebrity titles, which previously helped drive newsstand sales, have lost some of their appeal. While their combined unit sales were down 15.7 percent in the first half of this year, their market influence is still significant, with a massive 30 percent share of the audited consumer magazine market.

Men's magazine titles now represent only about 20 percent of total sales, down from 27 percent a decade ago. Three women's titles with bargain cover prices, *Woman's World, First,* and *All You,* have prospered in this down market. They now represent 15 percent of all audited publication unit sales—an indicator of price sensitivity in the current market.

Ads Up

According to Publishers Information Bureau, consumer magazines reported gains in both advertising revenue and pages. In the first half of 2011, revenue topped $5.21 billion, a 5.7 percent increase over the same period the previous year. Ad pages increased at 130 titles, as compared with 15 during the same period last year.

A number of magazines reported double-digit ad page growth during this period. Topping the list were *Conde Nast's Brides, Life & Style, Boys' Life, Playboy,* and *ESPN the Magazine.*

Magazine Health Watch noted that as of August 2011, the magazines it monitored showed a slight gain of 2 percent in advertising revenues. Nina Link, President of rhe Association of Magazine Media (MPA) predicts that advertising pages and revenue will continue to increase.

Martin S. Walker, Chairman, Walker Communications, sees a much closer connection now developing between the business and editorial sides of magazines. "It's not that advertisers tell editorial what to do, but there's no longer a wall between advertising and editorial," he told *MediaLife* at the beginning of the year. "But both sides understand the goal is to make money while respecting the integrity of the magazine." (www.medialifemagazine.com/art-man2/publish/Magazines_22/On-the-challenges-magazines-face-in-2011.asp)

Organization magazines and some children's magazines take no ads at all and rely on memberships, subscriptions, or other sources of income, which presents a special challenge in today's economy. "We as a group are trying to encourage use of children's magazines in the classroom for supplemental reading," says Marilyn Edwards,

~ Head in the Clouds ~

Print-on-demand is not anything new in the book industry, but Hewlett Packard's MagCloud (www.magcloud.com) brings this technology to magazine publishing. Anybody with an idea for a new magazine and a program that generates PDF files can use this one-stop shop to generate both print and digital copy for a reasonable cost, whether for one or 1,000 copies.

Andrew Bolwell, Chief MagClouder for Hewlett-Packard, explains that MagCloud is more than a print-on-demand service; it is a content publishing platform. "What our customers appreciate is that they can simply upload their content to MagCloud and make it available in a variety of formats—print and digital—at whatever price point they want," he says. "MagCloud manages all the heavy lifting and provides the publisher with royalty payments." Your publication is listed on their site and they handle the order taking, printing, and distribution.

MagCloud brings to the magazine table many services that vendors like Smashwords, Amazon, Barnes & Noble, and others have recently provided for book authors. Fledgling magazine editors can get into print without a large bankroll or a lot of risk. Established publishers can do small-run special interest publications or create custom content and still keep labor costs in line.

Editor in Chief of *Hopscotch for Girls, Boys' Quest,* and *Fun for Kidz.* "In those cases, I think magazines that don't contain advertising will have a greater chance to be accepted in many situations. We also rely on the home schooling market. These parents tend to be very particular as to what their children read, but will subscribe and use the periodical for the entire family."

Nancy Payne, Editor of *Kayak,* believes there's demand for ad-free magazines, but not necessarily a corresponding will to pay. "That means that, as in the case of *Kayak*, you need generous, open-minded donors who support the mission of the magazine—in our case, those donors give to Canada's History Society to further its mission through its magazines."

Move to Digital Mediums Continues

The year 2011 might be known for the invasion of the tablets, creating a larger beachhead for periodicals that want to establish themselves in the digitally. Tablet devices offer the best attributes of e-readers and up the ante by offering a variety of apps, Internet, and other computer capabilities in a compact and portable package.

Nancy Gibbs, Executive Editor of *Time*, suggests that tablets may be a more natural extension of print than the typical computer. "It is possible to have an immersive experience with tablets that I don't think is possible to have in the same way with websites," she said in an interview with Husni.

Publishers are looking to this new technology to help their bottom lines. "Conde Nast and the others are looking at the tablet market as the promised land that will deliver them from the plight that they are going through in print and online," Roger Entner told *The Wrap*. Entner is founder of the a research and consulting firm Recon Analytics. (www.thewrap.com/media/article/magazines-wrestle-best-app-strategy-30204)

Although electronic subscription numbers are increasing, publishing giants like Time, Hearst, and Conde Nast are not revealing revenues from their tablet apps yet. Subscription numbers remain relatively low in the big picture. Conde Nast reported 242,000 digital customers in the six weeks after they introduced iPad subscriptions, but that still makes up just 1.3 percent of its total print circulation.

Getting a magazine on an iPad is as simple as touching the iTunes icon, browsing the store, and buying the subscription app. For this convenience, Apple currently demands a 30 percent take on profits, which may give some publishers pause when they consider their bottom line. Competition from other digital delivery systems such as Zinio could become a game-changer, however. Zinio currently has hundreds of magazine titles accessible online in Windows, Mac, Linux, and Android compatible formats.

Changes

English novelist Arnold Bennett once said, "Any change, even a change for the better, is always accompanied by drawbacks and discomforts." This has been true of the publishing industry over the last few years.

Beginning on page 18 is a list of the start-up magazines that debuted in the past year. The following examples represent some of the recent shifts in the magazine market.

Newsweek merged operations with the *Daily Beast* in a joint venture called The Newsweek Daily Beast Company. The goal of the new Newsweek Daily Beast Company is to have the *Daily Beast* function as a source of instant analysis of the news, while *Newsweek* serves to take a look at the bigger picture and provide deeper analysis of the news.

In the trade magazine segment, Charles Thompson purchased *American Coin-Op, American Dry Cleaner,* and *American Laundry News* from Crain Communications. They will be published under American Trade Magazines (www.americantrademagazines.com). *Injection Molding Magazine* and *Modern Plastics Worldwide* ceased print publication, but will continue online (www.plasticstoday.com). BMP Media is merging *Meat & Deli Retailer* into *Refrigerated & Frozen Foods Retailer* and their newest publication, *The Deli Advisor.*

944 Magazine, a luxury lifestyle publication with regional editions, discontinued publication with the June issue. The 944 magazines had been acquired in 2010 by Sandow Media after 944 Media had filed for bankruptcy. The Las Vegas print edition may be revived and rebranded, however. In the meantime, the website continues at www.944.com. Sandow has also taken over *Surface*, which covers the contemporary luxury and design world (www.surfacemag.com).

~ Reality Checks ~

To keep your finger on the pulse of the magazine industry, here are a few sites that track the essential stats and goings-on.

~ **Association of Magazine Media** (MPA): www.magazine.org Established in 1919, MPA represents about 225 domestic magazine media companies with more than 1,000 titles, nearly 50 international companies, and has more than 100 associate members. The down-loadable *Magazine Media Factbook* gives information on trends.

~ **Cassell Network of Writers:** www.writers-editors.com. In addition to providing numerous writers resources, it publishes *Freelance Writers Report,* with up-to-date market news and a listing of new markets (paid membership).

~ **Magazine Health Watch:** www.mhw.ims.ca. If numbers are your thing, this is the right place to watch the U.S. magazine market. The database on ad pages and revenue in consumer and business publications is updated daily by Inquiry Management Systems, a publishing service company. It lets you evaluate listings any number of ways, and is especially handy if you are interested in finding out which magazine categories are on the rise.

~ **Mr. Magazine:** www.mrmagazine.com. Samir Husni is "the coun-try's leading magazine expert," according to *Forbes ASAP* magazine, and the *Chicago Tribune.* In Husni's blog, you will find news on magazine startups and quarterly stats about the market.

~ **Wooden Horse:** www.woodenhorsepub.com. Wooden Horse provides information about U.S. and Canadian consumer and trade magazines, including as addresses, phone, editors, URL, email addresses, circulation, frequency, subscription price. It summarizes changes in the market. Editorial concepts, writers' guidelines, reader demographics and editorial calendars are available by subscription.

In the world of vehicles, *Scoot!*, a magazine for scooter enthusiasts, suspended print publication. It will continue online with a digital version (www.scootmagazine.com). Bonnier's *Motorboating* is no longer in print, but a digital version is planned for early this year (www.motorboating.com). *Busch Sports Scene,* which covered NASCAR's Busch Series, also ceased publication.

Changes in entertainment magazines continue. Source Interlink, publisher of *Soap Opera Digest* and *Soap Opera Weekly*, cut staff by about 50 percent and turned over magazine operations to American Media, publishers of *National Enquirer* and *Shape.* American Media purchased the U.S. edition of *OK! Magazine* and plans to move it to AMI's new headquarters in New York. *Flex* will also move to the New York location from Woodland Hills, California.

Meredith Corporation acquired Eating Well Media Group, publisher of *Eating Well Magazine.* The magazine will stay at its location in Vermont and retain the current editorial staff.

Rodale Inc.'s *Prevention* unveiled an editorial makeover with its May 2011 issue to make it more in tune with readers' lifestyles.

Mothering ceased print publication and will have a website-only presence (http://mothering.com).

JAKES and *Xtreme JAKES*, from the National Wild Turkey Federation, have been combined and relaunched into one publication, *JAKES Country.*

Byte is resurfacing as an online publication (www.byte.com). This influential computer magazine was popular from the late 1970s through the 1990s and covered technical developments in the entire field of small computers and software. NewBay Media acquired five magazine titles from Penton Media: *Digital Content Producer, Electronic Musician, Mix, Radio Magazine,* and *Sound & Vision Contractor. Laptop Magazine* was acquired by TechMediaNetwork and will continue publishing in all its current formats.

Casualties

As the magazine market evolves, only the strong survive. It is

～ Is Digital the Answer for ～ Children's Magazines?

The children's magazine market has been affected by the economic downturn, despite its history of greater resilience to economic turmoil than many of its counterparts in adult magazine publishing. Fewer new magazines appeared on the market this year and established publications found themselves working harder just to remain status quo. Chris Rettstatt, Director of Digital Product Development for *Highlights for Children,* offers some thoughts on digital technologies and how they might play a role in the future of this market.

"Digital technologies offer a lot of possibilities that are exciting to think about, and it's easy to get caught up in that excitement, but the key is understanding how the technology can enable your editorial mission," he says. "Often it can, if it's incorporated thoughtfully. But sometimes it just gets in the way. And for all the fantastic digital products that will emerge and enrich the lives of children, there are always going to be those times when the ideal gadget for a particular experience is the print magazine."

Rettstatt thinks the *digital magazine* is a flawed concept. "The magazine evolved from the parameters of print, and staying too close to that layout prevents us from thinking about how our content is going to work best using the new tools, user experiences, delivery mechanisms, and business models provided by digital devices and delivery. So I do think that digital products that draw content and inspiration from print magazines are extremely viable for kids. The important thing is to pay close attention to how kids are using the devices you are interested in, what grabs their attention, what has staying power and sticking power, and what they remember about the experience afterward. Then line that up with what your company is trying to do for kids and families and see where the match is."

Depending on who you ask, digital delivery is either going to save or destroy the children's magazine market, according to Rettstatt. "The truth is neither of those extremes, but digital media will certainly change things."

inevitable that some publications will eventually end their runs for financial or other reasons. Among those that closed their doors is *Denver,* which sold its assets to 5280 Publishing (www.5280.com).

The *L.A. Times* closed the doors on *Brand X,* its weekly lifestyle magazine geared toward young, social-networking readers. Started in 2009 as a replacement for *Metromix,* it covered entertainment, technology, style, and other topics.

EQ, a publication in the contractor market that covered trucks and equipment, ceased publication. Continental Airline's in-flight maga-

> **"There is a place for both [magazines and e-readers] because there are things that are suited to print more than to reading on a screen, and there are things that are great on a screen. It's not as if television replaced radio. . . . It's not as though the Internet replaced movies or TV."**

zine *Continental,* is no longer being published. And after a 21-year run, Wisconsin business magazine *Marketplace* is closing.

Painting, Pack-O-Fun, and *The Cross Stitcher* all ceased publication. Their content merged into *Crafts 'n Things. Madame,* the French Canadian counterpart of the English-language *Homemaker's,* is being discontinued by publisher Transcontinental Media.

New Jersey Life Health + Beauty ceased print with the September 2011 issue. *Moms Like Me,* a Missouri-based parenting magazine, has closed but its website will remain as a networking site. connecting moms throughout the U.S.

Paper, Film & Foil Converter, a trade publication, ceased with the August issue after 84 years in print and also closed sister publication,

American Printer.

Meredith's DIY magazine, *ReadyMade*, folded, and 75 employees companywide were laid off.

Barnett's Magazine published its final issue in September 2011. It targeted the custom bike and modified Harley-Davidson enthusiasts. It is rumored that Barnett may now of launch a cafe racer magazine.

Staying the Course

Will paper magazines eventually go the way of the dinosaurs? Unlikely. Chris Cully, Editor of *Highlights for Children,* explains that none of the new technology comes close to the experience of reading a colorful, graphics-rich children's magazine. "Part of the fun of subscribing to a print magazine is finding it in your mailbox, addressed to you," she says. "For younger kids, each new issue is an invitation to snuggle with a parent or an older sibling to experience together the pleasure of turning the pages of an illustrated magazine."

Magazines still have a role in an e-reader world. "I absolutely think there's a place for both and partly because there are things that are suited to print more than to reading on a screen or experiencing on a screen, and there are things that are great on a screen," says Gibbs. "I don't by any means think that [e-readers will] replace print anymore, as everyone has pointed out. It's not as if television replaced radio. It's not as though cable television replaced broadcast television. It's not as though the Internet replaced movies or TV. Everything seems to be additional, rather than a replacement."

The MPA's Link suggests that a creative renaissance in the magazine industry is on the horizon, and expects bold new creative developments for magazine content. "Tablets and smart phones have sparked the beginning of a creative revolution in the magazine industry," she says. "Simply put, this revolution is transforming the way that magazine content is created and consumed."

~ New Magazines ~

~ *Arizona Golf Central Magazine:* http://golfcentralmagazine.com. This publication joins sister publication *Florida Golf Central Magazine,* highlighting golf courses, instruction, products and travel in Arizona. Monthly.

~ *Arlington Magazine:* www.arlingtonmagazine.com. This regional magazine covers Arlington, McLean, and Falls Church, Virginia. Content features people, parenting, health, shopping, schools, community issues, and entertainment. Bimonthly.

~ *ATX Man:* www.atxman.com. This lifestyle magazine for Austin, Texas men features articles on business, travel, style, technology, health, fitness, sports as well as profiles of Austin professionals and entrepreneurs. Quarterly.

~ *AKA Mom:* http://akamommagazine.com. *AKA Mom* focuses on the evolving roles of motherhood. Covers parenting, fashion, beauty, career advice, fitness, food, and pregnancy. Quarterly.

~ *Astonish:* www.astonishmagazine.com. *Astonish* showcases emerging artists in photography, fashion design and style, as well as interviews with industry pros. Quarterly.

~ *Best You:* http://mybestyou.com. *Best You* is an online publication with tips on looking great, staying healthy, eating well, and embracing life. From Reader's Digest.

~ *Black Socialite Magazine:* www.blacksocialitemagazine.com. *Black Socialite Magazine* is a luxury and lifestyle magazine targeting the elite black community of New Orleans. Content includes articles on fashion, beauty, entertainment, health, food, living and travel. Monthly.

~ *Brooklyn Magazine:* http://bklynmag.com. This regional culture and lifestyle magazine looks at home decorating, dining, fashion, local professionals, arts and entertainment. Quarterly.

~ New Magazines ~

~ *Chronogram:* www.chronogram.com. This regional arts and culture magazine serves the Mid-Hudson, New York, region and features poetry. Monthly.

~ *Commercial Integrator:* www.commercialintegrator.com. *Commercial Integrator* is a publication dedicated to address the business needs of professional integrators who serve the small and midsize business (SMB) market. The magazine tackles operational topics like job-estimating, project-bidding, big-picture market forecasting and more. 9 issues/year.

~ *Coffee Business Solutions:* www.coffeebusinesssolutions.com. This publication covers the specialty coffee and tea industry and features success stories, management and marketing strategies.

~ *Dirt:* http://dirt-mag.com. *Dirt* contains a broad range of articles to help people live a full, healthy life from the ground up while reducing their footprint. Bimonthly.

~ *Edible Indy:* www.ediblecommunities.com/indy. The magazine focuses on local food, farms, local chefs and cuisine. Quarterly.

~ *Emerge:* http://emergingfactor.com/magazine. *Emerge* covers the achievements of start-ups, small businesses, and success stories. It provides industry insights and credible solutions to small businesses. Bimonthly.

~ *Entra Magazine:* http://entramagazine.com. This online publication focuses on residences and buildings created by world's top architects and designers. Covers a variety of topical subjects, including contemporary design, visits to showrooms and artists' studios, humanitarian and preservation issues, antiques, market trends, and personality pieces. Bimonthly.

~ *Fairfield Living:* http://fairfieldlivingmag.com. The magazine joins *Westport Magazine, Stamford Magazine,* and several other Connecticut regionals from Moffly, covering the best of Fairfield. Bimonthly.

~ New Magazines ~

~ *Film Threat:* www.filmthreat.com. *FilmThreat* returns after 14 years of abandoning its print version. It delivers film reviews, news, film festival coverage, exclusive filmmaker interviews, and filmmaking education and inspiration. It includes material not available on the website.

~ *Foster Focus Magazine:* www.fosterfocusmag.com/index.html. *Foster Focus* offers and in-depth look at the foster care industry. Monthly.

~ *HGTV Magazine:* http://blog.hgtv.com/design/2011/04/07/big-news-hgtv-magazine. *HGTV* is a Hearst publication that offers readers personal tips, tricks and expertise, as well as a behind-the-scenes look at its shows. Content includes real estate, decorating, home renovation, gardening, entertaining and food. Monthly.

~ *I Am Entertainment:* www.iaemagazine.com. *I Am Entertainment* devotes each issue to music, film, TV, sports, health/fitness, and video game production from an industry viewpoint. Bimonthly.

~ *i.Business Magazine:* www.ibusinessmag.com/i.Business_Magazine/Home.html. This Apple-centric magazine focuses on business and enterprise solutions for the business end users who are using or changing to Apple computer technology. Bimonthly.

~ *Joy Magazine Memphis:* http://joymagazinememphis.com. *Joy* focuses on the black demographic, but its content reflects diversity. The magazine contains inspirational articles, profiles, and entertainment. Monthly.

~ *Kalamazoo Parent:* www.kalamazooparent.com. This regional magazine includes parenting tips and information, local activities, entertainment, and a monthly events calendar. Monthly.

~ *Knitting Today!:* http://knittingtodaymag.com. *Knitting Today* offers advice, patterns, instruction, with articles about fellow knitters and craft trends. Bimonthly plus two special issues.

~ New Magazines ~

~ *Kore Magazine:* www.koremagazine.com. This print and online urban lifestyle magazine focuses on entertainment, style and city life. Issues are dedicated to specific causes, like going green, education, etc. Quarterly.

~ *Kronicle:* www.kroniclemag.com. *Kronicle* is a backcountry snowboard publication tailored to riders with a thirst for untracked snow, untapped lines, and exploration. Articles cover people, locations, skills, and gear. Quarterly.

~ *Little Bit:* www.littlebitmag.com. *Little Bit* highlights children's spaces, birthday parties, modern stationery, cake designs, baby showers, lifestyle photography, and children's fashion. Bimonthly.

~ *Lucky Peach:* www.mcsweeneys.net/luckypeach Each issue of *Lucky Peach* explores a single food topic through essays, art, photography, interviews, rants and recipes. Quarterly.

~ *Lucky Kids:* www.luckymag.com/kids. *Lucky Kids* is a *kidified* version of *Lucky*, Conde Nast's grown-up shopping/fashion magazine. It is primarily geared toward parents. 3 issues/year.

~ *Maryland Physician:* www.mdpracticelife.com/about.php. Written for doctors practicing in Maryland, the magazine covers clinical and business topics, healthcare policy, practice liability and profiles successful physicians. Bimonthly.

~ *Mash Magazine:* http://mashmag.com. The magazine celebrates modernity and the parallels between beauty, fashion, design, and architecture. Quarterly.

~ *Mobile Bay Parents:* http://mobilebayparents.com. This regional parenting publication shares insightful parenting advice from local and national columnists, as well as providing a local calendar of family events for Montgomery, Alabama. Monthly.

~ *The New Guard:* www.newguardreview.com. *The New Guard* is an independent literary review that showcases newcomers alongside

~ New Magazines ~

established writers. It seeks literary and experimental fiction, as well as narrative and experimental poetry. Annual.

~ *Off Track Planet:* http://offtrackplanet.com. *Off Track Planet* is an unconventional travel magazine for college students and twenty-somethings who want to see the world.

~ *New York Tennis Magazine:* http://newyorktennismagazine.com. The magazine will feature previews of upcoming tennis events, player profiles, media coverage, and programs to promote tennis.

~ *Peloton Magazine:* http://pelotonmagazine.com. *Peloton* is about bicycle racing and the joy of riding. Topics covered include gear, technology, history, and other bicycle-related information. 9 issues/year.

~ *Phineas and Ferb:* www.phineasandferb.com. The 52-page bimonthly built on the TV series is among several new Disney offerings, which include a *Cars* monthly and other magazines based on Marvel movies, such as *Captain America.*

~ *Pynk:* www.pynkmag.com. This national glossy targets young, sophisticated, multicultural women. Coverage includes fashion, beauty, entertainment, celebrities, careers, and shopping. It is the sister magazine of *Bleu* magazine for men.

~ *Progressive Cattleman:* www.progressivecattle.com. *Progressive Cattleman* focuses on ranching and caring for livestock. Included are industry news and trends, as well as regional profiles. Monthly.

~ *Rebel Magazine:* www.rebelmagazine.com. *Rebel* is a contemporary men's publication that offers readers a fresh perspective on value-based living, spirituality, social responsibility, career and family challenges, relationships, entertainment and more. Monthly.

~ *Red Bulletin:* www.redbullusa.com/cs/Satellite/en_US/Red-Bulletin-USA/001243009873175. Published by the makers of Red Bull energy drink, this magazine covers sports, entertainment, food, travel, art

~ New Magazines ~

and culture for young men 18 to 34. Monthly.

~ *Renovation Contractor:* www.renocontractor.ca. This trade publication is written by and for Canada's small- and medium-sized home renovators. Issues feature reviews of the latest tools and building techniques, advice on expanding and improving a small-business, and tackles the issues that concern building tradespeople. Bimonthly.

~ *Sip Northwest:* www.sipnorthwest.com. *Sip* focuses on regional wine, beer, spirits, coffee, master chefs and culinary artisans in Washington, Oregon, and British Columbia. Quarterly.

~ *The Social Media Monthly:* http://thesocialmediamonthly.com. The magazine focuses on the continuing evolution of social media, its involvement in our lives, and how to use it more efficiently. Monthly.

~ *Sportsnet Magazine:* www.sportsnet.ca. *Sportsnet* is Canada's first national magazine source for in-depth perspective and inside reports on hockey, baseball, football, soccer, and mixed martial arts (MMA). Bimonthly.

~ *Timbuktu:* http://timbuktu.me. *Timbuktu* is the first iPad-based magazine specifically designed for children. The magazine engages youngsters in news and stories centered around interesting topics.

~ *Today's CNY Woman:* http://todayscnywoman.com. *CNY Woman* is a regional lifestyle magazine for central New York that covers health, art, fashion, family, and finance. 10 issues/yr.

~ *Ulster Magazine:* http://ulstermagazine.com. Joining sister publication *Orange Magazine,* this regional lifestyle magazine targets Ulster County baby boomers and visitors. Bimonthly.

~ *Uptown Professional:* www.uptownpromag.com. This career-focused magazine is written with the global urban professional in mind. Quarterly.

~ *Vibrant Living Magazine:* www.vibrantlivingmagazine.com. *Vibrant Living* is written for consumers ages 50 and over who are in the

~ New Magazines ~

Charlotte, North Carolina, region. Issues cover a variety of subjects and include articles on beauty, fashion, art, health and wellness, technology, home decoration, finance, travel, food, wine, entertainment, and more. Bimonthly.

~ *Viva Now Magazine:* http://vivanowmedia.com. Targeting Hispanics "living the American dream," this publication features celebrity interviews and articles on lifestyle, health and wellness, education, business, career development, beauty and fashion, sports, travel and entertainment. Bimonthly.

News from the Front Line

The Year in Books

By Patricia Curtis Pfitsch

T he revolution is gaining strength: More and more readers, publishers, and writers are hoisting the digital flag. A Harris poll taken in July reports that one in six Americans (15 percent) use an e-reader, up from one in ten (8 percent) a year ago. Among those who do not have an e-reader, one in six say they are likely to have one in the next six months. And it made news everywhere in May of last year, when Amazon announced that in the previous month, it *sold* 105 Kindle books for every 100 print books, soft or hardcover, including print titles that do not have Kindle editions and excluding free Kindle titles.

Most trade publishers are either already releasing ebooks or are planning to in the near future. Even J. K. Rowling, who retained her digital rights, begins selling ebooks and digital audiobooks of the Harry Potter series from her Pottermore website this year. The *New York Times* has created a new ebook bestseller list and the National Book Award committee now accepts ebook nominations, even accepting the first app book meant to be read on the iPad this year.

The Grassroots Gains Ground

Until recently, traditionally published writers garnered the most respect in the industry. Self-published authors were usually shunned by review journals, booksellers, and traditionally published authors. As new software made it possible for anyone with a computer to do layout and design, potential authors could bring their camera-ready manuscript to a printer and have bound books in a few weeks. But these writers still faced the problem of marketing, distribution, and reviews, and the process was expensive. Even though the writer usually received all the profits instead of the royalty that publishers offer, few self-publishers recouped their costs.

Enter the ebook with built-in distribution systems and customer reviews. Amazon and Barnes & Noble and other *e-tailers* (as in retailers) like Smashwords welcome self-publishers. For a nominal fee, a writer can upload a manuscript and have it converted to the ebook format and then distribute it through the online store. Thousands of writers have taken advantage of this new system. "In 2010, almost 2.8 million nontraditional books, including ebooks, were published in the United States," Fordham University publishing industry expert Albert Greco told Reuters, "while just more than 316,000 traditional books came out." To understand the significance of those numbers, compare them with the output in the United States in 2002, when "[f]ewer than 33,000 nontraditional books were published, while over 215,000 traditionally published books came out," Greco explained. ("Spam Clogging Amazon's Kindle Self-Publishing." Reuters, June 16, 2011, www.reuters.com/article/2011/06/16/us-amazon-kindle-spam-idUSTRE75F68620110616)

Marketing is still hard work for writers, with hours each day spent blogging, tweeting, emailing, and updating web pages. But in the last year, self-published authors have found that they can gather a following—sometimes a large following—and actually make a profit from their books. A few, like thriller writer John Locke and paranormal romance writer Amanda Hocking, sell hundreds of thousands of copies and have made millions. While most writers cannot expect those kinds of sales, the good news is that quite a few self published

∼ Alive & Kicking ∼

Perhaps the best news of all in this year of democratizing the publishing industry is that things are not as bad as they seem. On August 9, the Association of American Publishers (AAP) released the results of its *Bookstats* study, "the deepest, most comprehensive statistical survey ever conducted of the modern U.S. publishing industry," according to an AAP announcement. The survey, which drew on information submitted by 1,963 publishing companies, shows that the industry had grown in the preceding two years, 2009 and 2010. The latests figures showed that revenues increased by 5.6 percent and unit sales were also up by 4.1 percent. Ebooks brought in $1.6 billion and accounted for 5.8 percent of total industry revenue. "Americans, young and old, are reading actively in all print and digital formats," says the report. "Both Adult Fiction and Juvenile (non-fiction and fiction) have seen consistent annual gains."

Source: "New Publishing Industry Survey Details Strong Three-Year Growth in Net Revenue, Units." Association of American Publishers. Aug. 9, 2011.

writers sell as many as 20,000 copies of their ebooks each month, a figure that even most traditionally published writers will not see.

"Not only are these new midlisters selling a lot of books," writes Robin Sullivan, a small epublisher whose husband, Michael J. Sullivan, published six ebooks last year, "but they are also receiving significantly more money from each sale." Amazon pays 70 percent royalty for self-published authors who price their books between $2.99 and $9.99 each. "High volume combined with good revenue is providing self-published ebook authors five- and six-figure yearly incomes, allowing them to quit their *day jobs* and make a living by doing what they love most—writing." ("The New Midlist: Self-published E-book Authors Who Earn a Living," by Robin Sullivan, *Publishing Perspectives,* June 27, 2011. http://publishingperspectives.

～ The Legacy ～

Recently, *traditional* publishers have been given a new name by media sources, especially when they are reporting on the booming self-publishing phenomenon: *legacy publishers*. Whether these legacy publishers are a thing of the past, as the new term might suggest, the health of traditional publishing, and especially the health of the largest publishing houses, is still a strong measure of how the industry is doing. And on the whole, they are still doing well. Let's take a look.

Random House had the highest profits of the big-six publishers. In August, it reported that for the first half of 2011 profits went up 72.5 percent, to $99 million. It had a 200 percent increase in ebook sales, strong bestseller sales, and operational efficiencies. In announcing the good news, Chairman Markus Dohle said that the demand for "Random House content around the world continues to be enormous."

Hachette Book Group sales figures are still affected by, and reflect, the huge sales of the Twilight series in 2010. In the first half of 2011, sales fell 18 percent, even though ebook sales gained 115 percent. Given the fact that no new Twilight books were published in 2011, however, sales were flat, and Hachette hopes that as the comparisons with Meyer's sales fade, the numbers will improve dramatically.

Sales at both **Penguin** and **Simon & Schuster** were flat, but both

com/2011/06/self-published-ebook-authors-earn-living)

In an ironic twist, some traditionally published authors, like best-selling African American writer Omar Tyree—who has contracts with four major houses—have started self-publishing their books. And some extremely successful ebook self publishers have signed contracts with traditional publishers. Amanda Hocking, for example, signed a contract with St. Martin's Press for more than $2 million.

Bypassing the Watchdogs

In the past, the book review journals were the most trusted and powerful source for recommending, and thus selling, books. Today,

~ The Legacy ~

reported improved margins. Simon & Schuster's adjusted operating profit rose 13 percent, due to higher sales of digital content, but print sales declined, mostly due to the demise of Borders and the movement from print to digital.

HarperCollins reported that it "exceeded its plan for the year" but did not indicate whether sales rose or fell compared to the previous year. The report said that the children's division had its second best year ever in fiscal 2011, due to higher ebook sales. In a statement two weeks later, parent company News Corp. reported that HarperCollins had "lower book sales due to fewer new releases and lower licensing fees resulting from a settlement received in fiscal 2010." HarperCollins is part of Rupert Murdoch's empire and would be affected if Murdoch decided to sell off the newspaper division, as rumors were suggesting during the year.

Scholastic reported its second consecutive year of net income after reporting net losses in the previous two years. Its children's book publishing and distribution reported a one percent increase in sales, although operating income fell due to increased digital investments and higher promotional spending. Trade sales increased, driven by increased sales of ebooks, including the Hunger Games trilogy.

most book review journals still do not review self-published books. Alternatively, consumers now use sites like Goodreads (www. goodreads.com), recommendations from Facebook friends and Twitter followers, as well as reader comments attached to a book's entry on e-tailer sites to choose books. Writers have discovered that they do not need reviews from *Booklist* or *Kirkus* to sell their books.

Some literary agencies have even offered representation to self-published authors. When she announced that she would be working with self-published as well as traditionally published authors, agent Jane Dystel of Dystel & Goderich told *Publishers Weekly* that her agency "has always provided services for our clients that have gone far beyond selling their books to a traditional publisher." Possible services to self-publishers might include making sure they get paid, advising on creative decisions, and selling subsidiary rights. ("DGLM Elaborates on Plan to Rep Self-Published Authors." *Publishers Weekly,* June 29, 2011. www.publishersweekly.com/pw/by-topic/digital/ content-and-e-books/article/47813-dglm-elaborates-on-plan-to-rep-self-published-authors.html)

Another exciting development for all writers is OnDemand's Espresso Book Machine (EBM), which prints books "while you wait." Consumers purchase a title online or at a bookstore, retailer, or even library that has an EBM. Within three minutes, a paperback is printed on demand. The machine can print self-published books and books in the public domain, as well as books published by houses that have signed contracts with the company. OnDemand has strategic partnerships with Xerox for EBM sales, leasing, and service; with Google for access to public domain titles via Google Books; and with Lightning Source, a subsidiary of the distributor Ingram Group.

In September, HarperCollins announced that it had signed a contract with OnDemand—the first of the big-six trade houses to do so. Beginning in November, the publisher will make its trade paperbacks for adults and children available for printing on the Espresso Book Machine. Prices will be the same as for already printed books, and authors will receive their regular print royalties.

EBMs have not yet been installed in many bookstores, but if more big publishers get on board, this is likely to change. The advantage to readers is that they can immediately get books while at the bookstore without having to wait for an order to come in. The advantage to publishers and authors is that books can be kept in print while avoiding the need to store large inventories. Booksellers hope the machines will draw customers to their stores.

This decentralization of publishing has a dark side. While self-published authors can hire editors to help make a book the best it can be, many do not. Quantities of poor quality books on e-tailer sites make it more difficult for readers to find the good books. Even worse, spam books are showing up on ebook sites. Spammers can copy an ebook, give it a different title and cover and publish it as a new book. Other spammers reformat content they buy very cheaply online and sell that to unsuspecting customers.

Reuters reported in June that spammers can even buy Autopilot Kindle Cash, a video tutorial that teaches users "how to publish 10 to 20 new Kindle books a day without writing a word." This process involves copying already existing ebooks, and "repackaging" them to sell. Spammers also use Private Label Rights (PLR) content—bulk, prewritten, royalty-free content—for a minimal fee, and republish it however they want. The founder of ebook distributor Smashwords, Mark Coker, called PLR "one of the worst threats to ebooks today." "Ebooks: The Latest Frontier for Spam," by Mike Essex, *The Guardian*, June 23, 2011. www.guardian.co.uk/technology/2011/jun/23/ ebook-spam-problem-growing)

Amazon: Friend or Foe?

Amazon expanded its influence in the publishing world by launching its own book imprint a few years ago, becoming not only a bookseller but a publisher in the traditional manner. At the time, the move was almost unremarked in the industry. In 2011, the company hired New York Editor Larry Kirshbaum as head of Amazon's publishing unit and suddenly people began to notice, especially when he signed Timothy Ferriss, well-known author of *The 4-Hour Workweek* (Crown). By fall 2011, the publishing arm of Amazon had a list of 122 new titles, print and ebook. In October, it made a deal for the memoirs of actress and director Penny Marshall, reportedly for $800,000.

Amazon executive Richard Grandinetti told the *New York Times*, "The only really necessary people in the publishing process now are the writer and reader. Everyone who stands between those two has both risk and opportunity." ("Amazon Signs up Authors, Writing Publishers out of Deal," by David Streitfield, *New York Times*, October 16, 2011. http://www.nytimes.com/2011/10/17/technology/amazon

～ Legal Matters ～

The question of digital copyright has been a thorny one since the first byte of information appeared on the Internet. Publishers, agents, and authors have been blindly feeling their way through the maze of questions. In the past year, however, copyright holders have begun to take action against possible infringements and several high-profile suits have begun to define the answers.

The Google Settlement

In 2005, The Authors Guild and the American Association of Publishers sued Google for copyright infringement; Google had been scanning the library collections of large research libraries with the goal of making digital copies available for online searching. The Authors Guild case was a class action suit. Any author who had ever published a book was part of the class and affected by the result of the suit.

In 2008, the parties decided to settle the case; Google agreed to pay copyright holders for using the books two-thirds of the revenue it would receive, and keep one-third. A problem with the settlement was that by its rules, all authors gave permission for their books to be scanned and searched. An author who did not want a book in the database would have to contact Google and *opt out* of the settlement.

Another problem concerned the way *orphan works*—books for whom the author or copyright holder was unknown—were handled. Because even unknown authors were part of the class and bound by the terms of the settlement, Google could legally scan and use orphan works without compensating the authors since they were unknown. If an author was later found, he could then opt out and receive a check for the revenues associated with his book, but he could not sue Google. This would give Google rights over those orphan works that other companies were not awarded, a monopoly over books whose authors were unknown.

The law required that the court approve the settlement before it went into effect and after months of input from interested parties and

~ Legal Matters ~

deliberation by Judge Denny Chin, on March 22, 2011, the judge rejected the settlement. Among other things, he felt the settlement gave Google unfair advantages, too much control over orphan works, and not enough liability for future acts. The settlement raised issues of international importance, and Chin and others said the issue is one Congress should address, instead of the courts. Chin thought the settlement gave Google a monopoly over unclaimed works. He was also concerned that so many authors had already opted out of the settlement. He listed reasons from many of the objectors in his decision and suggested that many of the problems would be solved if it were an opt-in settlement instead of opt-out.

A further problem now is that even after the authors and publishers brought suit, Google kept scanning books. Now that the settlement has been rejected, the Internet behemoth faces potentially $3.6 trillion in fines for illegal copyright. Google could support an opt-in settlement, but that would leave out orphan works, which is the most valuable part of the database for the company.

Publishers and writers will also lose money, but for them the suit was from the beginning not about money but about control of copyright. In that light, they have made their point: "Don't scan our books without permission."

On September 15, it appeared that the case would go to trial. After several meetings with little progress towards a new settlement, Judge Chin presented the parties with pretrial schedule, even though both the Authors Guild and the Association of American Publishers said they were still hopeful about a new settlement. Perhaps it will be settled on the courthouse steps.

-rewrites-the-rules-of-book-publishing.html?pagewanted=all)

Some writers who have signed with Amazon praise the way the giant bookstore and publisher has treated them. In a blogged conversation between thriller writers Barry Eisler and Joe Konrath, they discuss the creative and publishing freedom they have with Amazon, along with the backing of a big distribution system. The blogs were later published for 99¢ as an ebook, *Be the Monkey: Ebooks and Self-Publishing, A Dialog Between Authors Barry Eisler and Joe Konrath,* on Amazon, Barnes & Noble, and Smashwords.

> **"The only really necessary people in publishing now are the writer and reader: Everyone who stands between those two has both risk and opportunity," said one publishing executive.**

While under contract to the Penguin division Riverhead Books for *The Chinese Soldier's Daughter,* author Kiana Davenport also gathered and published a collection of her award-winning short stories with Amazon called *Cannibal Nights, Pacific Stories.* Penguin accused her of a breach of her contract (which she denies), cancelled *The Chinese Soldier's Daughter*, and demanded she return her advance. She writes about it in her blog, "Sleeping with the Enemy: A Cautionary Tale" (http://kianadavenportdialogues.blogspot.com).

Some wonder if Amazon's publishing program is as beneficial as it seems. For its first ebook romance, Amazon released a preview chapter—with the editor's notes still attached. In the traditional publishing scenario of editors, copyeditors, proofreaders, fact-checkers, and production designers, that kind of error would not happen.

Brick-and-mortar bookstores have been reluctant to carry books published by Amazon. "We cannot do anything to support, help, or benefit Amazon," said the owner of Seattle Mystery Bookshop in a email to an Amazon author who requested a book signing. The owner later posted the series of emails on her blog, saying in part, "They're the enemy of independent bookshops and aiding them in any way—mainly ordering their books and selling them and promoting them—would be suicide. Things are tough enough without cutting our own throats." ("Can't Shake the Devil's Hand and Say You're Only Kidding," Seattle Mystery Bookshop Blog. June 22, 2011. http://seattlemysteryblog.typepad.com/seattle_mystery/2011/06/cant-shake-the-devils-hand-and-say-youre-only-kidding.html)

Publishers, booksellers, and others in the industry have raised fears that Amazon is already a monopoly and is moving to grab even more power. In July 2011, when Amazon moved to acquire U.K.-based online bookseller The Book Depository, the U.K. Publisher's Association and the Independent Publisher's Guild jointly opposed the merger, the first time those two organizations have acted together in this way. The move was investigated by the Office of Fair Trade and in late October Amazon's purchase was given official approval: The acquistion did not create a de facto monopoly.

The King is Dead

The changing face of bookselling is clearly read in the story of Borders. In the 1990s, Borders was one of the first chains to take significant business away from smaller, independent bookstores. Now, after filing for bankruptcy in February 2011, Borders is no more. In July it went to court to liquidate the remaining stores. Its closing highlights the difficult climate for bricks-and-mortar bookstores, but the answer to the question of why Borders has closed and other stores, like Barnes & Noble, have so far survived, is directly related to the Internet and the digital revolution.

When bookstores first realized they needed a web presence, Borders outsourced online book sales to Amazon rather than develop its own program. It became clear that the biggest advantage of a physical bookstore was no longer in buying books, which could be

~ People News ~

~ **Gillian Blake** started as Editor in Chief at Henry Holt in September. She has been at Holt since 2009; among the authors she has edited are Rob Lowe and William Boyd. Before taking her first job at Holt, she worked at Scribner, Bloomsbury, and HarperCollins. She replaced Jill Lamar who became Editor in Chief in February.

~ **Phyllis Grann** retired as Senior Editor at the Doubleday division of the Knopf Doubleday Publishing Group, ending a 40-year career in publishing. She joined Doubleday in 2002 after stepping down as CEO of Penguin Putnam in 2001.

~ **Elise Howard** is launching a new middle-grade and young adult line for Algonquin Books in Chapel Hill, North Carolina. She had been Associate Publisher at HarperCollins Children's Books.

~ Several changes took place at Penguin Young Readers in a major restructuring. **Jennifer Hunt** became Vice President of Acquisition and Development and Editor at Large. She had been at Little, Brown. **Julie Strauss-Gabel** was promoted to Vice President and Publisher of Dutton Chidren's Books and **Lauri Hornik** became President and Publisher of Dial Books for Young readers.

~ **Larry Kirshbaum** was named Vice President and Publisher for Amazon Publishing's New York office. Kirshbaum was formerly CEO of Time Warner Book Group and a literary agent. Amazon executive Jeff Belle said that Kirshbaum will focus on acquiring literary and commercial fiction, business, and general nonfiction.

~ **Philip Levine** was named the new U.S. Poet Laureate by the Library of Congress in August. He is best known for his poems about working-class Detroit. James Billington, Librarian of Congress, said of Levine, "He's the laureate, if you like, of the industrial heartland. It's a very, very American voice." Levine is 83, one of the oldest laureates.

~ **Betsy Mitchell,** Editor in Chief of Del Ray, Random House's science fiction and fantasy imprint, took early retirement and left in December. She was at her post for the last decade and edited such

~ People News ~

well-known authors as William Gibson, Terry Brooks, Marion Zimmer Bradley, Dean Koontz, Diana Gabaldon, and Octavia Butler.

~ **Elizabeth Van Doren** became the Executive Editor at Boyds Mills Press and *Highlights for Children*. Her mandate was to "play a key role in the publishers' expanding book-publishing initiatives." Van Doren had been Editor in Chief at Black Dog & Leventhal and Editorial Director at Harcourt Children's Books.

~ **Linda Zecher** was appointed president and CEO of Houghton Mifflin Harcourt. She was most recently a corporate vice president at Microsoft. She succeeded Barry O'Callaghan, who resigned in March.

Deaths

~ **Margaret K. McElderry,** renowned children's book editor and publisher, died on February 14. The *New York Times* called McElderry "the last of her class of editors who brought American children's books into the post-war world." She was 98.

~ **Janet Schulman**, longtime children's book editor and publisher, died on February 11. She worked for 30 years at Random House where, among other things, she was the last editor there to work with Theodor Geisel, Dr. Seuss.

~ **William Sleator,** well-known science fiction writer and author of more than 30 books for children and young adults, died on August 2. His ground-breaking YA novel *House of Stairs* was named one of the best novels of the twentieth century by the Young Adults Library Services Association (YALSA). He was 66.

done more easily online, but in the pleasure of sipping coffee and browsing the shelves. But Borders lost a contract with Starbucks to Barnes & Noble. Barnes & Noble developed and released its own e-reader, the Nook, while Borders did not even try to compete in that venue. Bad business decisions put Borders behind other chains, and the increasingly bad economy made it impossible for it to catch up.

Will Borders's fall bring down other stores? Some independent bookstores are worried that Borders's store closings and the resulting steep discounts in books will make their situations even worse in the short run. However, independents that survived the growth of the big chains have carved their own niches and their customer bases may not overlap to any significant degree. Some industry watchers hope that the company's demise will make opportunities for new stores to open, and that is already happening in some cities with new independents opening in former Borders' locations. National chain Books-a-Million, however, has taken over 14 Borders leases, both superstores and smaller airport locations, which does not help independents.

Everyone agrees that a reduced number of locations for book sales is not good for either authors or publishers. Fewer books sold means lower royalties and smaller print runs in the future. Publishers also lost money because Borders was unable to pay its bills. It owed Penguin more than $41 million and Hachette Book Group $36 million. The aftershocks of the Borders fall will be affecting the industry for some time to come.

A 2011 study from the Association of American Publishers (AAP) called *Bookstats* indicates that more people are buying trade books online, and fewer frequent bookstores. Publishers, who have traditionally relied on bookstores to do much of the marketing for their books, are scrambling for new marketing venues. For example, most of the biggest publishers have created their own social networking sites where readers can share favorite books, find book lists, and on some sites even upload their own manuscripts to be read and reviewed by the community. Random House has "The Conversation," a website to facilitate discussion about current events and books and links to all major retailers for book sale opportunities. Macmillian's "The Daily Reader" is also designed to link current events with books, and they maintain "Criminal Element" and "Heroes And Heartbreakers" for mystery and romance readers respectively. Penguin's "Book Country" is designed to support both writers and readers and plans to offer self-publishing services in the future. At this point readers can find traditionally published books

Publishers, reviewers, and booksellers must find new reasons for their existence. If they succeed, the future will be golden.

and manuscripts by category, add reviews, and upload their own manuscripts. When it launches, "Bookish," maintained by Simon & Schuster, Hachette, and Penguin, will provide readers with breaking news, author interviews, reviews, and other marketing materials to help readers choose books. All the sites will include books from various publishers' lists.

Change will always be difficult to accept, especially by those who enjoyed or benefited from the status quo. And the changes happening now in the publishing industry are huge. Digital technology in general, and the Internet in particular, encourage decentralization. They put the means of communication in the hands of the many. Anyone can use the power of the Internet to publish and distribute a book, magazine, or newspaper. This does not necessarily mean we do not need publishers, reviewers, or physical bookstores. What it does mean is that publishers, reviewers, and booksellers must find new reasons for their existence. It is too soon to know for sure if they are succeeding, but we are all holding our breaths and crossing our fingers. If they succeed, the future will be golden.

~ New Imprints & Start-ups ~

~ **Signal**, a new nonfiction imprint from Canadian publisher **McClelland & Stewart** launched in the fall. It showcases books by Canadian and international authors on important issues in politics, religion, culture, history, business, and the environment. Books on the first list include *In Other Worlds: SF and the Human Imagination,* by Margaret Atwood, and *Damned Nations: Greed, Guns and Aid,* by Samantha Nutt, and *Arguably: Selected Essays,* by Christopher Hitchens. Books in the line will be "issue-shifting, usually by very iconic voices, sometimes quite contrarian," President and Publisher Doug Pepper has said. He explained that the company has already been publishing this type of nonfiction, but wanted to "put an umbrella over the program to give it more focus and prominence."

Fenn/McClelland & Stewart is a second new imprint that focuses on hockey books, headed by Publisher Jordan Fenn, formerly of Key Porter Books. Fenn brought the line from Key Porter, where it was built with ties to the NHL, the NHL Players Association, Hockey Canada, and the International Hockey Federation.

~ **Jericho Books**, a faith-based imprint, was launched by **Hachette Book Group**. Wendy Grisham, who has served as director of publishing for Hodder Faith, a Hachette U.K. company, has been named Publisher and Vice President.

~ **Splinter**, a new teen imprint from **Sterling**, began publishing in January 2011. The list will embrace multiple genres and publish across print, digital, mobile, and multimedia platforms. Hardcover and ebook formats will be released at the same time and print editions will have TAG codes to allow readers with smartphones to scan the codes to access web-only material. On the debut list is *Tiger's Curse,* the first installment in a fantasy-romance saga by Colleen Houck.

~ **Downtown Bookworks** is a book packager that launched its own line of children's books a little over a year ago. "I felt the big publishers

~ New Imprints & Start-ups ~

weren't taking chances," President and founder Julie Merberg told *Publishers Weekly.* "They were doing more of what they'd done—established authors and illustrators and a lot of licensed stuff." Merberg's experience in packaging for clients such as Time Inc. and Scholastic enabled her to create affordable titles. Simon & Schuster is distributing the new line.

~ **Electric Monkey**, a new imprint aimed at 12 to 15 year olds, has a February 2012 launch by Egmont UK. It plans to publish 10 young adult titles in its first six months and then one or two titles per month thereafter. Titles like its Gone series, by Michael Grant, will have electronic components like video games and interactive websites.

~ **Scholastic Ruckus** is a joint venture between new children's digital developer Ruckus Media and Scholastic. It plans to publish a wide range of children's and teen content across all platforms, from interactive content and transmedia projects to ebooks, enhanced ebooks and print. The first titles will be released in 2012.

~ **Albert Whitman Teen**, a new young adult imprint, launched in August. The first list included *Guantanamo Boy*, by Anna Perra, a novel set six months after September 11, 2001, that centers on a teen who find himself incarcerated as an enemy combatant; and *The Poisoned House*, by Michael Ford, a ghost story set in Victorian London.

~ Another new YA imprint is **Kensington Teen**, or KTeen, whose first list appeared last spring. Its books "reflect the emotionally authentic teen experience by featuring unique voices and imaginative storytelling, all with an underlying, universal theme of self-discovery." Titles have included *Mythos Academy*, by Jennifer Estep.

~ **Confluence Books**, the third imprint from **White Cloud Press**, signed three titles by August 2011, and plans to do four or five in 2012. The division was formed to accommodate the high number of self-published authors White Cloud was finding that were not suited for its

~ New Imprints & Start-ups ~

core spirituality and religion lines. Publisher Steve Scholl explained that authors will be able to buy books in advance or help pay for printing and marketing costs and receive higher royalties. The **RiverWood Books** imprint publishes books on cultural awareness, historical fiction, and West Coast regional topics; it has, however, stopped publishing children's and YA books.

~ **Chalberg & Sussman** is a new literary agency started by Terra Chalberg and Rachel Sussman. Chalberg has been an agent and foreign rights director at the Susan Golomb agency, and Sussman spend six years as an agent at Zachary Shuster Harmsworth. They will work with authors of literary and commercial fiction and nonfiction.

~ **Red Fox Literary**, a new literary agency based in Shell Beach, California, opened in June. Karen Grencik and Abigail Samoun will represent children's book authors and illustrators. Grencik is looking for real-life stories with an emphasis on character development. Samoun will focus on illustrators.

~ The **Leshne Agency**, founded by Lisa Leshne, opened for business in August. It will represent authors of narrative and prescription nonfiction, especially sports, wellness, business, political, and parenting topics, as well as commercial fiction and middle-grade and YA books. It will also offer services to self-published authors.

Murder & Mayhem, Crimes & Clues

The World of Mystery Writing

By Chris Eboch

B y nature, people like to have all the answers, but they also naturally love a mystery. Mysteries allow readers to ponder options, follow clues, and test their wits, and ultimately, to have all the answers.

Mystery writing is a category containing many subgenres, from gritty *hard-boiled* to light and humorous *cozies*. Some fans read across subgenres, but many have decided favorites. Claire Eddy, Senior Editor at Tor/Forge Books, says, "I am a sucker for a well-crafted *noir* tale and also historical mysteries, but only if the author has really done the research."

The research that goes into writing a mystery is not likely to stem directly from personal experience. Robert Kresge's *Murder for Greenhorns* (ABQ Press) is about a young schoolteacher and a Texas cowboy who join forces to solve a murder in 1870 Wyoming. Kresge comments, "They say 'write what you know.' So with 30 years in the CIA, should I be writing spy novels?" Perhaps, he says, the traditional writing advice should be to "'write what you read the most of.' I found myself reading or listening to [historical mystery heroes] Brother Cadfael, Marcus Didius Falco, Amelia Peabody, and Phryne Fisher."

~ Mini-Mysteries ~

Jenny Milchman is an aspiring mystery novelist whose first publication is a short story, "The Very Old Man," in *Lunch Reads,* Volume I (Istoria Books). "It can be hard to craft a whole and complete puzzle in a short number of words," Milchman says. "On the other hand, maintaining tension for a short while can be relatively easy compared to when a story is drawn out."

Authors may find more opportunities for short stories today than in the past. "Although many of the print outlets have dried up, the online world presents more opportunities than ever for shorts to appear," Milchman says.

While traditional publishers often expect or require manuscripts to fall within a certain word count, electronic publishing welcomes different lengths, from short stories to novellas. Istoria Books's Lunch Reads series publishes short stories with no word count restrictions. According to Editor in Chief Libby Sternberg, the ebook revolution has "opened up the field to new voices and stories that might not have fit neatly into traditional publishing niches. No short is too short or too long when you're epublishing. You don't need to think about the number of pages to fill, just whether it's a good story."

Whether historical or modern-day, mysteries feature heroes ranging from police officers and private eyes to nosy amateurs and innocent victims who get swept into trouble. Thrillers and suspense novels may also be mysteries, even if the hero is not trying to solve a crime in a traditional sense. For example, my own Southwestern adventure, *Rattled* (Pig River Press), features a heroine and hero trying to elude villains while they hunt for a long-lost treasure. Romantic suspense novels like these find favor with many mystery fans if they have enough action.

Each subgenre has particular challenges, and aspiring authors better know each one's traditions. *Cozies* tend to avoid sex or on-stage violence, and have an educated (most often female) detective (think Miss Marple). *Hard-boiled* mysteries delve into the seamy side of life. *Police procedurals* must get the police work right. *Techno-thrillers* focus on the latest technology. As for *romantic suspense*, dealing with this subgenre "means fitting a mystery or a suspense into the romance reader's expectations," says Terry Odell, author of *Where Danger Hides* (Five Star). "In mystery series, relationships can develop over the course of many books; in romantic suspense, it's one." Reading widely in a given subgenre is the best way to identify the important differences and qualities inherent in each.

But genres, like rules, are made to be broken. Pari Noskin Taichert calls her Agatha Award-nominated Sasha Solomon series (University of New Mexico Press) *"whodunits* with a humorous New Mexican flair. They're not your standard cozies because they have an edge to them. Some of my readers think they're beach reads while others find the deeper themes. I'm happy to satisfy both ends of the spectrum."

Mixing genres can be fun for the writer and the audience, but may also make it harder to sell a manuscript. Kresge received about 200 rejections for *Murder for Greenhorns,* often hearing, "This is just a Western and we don't publish Westerns." He was about to give up when he found a small local publisher that shared his vision. The book became a finalist for the 2011 Bruce Alexander Award for Best Historical Mystery of the Year.

Starting Young

Children may become mystery fans at an early age. Juliana Hanford is Senior Editor at Kane Press, which publishes illustrated books for ages 3 to 10. She says, "I vividly remember the very first time I was reading a mystery on my own and had that *can't put it down* feeling. I think that feeling can make kids not just mystery lovers, but book lovers for life."

"I guess children enjoy reading mysteries for the same reason adults do," says Mara Rockliff, who writes a humorous chapter book mystery series under the pen name Lewis B. Montgomery. "They're fun, they're exciting, they're full of surprises and suspense. And a mystery series offers the chance to keep coming back to characters we love."

As a bonus, mysteries stretch the way readers think, especially when they are written for children. Of her Milo and Jazz Mysteries (Kane Press), Rockliff says, "Kids read these books for fun, but teachers like them because the detective lessons teach critical thinking skills. For instance, setting a trap for a culprit equals predicting and testing; circumstantial evidence equals making inferences. And the back of every book includes puzzles and games to help the reader hone those skills."

Mysteries for kids are not quite the same as mysteries for adults, of course. "Practically all adult mysteries are murder mysteries, but in a realistic chapter book, you can't have kids knocking each other off," Rockliff says. "One of the big challenges is thinking of new crimes that are serious enough to be investigated, but not too serious. If it's theft, it needs to be a funny and unusual theft, as in *The Case of the Stinky Socks* or *The Case of the Missing Moose.* Or it might be something off the wall: figuring out how the public pool turned purple overnight, or trying to prove a pet psychic is a fake."

By the time readers reach the teen years, fewer crimes are off-limits. Sara Beitia calls her *The Last Good Place of Lily Odilon* (Flux) "a noir-ish contemporary YA." She continues, "In reality, kids can and do encounter the heavy stuff—love and death and people with bad intentions—and like anyone, they mull these things over and try to digest the implications. They expect to encounter the heavy stuff in literature, too. Perhaps it helps with the digesting. In dealing with these darker matters, it's rather amazing what can be covered in kid lit; kids often shock adults with a frank interest in the lurid. Still, everyone has an opinion as to how much kids can and should be exposed to in books."

Most children's book publishers are open to mysteries, but do not specialize. Brian Farrey, Flux Acquisitions Editor, says, "I've heard from countless librarians at the American Library Association conferences that their teens are looking for more mysteries, to the point where librarians direct them to adult books to satisfy the need. My ears perk up a bit if I'm presented with one in submissions. But I don't acquire based on fads or trends."

Putting It All Together

Whether the audience is children or adults, a solid mystery requires a clever and believable puzzle. Taichert says, "For me, with traditional mystery series, there are three big challenges: telling a really good story; making the puzzle interesting and believable

> **"H**aving a great premise is meaningless if the writing is phoned in and reads like anyone could have written it. I look for authors who have a pronounced sense of voice."

enough that the reader wants to work with my amateur-sleuth protagonist to figure out the crime; and not giving too much away with the hints I put in the story."

Odell lists the keys to a good mystery as "providing clues, being fair to the readers with red herrings, and for anything current, keeping on top of the latest technology. Things are out-of-date before you finish writing, and the public has a skewed perception of reality based on television."

A good puzzle is not enough. Editors judge mysteries by the same standards as other books. "What I've seen a lot lately is a great premise, a terrific pitch, and then a mediocre manuscript," Farrey says. "Having that great premise is meaningless if the writing is phoned in and reads like anyone could have written it. I look for authors who have a pronounced sense of voice."

At Kane Press, Hanford says, "We always look for great characters.

~ Mystery Authors ~

~ Sara Beitia, *The Last Good Place of Lily Odilon* (Flux). www.sarabeitia.com

~ Robert Kresge, *Murder for Greenhorns*, a Warbonnet mystery (ABQ Press). www.robertkresge.com

~ Jenny Milchman, "The Very Old Man," *Lunch Reads* (Istoria Books). jennymilchman.com

~ Terry Odell, *When Danger Calls* and *Where Danger Hides*, the Blackthorne, Inc. series (Five Star); *Nowhere to Hide* (Wild Rose Press). www.terryodell.com

~ Mara Rockliff, The Milo and Jazz Mysteries (Kane Press). www.mararockliff.com

~ Pari Noskin Taichert, The Sasha Solomon mystery series (University of New Mexico Press). www. parinoskintaichert.com

And when authors can balance humor with nail-biting, on-the-edge-of-your-seat suspense, and can come up with a final twist that surprises even the readers who think they know everything, then we're sold!"

Libby Sternberg, Editor in Chief of the digital publisher Istoria Books, says, "We look for the same thing we want in all submissions: a good story, well told. Do I want to keep turning or clicking through the pages, and do I want to keep hearing this author tell me the story? I know that seems simple, but you'd be surprised how hard it is to write a page-turning story that has a great voice attached to it. With mystery, I'd also add this requirement: The mystery itself must be well-constructed with a resolution that does not rely on a *deus ex machina* or anything similar. I hate reading mysteries where suddenly a strange character, never encountered in the story previously, shows up and turns out to be the criminal. The reader should be able to reread the story and see how the clues add up to the denouement."

"In writing mysteries, one has to come up with a crime, figure out who did it, create a sympathetic sleuth or sleuths, manage subplots,

~ Mystery Publishers ~

~ **Flux:** Llewellyn Worldwide, 2143 Wooddale Dr., Woodbury, MN 55125. www.fluxnow.com. Brian Farrey, Acquisitions Editor. Agented submissions by email only.

~ **Kane Press:** 350 Fifth Ave, Suite 7206, New York, NY 10029. www.kanepress.com. Juliana Hanford, Senior Editor. Agented authors. Specific needs only; titles are series-based for ages 4 to 11.

~ **Istoria Books:** 1125 Old Eagle Road, Lancaster, PA 17601. www.istoriabooks.com. Libby Sternberg, Editor in Chief. An epublisher. "We are open to unagented submissions. Authors should query us through email about novels, giving us a brief (one-paragraph) summary of the book, its genre and word count, plus their writing credentials. Short story authors can go ahead and send the story as an attachment with a description of it and the author's writing credentials in the email. You can read more about our submission guidelines in the About Us section of our website. We publish only fiction, but in a variety of genres."

~ **Tor/Forge Books:** 175 Fifth Ave., New York, NY 10010. http://us.macmillan.com/TorForge.aspx. Claire Eddy, Senior Editor. "We do in fact take unagented material. You can find our submissions guidelines at our website."

~ For more mystery publishers, see http://www.overbooked.org/genres/mystery/links/mystpub.html or http://publishers.omnimystery.com/mystery-publishers.html

plant clues, play fair with your readers, and—usually—come to a satisfying conclusion," Kresge says. That is in addition to the challenges present in all types of fiction: "Creating and sustaining believable characters, plotting, pacing, setting, research. Piece of cake juggling all those elements, right?"

How does a writer deal with all these challenges? Taichert says, "I've written all my life. That's part of the way I've developed it. Reading voraciously is another. Studying writers—the popular ones who tell stories really well—makes a difference in my own writing. I've also taken a few workshops here and there, but the biggest result has come from committing to writing, every single day."

Writing a great mystery that is also a great book is not easy, but it has its rewards. "I've read various reports that indicate the mystery market remains strong," Sternberg says. "Certainly, its fans are loyal and intelligent, always willing to look at new authors and material. Well-written mysteries take a tremendous amount of talent, and what I love about mystery fans is that they appreciate the skill level of mystery writers."

Finding an Audience

Mystery fans show great loyalty to favorite authors, but reaching potential fans can be a challenge for newcomers. Epublishing is providing new opportunities. At Tor/Forge, Eddy has noticed a jump in ebooks sales for genre fiction, especially science fiction, fantasy, and mysteries. "As the devices proliferate I think we will see this continue," she says. "People love to read about murder and mayhem. The way they read [mysteries] might change; the desire for the genre will still be there."

"It also gives authors a way to keep [out-of-print] books alive," Odell notes, "and to get things published that straddle or cross genres, or don't fit into the narrower confines of traditional publishers."

"I'm launching an original ebook mystery soon," Taichert says. "More and more writers are taking this chance partly because of economics, but for me it's mostly about artistic freedom and control. If I write a protagonist who editors at the major publishers say mystery readers aren't ready for—like my new one who can communicate with insects and other nonhumans—I have the freedom to give her life even though she may not fit the mold that New York City houses are looking for right now."

The time has never been better for mysteries, whether for children or adults, traditionally or independently published, and in whatever subgenre. As Hanford says, "Good mysteries never go out of style."

Profiles: Endless Possibilities

By Patricia Curtis Pfitsch

T ake a look at the indexes of the latest editions of market directories like *Magazine Markets for Children's Writers* and *The Best of the Magazine Markets for Writers* and one fact stands out: Magazines of every type—secular and religious, national and regional, juvenile and adult—and their readers, like the tightly focused, human interest, accomplishment-oriented articles called profiles.

Common Ground

Editors of all kinds of magazines agree on the characteristics of a good profile. Unlike a biography, which looks at a person's entire life, "a good profile offers a window into the life or mind of its subject," says Debra Hess, Senior Editor at *Highlights for Children*.

"There's a particular take-off point" that makes a profile work, says Bruce Murphy, Editor of *Milwaukee Magazine*. "We ran a story about a judge, the Honorable M. Joseph Donald. It was a kind of a hybrid—partly about him and partly about the drug court that he helped create in Milwaukee." Readers learned about the judge's life, Murphy explains, but always in the context of his role as a judge who changed the way the court dealt with drug offenders in Milwaukee.

51

"A successful profile makes you feel as if you've peered into this person's life for a short time," says Jessica Kellner, Editor of *Natural Home and Garden*. "It's important to include very specific, personalized details along with the broader information about what they do and why."

Lonnie Plecha, Editor of the literary magazine *Cricket*, whose readers are ages 9 to 14, agrees. "In *Cricket*, a profile gives a strong sense of the subject's personality, character, challenges, and thought processes. It needs a focus and, like a work of fiction, tells a great story that is vivid, detailed, and evocative."

A profile, "like a work of fiction, tells a great story that is vivid, detailed, and evocative."

"Good profiles show instead of tell," says Natasha Kassulke, Assistant Editor of *Wisconsin Natural Resources*. "We want action and depth of feeling. Use all five senses when you interview someone. What are they wearing? What body language do they use?" She continues, "The strongest profiles include interviews with the subject and/or those who know or knew the subject well. Let the subject tell the story, and [you] step back as the writer. Learn to ask open-ended questions that will elicit answers about what is most interesting or vivid in their lives."

Plecha cautions that "the best profiles are not usually in the format of an interview, but integrate what was learned in the interview into a coherent story.

While it is never the optimal situation, Murphy has found that it is possible to do a profile from secondary research alone. "It's a lot harder, but on occasion *Milwaukee Magazine* has done profiles of someone who didn't cooperate. If we think they're an important person in town with an impact on the community, we would want to do a profile regardless of whether they cooperated."

Other magazines have different policies with regard to interviews and cooperation, so be sure you know a magazine's guidelines before submitting a query or a manuscript.

Who Cares?

A good profile writer thinks about what the audience will truly find interesting about a person. An essential element in children's magazine profiles, for instance, is the subject's childhood. "We want to know something about what profile subjects were like as children, so our readers can envision themselves emulating their success," says Plecha. "What were some turning points as they chose their career? Did they face special challenges?"

In "A Pirate's Life For Me" (*Cricket*, August 2008), Shannon Hitchcock profiled underwater archaeologist Wendy Welsh, who was working on the wreck of Blackbeard's ship *The Queen Anne's Revenge*. When she interviewed Welsh, Hitchcock asked her which subjects she liked in elementary school and whether they played into her work as an adult. Welsh answered that math had been a favorite, and now she has to know all the units of measurement to make the concoctions she uses to clean the items [found in the wreck]. And she has to maintain a budget for the lab. Hitchcock's profile also describes activities that appeal to kids. "For example, Wendy likes to get messy and grungy. We talked about how one of the tools she uses is like a big vacuum cleaner. She has actually found some of her own relics and these are her favorites."

Audience is crucial in magazines for adults too. "Like a lot of city magazines," Murphy says, "the readership of *Milwaukee Magazine* skews older. The general theory is that people don't subscribe to a magazine like this until maybe they're married with kids and a house." The subjects it chooses for profiles obviously should interest this demographic, in this region. The magazine's First Person series, for instance, has included a short profile of an Austrian cook in America. Murphy says, "We did one on a guy who is a lake surfer who described the difference between surfing in Lake Michigan and surfing in the ocean."

~ The Necessary Research ~

Shannon Hitchcock was immediately intrigued when she read about underwater archaeologist Wendy Welsh in her college magazine. "I had to be," she says. "I knew nothing about underwater archaeology. If I hadn't been fascinated I don't think I would have been able to stick it out [and approach Welsh to create a profile]. It took me forever before I felt like I knew enough to ask her any questions."

Hitchcock read three years' worth of newsletters Welsh wrote about her work on Blackbeard's sunken ship, the *Queen Anne's Revenge*. "I looked at the history, what items they've pulled up and how they treated them." She made lists of unfamiliar terms, checked definitions, and read other articles about the project. "I tried to read everything that had been published so that when I contacted Wendy she would take me seriously and I would know what to ask her."

Hitchcock also found hundreds of photos on the project's website. She picked out the most interesting photos and then geared the discussion in her profile to the photos. "When I found a really cool picture, then I wanted to illustrate it—that was key."

Not all profiles need as much research. Among Hitchcock's other credits are "Helping Hearts," which profiles some New Jersey children who financed heart surgeries for children in India, and "Nothing but Nets" about a seven-year-old who saved the lives of more than 6,000 people by raising money for malaria nets. Both were published in *Pockets*. "The church I attend has a very active youth group," Hitchcock explains. "So when they're doing a project I think is particularly appealing, I go to some of the youth group meetings and snap pictures." She interviews the young people and gets permission from their parents to quote them and to use their photos.

When you write profiles, Hitchcock says, "All you have to do is keep your eyes open and listen. You'll see ideas on family trips, you'll read about them in your church newsletter, you'll take a trip to the historical society and see lots of people you could write about. They're just everywhere."

The Perfect Fit

Knowing the slant of your intended magazine, as well as the audience and its interests, will help you sell a profile. "Study the magazines you want to submit to," Hitchcock advises. "And if the first one turns you down, don't send it out in that [same] format. Make sure it fits the second magazine on your list. There are all kinds of differences and you don't know that unless you study the magazines."

It is crucial that writers follow the magazine's guidelines, and know it well enough to pitch a piece that reflects the publication. "It shows a respect for the editor and a professional approach to writing," *Highlights*'s Hess says.

Murphy's experience at *Milwaukee Magazine* is the same. "It's so common for people to pitch you, and they know nothing about your magazine. So they pitch you on stuff that makes no sense. If they bothered to take a look at the magazine they would know that."

Although most regional magazines use profiles, you cannot take a generic approach. Read back issues to understand each one's unique slant. *Milwaukee Magazine* is a good example of a tightly focused regional magazine. "We typically cover the four-county area, the metro area of Milwaukee," explains Murphy. Writers often ask him if he would consider a profile of a famous person who grew up in Milwaukee but now lives elsewhere. "What it boils down to is whether the person has some strong connection to the city." He points to a profile of the Zucker brothers, makers of the hit comedy film *Airplane*. "They still identify strongly with Milwaukee. They come back here for fundraisers at their high school. That's an example of a profile that felt local, even though they've gone on to fame and fortune."

Wisconsin Natural Resources has a completely different slant. Its geographic focus includes the entire state, but its subject focus is narrow. "Our readers are interested in profiles of people doing good work in environmental protection and restoration or recreation," says Kassulke. "They enjoy meeting colorful people who are doing meaningful new research about Wisconsin's resources."

While *Wisconsin Natural Resources* might profile scientists and others doing environmental research in Wisconsin, it is not a technical journal. That is important to know when pitching and writing articles for this bimonthly. "Only cite research results to make a point and give readers some insight. Cut through years of research and give them the gist," says Kassulke. "Get specific, but not pedantic."

The slant of a magazine with a national audience can be just as individual. "For *Natural Home and Garden,* we love profiles that really showcase how a person's life ties with, and is bettered by, their work in sustainability," says Kellner. "Whether it's a home profile in which we delve into the ways that home has improved the family's life or a profile of a community garden organizer, we love to tie the work the person is doing in their life and community with their own personality and feelings."

Subtle Differences

Cricket and *Highlights For Children* aim at similar audiences, and both cut a broad swath with subjects. Plecha reports that *Cricket* has published profiles of a dancer with the Joffrey Ballet ("Born to Dance," by Ellen Seiden); of violinists Rachel Barton and Itzhak Perlman ("Rachel, Violinist" and "Master of Beautiful Music," by Ellen Seiden) and of an airline pilot ("Getting There Is Half the Fun," by Heather Delabre and Julia Messina.) Plecha adds, "I suppose "Beyond the Call of Duty," by Brenda Moore, was a kind of profile of a heroic dog, Gander, who won the Dicken Medal for conspicuous bravery during the defense of Hong Kong in World War II."

The subjects of *Highlights*'s profiles are equally wide-ranging. "We run a Gallant Kids feature five or six times a year in which we profile kids who have done something to make the lives of others or their communities a better place," Hess says. "We also profile experts in our feature, What a Pro Knows. These profiles are career-specific and contain something concrete that the reader comes away with. An example of this would be the pastry chef we profiled; we included a recipe for buttercream frosting. When we profiled a magician, we

∼ Submitting Profiles ∼

∼ **Cricket:** Submissions Editor, 70 East Lake St., Suite 300, Chicago, IL 60601. www.cricketmag.com/25-Submission-Guidelines-for-CRICKET-magazine-for-children-ages-9-14. Editor Lonnie Plecha says, "Don't query, please. We need to see a complete manuscript, most likely in the range of 1,200 to 1,500 words with SASE for our reply. Include a brief cover letter stating any relevant experience you may have, and why you were interested in profiling this person. Why did this person fascinate or amaze you? And perhaps a hint of the insights you gained from a personal interview or other research. For profiles of historical figures, please include a bibliography that attests that you have done solid research, including books you consulted by experts in the field."

∼ **Highlights for Children:** Manuscript Coordinator, 803 Church St., Honesdale, PA 18431. www.highlights.com/contributor-guidelines. "I always prefer seeing a manuscript rather than a query," says Senior Editor Debra Hess. "All nonfiction must be accompanied by a bibliography, and if possible, an expert review."

∼ **Milwaukee:** www.milwaukeemagazine.com. "Send a query," says Editor Bruce Murphy. "The shorter the better. Get across what you think the story is going to be—that's really all I need. If I'm interested in the pitch, then I'll want to check a writing sample. If I feel like I want to know more, I'll ask questions. The easiest way to query us is email." Send to bruce.murphy@milwaukeemag.com.

∼ **Natural Home and Garden:** 1503 SW 42nd St., Topeka, KS 66609. www.naturalhomemagazine.com. "Definitely queries; never send complete manuscripts," says Editor Jessica Kellner. Send by mail or email to editor@naturalhomemagazine.com.

∼ **Wisconsin Natural Resources:** http://dnr.wi.gov/wnrmag/freelance. "Articles that are accompanied by color digital photos, slides, drawing charts, or black-and-white prints are more likely to be used. Photos of people and places described in your article are essential. Caption, and tell us who took the images and how to reach that person via email, mailing address and phone number in case we have follow-up questions," says Editor Natasha Kassulke. Email query to natasha.kassulke@wisconsin.gov.

included magic tricks." Submissions should be under 800 words.

These magazines have differences that are as important as their similarities. "*Cricket* is interested in people in any area of innovation and accomplishment . . . any area where people are pushing knowledge or human experience to a different level," says Plecha. Profiles run between 1,200 and 1,500 words.

Hess explains that for *Highlights*, "a good profile should reflect the values of the magazine." It avoids even a suggestion of crime or violence in any piece.

Hitchcock first submitted "A Pirate's Life For Me" to *Highlights*. She received "a wonderful three-page critique from editor Linda Rose even though they didn't buy it," Hitchcock says. The profile did not focus on Blackbeard's well-known stealing and plundering of merchant ships, but because of the its policy not to refer to guns or violence, *Highlights* editors felt they couldn't do a piece on pirates.

Hitchcock then submitted the piece to *Cricket*, but only after a major revision. "*Cricket* has a much bigger word count. Linda's critique gave me a lot of food for thought about things she thought should be included, and I think it got more interesting when I was able to make it longer." Hitchcock's profile nearly doubled in size before she submitted to *Cricket*. "It wouldn't have sold otherwise."

That is the key. Understand the specific needs of the magazine you are targeting. Open the appropriate window into your profile subject's life. Let readers get to know that person intimately, using fictional techniques, dialogue, description, and action. Soon you will have a list of sales to add to your nonfiction résumé.

Go Local (Publishers)

Regionally Speaking

By Peggy Thomas

"**L**ocal is the rage in reading," says Gary Luke, Publisher of Sasquatch Books. For a writer, it should be all the rage in submitting. While big trade publishers flounder under their own weight making it hard for new writers to break in, regional independent presses are flourishing, and offer writers an important market to tap into. Sasquatch, for example, formed in 1986 with only one title. Now it has more than 200 books on its list, all of which celebrate the Pacific Northwest, California, and Alaska.

Regional publishers produce books and magazines about and for a particular area of the country. Writers of history, biography, travel, nature, food, and fiction with a geographical take can all find safe harbor at a regional press instead of getting lost in the mid-list of a conglomerate. "The major league publishers are in the business of bestsellers," says Luke. "As a regional press, we recognize the value of the *literature of place* in all its forms."

Place is important because many regional book publishers are owned and operated by families with strong ties to an area. Bobby and Lee Byrd, founders of Cinco Puntos Press, fell in love with El Paso, Texas, and have developed a list of more than 130 titles for children and adults that reflect the unique culture along the U.S. and Mexico border. For 30 years, the Bess family has been publishing books about Hawaii and the Pacific. They started with two textbooks and today, Bess Press produces two lines—general interest titles and books for the educational market—and recently acquired another local publishing company.

These businesses tend to be labors of love, and they pay attention to quality. As a result, many have won awards and have had their fair share of bestsellers. One of the first titles published by Cinco Puntos Press, Joe Hayes's *La Llorona*, has sold more than 300,000 copies, and the publishers received the American Book Award for Excellence in Publishing and were inducted into the Latino Literary Hall of Fame. Black Dome Press, which focuses on the Adirondacks, Catskills, and the Hudson River Valley of New York State, received the first Barnes & Noble Focus on New York Award for Outstanding Regional Literature. Even its name is regional: Black Dome Mountain looms over the company office in the Catskills.

Regional magazines may not be family run as often, but they do display a similar geographical love affair. For nearly every city, county, and state at least one magazine highlights the regional lifestyle, food, music, and politics. One of the largest covers 12 states: The bimonthly *Midwest Living* has a circulation of 925,000 and considers itself a service magazine that provides detailed information specific to the Midwest. Families of Jackson, Mississippi, get their information from the regional magazine *Parents & Kids,* and *Buffalo Spree* targets readers in and around Buffalo, New York. The list goes on and on. You can find more information on many of them through the Parenting Media Association (formerly the Parenting Publications of America) at www.parentingpublications.org.

Whether they produce books or magazines, regional publishers offer writers many advantages over larger, national companies. Regionals provide new writers a way to break into the business; seasoned writers a place to build a career; and every writer a ready-made audience.

Begin At Home

Because their primary goal is printing the literature of place, regional editors tend to focus more on the project than the writer's publishing credits. That does not mean their standards are any lower than other publishers'. It can mean that they are willing to take a risk on an unpublished writer with a great idea. David DeLuca, Director of Bess Press, says, "Each year half of our new releases are from new authors." Last year, 30 percent of Sasquatch's list consisted of debut titles. Sasquatch editors also seek out writers for ideas that are generated in-house. Luke says, "We hunt them down by reading newspapers, magazines, blogs, and books." So, if you have a passion for local history, art or food, an outlet waits for you.

Kendra L. Williams, Travel Editor of *Midwest Living,* recently took on five new writers after speaking at a Midwest Travel Writers Association meeting, and says, on average, she uses a new author once or twice a month. That was not always the case. *Midwest Living* used to fly a small stable of writers across 12 states. Today, it makes more sense fiscally and culturally to hire writers from each state that the magazine represents. As Williams says, "The culture of western North Dakota—the way they talk, the dishes on the menu, the amenities offered, the vacation experience—is inherently different from Cincinnati, Ohio."

You already have a leg up over the competition if you want to write about your hometown because resident writers are better able to reflect the voice and social mores of their own culture. In Mississippi, for example, two editions of *Parents & Kids* are published. Editor Gretchen Cook explains, "One edition is in a market that is noticeably more liberal than the other. An article that might garner negative response in one area would not even be remarkable in the other."

Similarly, Elizabeth Licata, Editor in Chief of *Buffalo Spree Magazine,* prefers queries from writers familiar with western New York State. "Our readers know the difference." Book publishers feel the same way. Almost all of the titles published by Bess Press are

~ Sample Titles ~

~ **Bess Press:** *There's A Monster in My Opu,* by Karyn Hopper (children's book); *Duke: A Great Hawaiian,* by Sandra Kimberley Hall; *50 Simple Things You Can Do to Save Hawaii,* by Gail L. Grabowsky.

~ **Black Dome Press:** *Landscape Gardens on the Hudson, A History* by Robert M. Toole; *Bloody Mohawk: The French and Indian War & American Revolution on New York's Frontier,* by Richard Berleth

~ **Cinco Puntos Press:** *La Llorona,* by Joe Hayes (children's book); *Incantations: Songs, Spells and Images by Mayan Women,* edited by Ambar Past.

~ **Sasquatch Books:** *Book Lust,* by Nancy Pearl; *The Wisdom of the Radish,* by Lynda Hopkins; *1, 2, 3 Moose,* by Andrea Helman and Art Wolfe (children's book).

created by authors and illustrators who live in, travel in, or care deeply about Hawaii and the Pacific Islands.

Built-In Readership

Regional publishers cater to readers who are already interested in the place where they live, work, or vacation. But no audience is a homogeneous market, even if it is localized. According to Debbie Allen, Publisher at Black Dome, "The material must appeal to multiple constituencies, including residents, second-homeowners, and visitors, as well as satisfy the academics/experts." So when she chooses a manuscript about the mountainous regions of eastern New York, she keeps all of her readers in mind.

The target audience of so-called regionals may sometimes be national. Cinco Puntos prefers to be called an independent, or indie, publisher, rather than regional. "The *regional* term marginalizes the work we do and creates unnecessary barriers that push people away from our books," says Byrd. Its audience does not live just in Texas; the company sells to a much wider audience through a national

～ Regional Publishers ～

Book Publishers:

～ **Bess Press:** 3565 Harding Ave., Honolulu, HI. www.besspress.com. David DeLuca, Director. General interest and educational material specific to Hawaii and the Pacific Islands. Accepts queries, proposals and manuscripts to submission@besspress.com.

～ **Black Dome Press:** 1011 Route 296, Hensonville, NY 12439. www.blackdomepress.com. Debbie Allen, Publisher. Query with proposal and résumé. Nonfiction that addresses the history, culture, and natural sciences of New York State, specifically the Catskill Mountains and Hudson River Valley.

～ **Cinco Puntos Press:** www.cincopuntos.com. 701 Texas Ave., El Paso, TX 79901. Lee Byrd, Co-publisher, Senior Editor, and President. After a careful examination of their books, query via telephone before sending a manuscript.

～ **Sasquatch Books:** 119 South Main, Suite 400, Seattle, WA 98104. www.sasquatchbooks.com. Gary Luke, Publisher. Accepts queries and proposals for adult and children's books connected to the Pacific Northwest, Alaska, and California.

Magazine Publishers:

～ **Buffalo Spree:** 100 Corporate Parkway, Ste. 220, Buffalo, NY 14226. www.buffalospree.com. Elizabeth Licata, Editor in Chief. Query with sample clips and résumé.

～ **Midwest Living:** 1716 Locust St., Des Moines, IA 50309. www.midwestliving.com. Kendra L. Williams, Travel Editor. Most articles are written on assignment. To submit an idea, query with several clips.

～ **Parents & Kids:** 785 N. President St., Suite B, Jackson, MS 39202. www.parents-kids.com. Gretchen W. Cook, Editor. Query article ideas first. Reprint articles may be sent in full via email.

distributor. "One of our goals is to help readers [outside this area] find enjoyment in stories that may seem foreign to them at first glance." And they have succeeded. Cinco Puntos's colorful line of bilingual books for children has received international attention.

Similarly, the children's books that Sasquatch puts out can be purchased in specialty stores as souvenirs or gifts, and titles like *O Is for Orca* and *1, 2, 3 Moose*, both by Andrea Helman and Art Wolfe, can be found in many schools and libraries across the country. "Particularly within the digital age," says De Luca, "we are now able to reach the same audiences [as national companies] and now beyond."

A Partnership in Publishing

At a large publishing house, the bulk of the promotional budget benefits only a small percentage of titles. At a regional press, all titles are equal, and the author is integral to the process. "Marketing," says Allen, "starts at manuscript selection and continues straight through to promotion of the published book and beyond." She believes that if you see a strong, sustained regional title, you can be certain that the writer has been actively involved in planning the promotion. Other than maintaining long-standing relationships with bookstores and libraries, Allen encourages Black Dome authors to speak at museums and contribute to journals because all of these opportunities generate sales.

"It is important these days for a writer to play an active role in marketing their books," says Byrd. "And we focus on reaching readers through nontraditional outlets." Communities that do not have a bookstore can find Cinco Puntos titles at hardware, grocery, and feed stores.

Bess Press relies on word of mouth, book sampling, sales incentives, and coupling new books with best-selling backlist titles on similar subjects. The company also uses social networking. "We can cover the broad-based outlets," says DeLuca, "but it is with the help of the author that we can target the special interest groups." Similarly,

Sasquatch authors are encouraged to blog, tweet, and use Facebook. Each book's web presence is fine-tuned to optimize "discoverability."

Such dedication to every book means a longer shelf life. "Our backlist is critically important to us," says Allen. "We have some titles that have been in print for close to 20 years." Only classics and best sellers can claim that fame at bigger houses. At Cinco Puntos, Byrd says, "We want our books to live, and sell, forever."

Study the Market

Each book publisher and every magazine not only has its own regional focus, but also has its own style and preference for genre or subject matter. If you are going to target these markets, know them well. Black Dome only publishes nonfiction. It specializes in history, folklore, art, and natural history of the Catskills and nearby regions. When Allen looks through the submissions, she hopes to find, "Well-researched, well-organized, beautifully written books." The writer should be "collegial" and willing to "enthusiastically cooperate in the promotion and continued marketing of the title."

Bess Press focuses on Hawaii and the Pacific, but DeLuca reminds writers, "Our titles reflect the hodgepodge of varied ethnicities and cultures that make up Hawaii. Our backlist ranges from titles concerning languages and history, to cooking, memoirs, and culture—all targeted to kids, young adults, and adults." Writers can submit ideas to either the general interest or the textbook line, but most of the educational titles are developed in-house. A query for educational work, particularly those that concern early childhood education, should include the writer's résumé and biography that indicates the writer's qualifications. DeLuca also suggests tightening a book's focus even beyond the geographical. Strive for unique content and target particular special interest groups within the region. "This is very important with kid's books where themes tend to run similarly among titles, but [a theme] becomes more special when localized."

Cinco Puntos publishes a full range of fiction and nonfiction for adults and children, but Byrd says, "I'm always hoping to get a few more adult nonfiction manuscripts in the door. That's probably the area [in which] we get the fewest submissions."

When submitting to a regional magazine, think about style. "Our tone is conversational," says Cook about *Parents & Kids.* "Write as if you were telling a neighbor all about the topic of the article." Do not forget the local angle. Cook, who considers reprint articles, needs to know how you will adapt the story to benefit her readers specifically. Articles about universal issues like bullying, bedtime angst, or choosing a babysitter are best for reprinting, but you need to localize. If you are not from the area of the magazine you are targeting, read back issues for tone and style and research local authorities to set up interviews. Send the complete manuscript with a cover letter naming specific agencies you plan to contact.

At *Midwest Living,* the pitch is more important than the résumé. "I look at how they craft their pitch," says Williams, "what kind of language they use, how familiar they appear to be with the magazine and its travel content." Keep your query short, lively, and focused more on why you should be hired rather than details about a specific idea. Williams admits, "It is extremely rare that a new writer sends us a query about a destination we haven't already covered fairly recently or didn't already know about."

Timing is another consideration when submitting to a magazine. Each June, Licata plans out the theme calendar for the next year's issues of *Buffalo Spree.* "I assign stories three months prior to the publication date, sometimes further in advance." Think ahead and query early. "I'd love to see a story idea that is relevant to western New York but has not been covered to death—an exciting story from the past or the present."

So, go local. Steep yourself in the culture that you inhabit and write the literature of place. For regional books and magazines, the mantra is not just write *what* you know, but *where* you know.

Flash Fiction

Stories in Brief

By Mark Haverstock

In a world of tweets, texts, and sound bytes, stories were bound to evolve into shorter forms. Flash fiction is this decade's relatively new phenomenon, although it has roots in the venerable short-short story. It is a mode of writing that is well-suited to those who still crave good literature yet have trouble finding enough reading time in their fast-paced, hectic lives.

Flash fiction is also well-suited to the concise content necessary for Internet publications. It is not only appealing reading in its own right, but its length is also perfect for reading on computer screens, ebooks, and mobile devices. Short works are much easier to read on screen, and many people today prefer not to deal with large chunks of text, no matter what the medium.

Prose by Any Other Name

A relative of the conventional short story, flash ficition is somewhat difficult to define by word count, sentences, or pages. Most agree that it should be less than 1,000 words. That is where the consensus ends.

Some variations specify an exact number of words. Examples

~ In Essence ~

Know what flash fiction is not. It is not a novel. While a story can suggest wide-ranging and complex implications, flash fiction has a specific, hard-core focus.

The classical epics like the *Odyssey*, perhaps the longest narrative form in literature, often began *in media res*—in the middle of the action. This shortest form of narrative can do the same. Backstory must be implied, not told in flash fiction. Character brush strokes must be broad.

Flash fiction might also be compared to other short forms, such as haiku or sonnets. They are all brief, highly concentrated, can be evocative and/or intense. Language is not wasted. Imagery and flash fiction may make use of allusions, and be indirect in the best sense, without being confusing. The payoff may come in a strong way with a surprise.

include *nanofiction*, the *drabble,* and the *69er*. Nanofictions are complete stories that have at least one character and a discernible plot, and are exactly 55 words long. A Drabble is a story of exactly 100 words, and a 69er is a story of exactly 69 words (not including titles).

Flash fiction also has many aliases. Pamelyn Casto has been teaching online courses in this fiction form since the 1990s, writes about it, and blogs about it at http://flashfictionblog.blogspot.com. She speaks of sudden fiction, postcard fiction, minute fiction, fast- and furious fiction, quick fiction, skinny fiction, and microfiction. She points out that it is called nouvelles in France, and reports that it is very popular in China, where along with many other names, it is sometimes called smoke-long story, for the length of time it takes to smoke a cigarette. Casto suggests that Aesop, Ovid, Guy de Maupassant, Anton Chekov, O. Henry, and Franz Kafka are the short genre's precursors. ("Flashes on the Meridian: Dazzled by Flash Fiction." www.heelstone.com/meridian/meansarticle1.html)

~ Learn by Example ~

Many renowned writers have written flash fiction, whether it was called that or not, and many writers are making a name for themselves in the form as it evolves today.

Aesop	Franz Kafka
Donald Barthelme	Yasunari Kawabata
Jorge Luis Borges	H. P. Lovecraft
Ray Bradbury	Joyce Carol Oates
Italo Calvino	Ovid
Raymond Carver	Grace Paley
Anton Chekhov	Bruce Holland Rogers
Arthur C. Clarke	Paul Theroux
Julio Cortazar	Melanie Rae Thon
Katie Farris	John Updike
Ernest Hemingway	Kurt Vonnegut, Jr.
O. Henry	John Edgar Wideman

Find other authors listed at http://flashfiction.net/authors.

Anatomy of the Flash

Like any short story, flash fiction contains four distinct elements: setting, characters, conflict, and resolution. But flash fiction has a fifth element: suggestion. In *The Art of Writing Flash Fiction* (Smashwords), Harvey Stanbrough writes, "Suggestion or implication is the fine art of letting the reader know what you're talking about—or letting him think he knows what you're talking about—without telling him directly. When she uses suggestion, the writer hints at an emotion or an occurrence and lets the reader invent it himself rather than telling him about it outright."

Ernest Hemingway somewhat famously wrote flash fiction as well in a story apocryphally written as part of a bet: "For Sale: Baby shoes, never worn." This remarkably short but complete work of fiction is

~ And the Winner Is ~

Author Robert Laughlin founded the Micro Award (www.micro-award.org) to recognize outstanding flash fiction. The first award was given to Bruce Holland Rogers for "Reconstruction Work," published in the inaugural issue of *Flash Fiction Online* (December 2007). Laughlin served as the Micro Award's administrator and primary financial supporter until 2010, when Alan Presley succeeded him.

Award guidelines say that works of English prose fiction in any genre, and not above 1,000 words, are eligible. Works may have appeared in print, electronically, and may be self-published. An author may submit one story; the editors of a magazine or anthology may submit two stories from the publication, if neither is self-written.

Mailed submissions must be postmarked from October 1 to December 31 and received by January 15, or emailed to admin@ microaward.org by December 31. The text of the story must be copied into in the body of the email, attached as a Rich Text File (RTF), or accessible through a URL.

an example of Hemingway's economical writing style with its simple nouns and verbs used to capture a scene precisely. Despite the clarity, it also works on the level of implication.

Stanbrough also says that misdirection is an important function of suggestion. Flash fiction also uses twists of conflict, character, image, or point of view to make an impact—the *flash* is not just the brevity, but the sudden turn of events. Short fiction can be highly experimental writing that pushes the boundaries of traditional reader expectations, or even traditional forms used to a different end. In Casto's view, flash fiction can even take the form of a magazine quiz, a survey, acknowledgments in a book, or a posted ad or message. In 2012, tweets and text messages should surely be included on that list. Even within this minimalist genre are variations of form. Some stories are written in one or two sentences, others use dialogue only, others use the second person.

By whatever name you call it, this genre covers a large range forms and styles—perfect for today's short attention spans. It runs the gamut: It can be clever, entertaining, literary, ironic, or satirical in nature. Sometimes it is funny; sometimes controversial or unconventional. But it's always short and to the point.

Examples of flash fiction can be found almost everywhere. They appear print journals, magazines, anthologies, collections. You will also find examples of flash fiction on the Internet, in all its many forms and under all its various names.

"Flash fiction is fiction with its teeth bared and its claws extended, lithe and muscular with no extra fat," says Kathy Kachelries, founder of 365 Tomorrows, a science fiction flash fiction website. "It pounces in the first paragraph, and if those claws aren't embedded in the reader by the start of the second, the story began a paragraph too soon. There is no margin for error. Every word must be essential, and if it isn't essential, it must be eliminated."

Flash fiction's deceptive simplicity can provide a thought-provoking read that satisfies long after you have finished the story.

~ Sources ~

~ Pamelyn Casto. "Flashes on the Meridian: Dazzled by Flash Fiction." www.heelstone.com/meridian/meansarticle1.htm

~ Jason Gurley. "Flash What? A Quick Look at Flash Fiction." www.writing-world.com/fiction/flash.shtml

~ William Highsmith. "Flash Fiction FAQs." www.writersdigest.com/article/flashfiction-faqs

~ Index of Flash Fiction Markets. http://www.absolutewrite.com/forums/showthread.php?t=59234

~ The Micro Award. www.microaward.org

~ Harvey Stanbrough,.The Art of Writing Flash Fiction (Smashwords).

~ G. W. Thomas. "Writing Flash Fiction." www.fictionfactor.com/guests/flashfiction.html

sh Fiction Markets ~

~ **⟩ex:** www.abyssapexzine.com. Quarterly. Flash
⟩vords. Pays 5¢ a word. Guidelines available.

~ **Apple Valley Review:** www.applevalleyreview.com. Accepts
literary and mainstream stories to 3,000 words. No payment.

~ **Bound Off:** www.boundoff.com. Literary fiction, 250 to 2,500
words to be read aloud for a podcast. Pays $20 a story.

~ **Drabblecast:** http://web.me.com/normsherman/Site/Podcast/
Podcast.html. Audiofiction podcast of "short stories at the far side of
weird," including science fiction, fantasy, horror. Short fiction, 500–
2,500 words. Drabbles, exactly 100 words. Twabbles, exactly 100
characters. Poetry, 1,000 words or less. Pays $1^1/2¢$ a word.

~ **Every Day Fiction:** www.everydayfiction.com/stories. Flash fiction
to 1,000 words. Nominal payment, and links to your blog or website.

~ **Flashshot:** www.gwthomas.org/guidelines.htm. Fiction to 100
words. No payment; includes author bio and opportunity to promote
your publications.

~ **Flashquake:** www.flashquake.org. A literary and art journal. Flash
fiction, to 1,000 words. Nonfiction, to 1,000 words. Poetry, to 35 lines.
Prose poetry, to 300 words. Temporarily suspending payment;
includes author bio.

~ **Funny Times:** www.funnytimes.com www. Monthly. Humor, satire.
Stories, 500-700 words. Pays $60 for a story.

~ **Glimmer Train:** www.glimmertrain.com. Fiction, 2,000–20,000
words. Holds two Very Short Fiction competitions in January and July,
to 3,000 words. Payment, to $700.

~ **GUD: Greatest Uncommon Denominator:** www.gudmagazine.
com. Literary journal. Fiction, 20–15,000 words. Pays $5 a piece, or
3¢ a word.

~ **Ideomancer:** www.ideomancer.com. Speculative fiction, to 7,000
words. Pays 3¢ a word.

~ **Inch:** http://inch.bullcitypress.com. Highlights the smallest fiction
and poetry. Fiction, to 750 words. Pays in copies.

~ **Literary Potpourri:** www.literarypotpourri.com. Literary journal.

~ Flash Fiction Markets ~

Flash fiction, to 1,000 words. Other fiction, to 5,000 words. Pays $10 for a flash fiction story.

~ **Mslexia:** www.mslexia.co.uk. Writing from women in the U.K. and beyond. Accepts many forms and word counts, including Monologue (to 200 words) and A Week of Tweets (7 tweets, 140 characters each). Payment varies.

~ **Night Train:** www.nighttrainmagazine.com. Firebox fiction, to 1,500 words. Has been on a hiatus that is scheduled to end in early 2012.

~ **Pedestal Magazine:** www.thepedestalmagazine.com. Guidelines vary by issue. Publishes fiction of varying lengths, poetry, reviews, interviews. Fiction payment, 5¢ a word.

~ **The People's Friend**: www.jbwb.co.uk. U.K. story magazine publishing since 1869. Short, short stories, 500–1,000 words. Other stories, 1,000–4,000 words. Publishes for children and adults. Pays on acceptance.

~ **Shimmer**: www.shimmerzine.com. Contemporary fantasy, to 5,000 words. Some science fiction amd other speculative genres accepted. Pays 1¢ a word, minimum of $10.

~ **SmokeLong Quarterly:** http://smokelong.com/sub_guidelines.asp Specializes in flash fiction, to 1,000 words. No payment.

~ **Sniplits**: www.sniplits.com/authorsroom.jsp. Stories of many lengths in MP3 audio form "that take just a snip of time." Pays advance, royalty. Worked through a backlog of stories in 2011. Check website for updates.

~ **Strange Horizons**: www.strangehorizons.com. Speculative fiction, and looking for "more inclusive" writers and stories. Accepts stories to 9,000 words, prefers fewer than 5,000 words, and has no minimum word count. Accepts short-short stories. Pays 7¢ a word, minimum payment, $50.

~ **Vestal Review:** www.vestalreview.net. Tag line is "the most intense flash fiction in America." To 500 words. Biannual with themes; a recent example is a twist on classic fairy tales.

～ Flash Fiction Markets ～

～ Tweet the Meat: http://tweetthemeat.blogspot.com. A Twitter-based horror ezine. 140 characters or less, theme-based. Pays $1 per story tweet.

～ WOW! Women on Writing: www.wow-womenonwriting.com. Runs a quarterly flash fiction contest. Fiction, 250-750 words.

Bright Futures: Children's Nonfiction Series

By Barbara Kramer

T he future of children's nonfiction series looks bright, even in a time of uncertainty in the publishing world. "Book buyers like to see a commitment, like a series, from a publisher," says Allison Shaloum Brydon, Editor at Sterling Children's Books. "They want something that will bring their customers back, looking for the next installation."

The Creative Company Senior Editor Aaron Frisch is also optimistic. "Kids have access to encyclopedias and increasing numbers of online sources on nonfiction subjects," he says, "but nothing combines the conciseness, visual appeal, and information accuracy of a good nonfiction series."

Many companies publish nonfiction series, some producing more than 200 new titles a year. That is encouraging news for writers in a slow economy, but writing nonfiction series is not for everyone. Writers should think about what is important to them in a working relationship with a publisher before attempting to embark on a career in nonfiction series.

~ Resources ~

~ **Evelyn B. Christensen** provides an updated list of educational publishers with links to their guidelines on her website at: http://evelynchristensen.com/writers.html.

~ **NFforKids.** This Yahoo Group is for people who write nonfiction for kids. Although it is for all children's nonfiction writers, it often includes discussions about writing nonfiction series. You can join at: NFforKids-subscribe@yahoogroups.com.

~ **Laura Purdie Salas** teaches classes both online and in person about writing nonfiction series. She has also created a self-guided workbook based on her classes. Learn more at: http://www.laurasalas.com/present.html.

For Your Consideration

One advantage of writing for a nonfiction series is that authors can feel confident they are working on marketable projects because the publishers have already established the need for books on particular topics. Of course, for writers who want to select their own topics that can also be a disadvantage.

Nonfiction series publishers seek out writers with skills that match their needs; the authors then often choose from a small list of ideas provided by the publishers. Mary Meinking chose from such a list when she got the opportunity to write two books on origami for Capstone Press. Since she works full-time as a graphic designer and artist, the books were a good match for her talents. Nancy Furstinger, whose favorite topic is animals, was contracted to write a series about dogs and cats for Checkerboard Library, an imprint of ABDO Publishing Company.

Before taking on an assignment for a nonfiction series, writers should consider how much time they will have to work on a project. Some publishers allow a few months. "We try not to schedule books so that people are working a crash schedule," Sterling's Brydon notes. But there are exceptions. "If a specific anniversary is coming up or there is a special promotion we want the book to be considered for, the deadlines might be tighter."

For other publishers, the deadlines can be more rushed. Authors may have only a couple of weeks to research and write a book. Although that may seem like an impossible amount of time, experienced writers of nonfiction series make it work by putting writing ahead of everything else for a few weeks. Meinking recalls nights that she wrote until 4:00 AM and then got up by 6:30 AM to get ready for her day job. She also avoids watching television when she is working to meet a deadline. "My reality shows have to go on without me," she jokes.

Laura Purdie Salas, who has written more than 75 nonfiction series books, finds it helpful to follow a schedule. If a book is due on September 15, for example, she manages her time so that she can finish by September 5. "That way, I've got a little time built in for unexpected delays," she says.

Even with planning, it can be overwhelming to research and write a book in a short amount of time. "Nonfiction series writing is not for people who agonize over every sentence and are slow to research and write," notes Marcia Amidon Lüsted, who has written almost 60 nonfiction books, most of them part of series.

Deadlines are tight because publishers are working on schedules themselves—to publish in time for the school year, for example, for the many series books that target the school and library market. Editors need authors who can be depended on to deliver their work on time. Failing to meet a deadline could mean that a publishing door will slam shut.

Payment is another consideration. Many nonfiction series assignments are on a work-for-hire basis. Instead of royalties based on the number of copies sold, the author is paid a predetermined fee. For some writers, that can be an advantage. "You get paid promptly, and you know exactly how much you're going to make," says Salas.

The downside is that even if a book does well, the author cannot expect additional income from that project. Note, however, that some nonfiction series publishers pay royalties on a least some projects.

Getting Started

The nonfiction series market is competitive, and writers who hope to break into it should create a battle plan. The first step is to build a résumé, since book publishers want to know a writer has strong skills, and credits show that. Meinking had written dozens of articles for more than a dozen magazines before she started contacting book publishers. She included those magazine publishing credits on her résumé to help her get book assignments.

Writers with no publishing credits should highlight other skills that could make them good candidates for writing nonfiction series. Think about your interests and your work experience. Are you a teacher? A publisher might be willing to work with teachers even though they do not have writing experience because teachers are familiar with school curriculums. Library work is another plus because librarians know how to research. Do you do any writing at your current job? That experience is worth mentioning even though it is a different type of writing. A nurse might be able to write on medical topics. Do you have a background in history or science? Publishers need writers who are experts in those areas.

Next, spend time reading nonfiction series and becoming familiar with the types of series produced by various publishers. When you find series that match your interests, study the publishers' catalogues, many of which are available online. "We are impressed when we are contacted by writers who have researched our titles and have found a way to correlate their expertise with our series," says Adrianne Loggins, Associate Editor at Morgan Reynolds Publishing.

Note if the publishers' series are open or closed. An open series continues to add a few new books each year. If all the books in a series were published about the same time, and that is more than a couple of years ago, the series is probably closed. The publisher may have intended from the start that the series would consist of a limited number of titles. Another sign that a series is closed is if all the books are written by the same author. If new titles are added later, they will most likely be written by that same author.

Then study the latest writers' guidelines for each publisher and prepare a submissions package. Follow the guidelines carefully as each publisher has different requirements for what they want to see from writers for the initial contact. Some create series in-house and then look for writers. They may want to see a résumé, publishing credits, and writing samples. Other publishers prefer queries, with a proposal package that may include a table of contents and a sample chapter, or chapters and an outline.

Some publishers are open to receiving series ideas from writers. Morgan Reynolds is one. "Initially, we'd like to receive the writer's résumé, samples of his or her writing, and a one-page summary of their book proposal," says Loggins.

Even though most of its series are created in-house, The Creative Company is open to ideas for new series. "There is always the possibility someone will pitch a terrific idea that hadn't occurred to us," Frisch says. "But the truth is that the vast majority of our nonfiction series originate in-house. Our company has been around a long time and published on a wide array of topics, and our staff is best able to determine which subjects will fill a niche on our lists."

Salas recommends sending submissions packets to five to ten publishers. "It's a lot of work," she admits, "but it really increases your chances of getting that first assignment."

Continue to hone your writing skills. "Get as much experience writing as you can," Loggins advises. Spending time networking with other writers and with editors is another way to find work. "Keep up with what's going on in the publishing industry through newsletters, magazines, blogs, and websites," Brydon suggests. She also urges writers to go to conferences to meet editors and agents and learn more about what they want.

Building a Career

Getting an assignment from a publisher is exciting, but it is only a first step. The key to building a successful career in nonfiction series is to do a great job on the first assignment by paying attention to details. Books in a series need to be a cohesive set. That means they all have a similar word count and may have the same number of chapters. If a writer is assigned a book for an existing series, the publisher will send a sample book for the author to study. "I enjoy

> The key to building a successful career in nonfiction series is to do a great job on the first assignment by paying attention to details.

looking at the sample books and figuring out how to match them," Salas says. "That's a key skill for series writers."

If the writer is to work on a new series, the editor will provide guidelines. "The writers we work with a second time are the ones who really pay attention to the guidelines, and therefore make our editing work easy," Frisch says. "If in the course of our edits we have to keep saying 'refer to the series guidelines,' then the writer probably has not been attentive enough."

Success with a first project may open the door for future assignments from a publisher. That continuing relationship with editors is perhaps the biggest advantage in writing nonfiction series. But continue to build new relationships, rather than work with just one publisher. "Things change all the time," Lüsted says. "The editor might leave the company and you'll lose your contact there, or they might change focus, or cancel a series you were working on." Lüsted spends time each month sending out résumés and writing samples to make new contacts. About once a year, she follows up with editors

~ Markets ~

~ The Creative Company: P.O. Box 227, Mankato, MN 56002. Aaron Frisch, Senior Editor. Writers who want to propose series should query with an outline and sample pages. Their series are 4–8 books.

~ Morgan Reynolds Publishing: 620 South Elm St., Suite 387, Greensboro, NC 27406. Adrianne Loggins, Associate Editor. Authors should query first with ideas for existing series.

~ Sterling Children's Books: 387 Park Ave. South, New York, NY 10016. Allison Shaloum Brydon, Editor. Most of Sterling's nonfiction series are developed in-house, but they do keep a "freelancer file" from writers who send in their work. "A writer can send in a cover letter stating that he or she would like to be considered for future nonfiction writing, samples of their nonfiction writing, and samples of any previous publications," Brydon says, "and we will put it in our freelancer file for future reference."

More Markets

~ ABDO: 8000 West 78th St., Suite 310, Edina, MN 55439. www.abdopublishing.com

~ Barron's Educational: 250 Wireless Blvd., Hauppage, NY 11788. www.barronseduc.com

~ Capstone: 151 Good Counsel Dr., Mankato, MN 56001. www.capstonepress.com

~ Greenhaven, Kidhaven, Lucent Books: 27500 Drake Road, Farmington Hills, MI 48331. www.gale.com

~ Lerner Publishing Group: 241 First Ave. North, Minneapolis, MN 55401. www.lernerbooks.com

~ Marshall Cavendish Benchmark: 99 White Plains Road, Tarrytown, NY 10591. www.marshallcavendish.us

~ Sourcebooks: 1935 Brookdale Road, Suite 139, Naperville, IL 60563. www.sourcebooks.com

~ Workman Publishing: 225 Varick St., New York, NY 10014. www.workman.com

who have shown interest in her work. She sends them reminders that she is still available for assignments.

Writing nonfiction series is not for everyone, but for those who are willing to work hard, if offers rewards. "I get to learn about all sorts of things, which is always fun!" Salas says. It can also mean steady work for writers who research and write well, pay attention to publishers' guidelines and are punctual in meeting due dates.

ABCs of Early Readers

By Casie Hermansson

E arly readers are children and *early readers* are books that young children read. With both children and books, word choice and syntax are limited but progressing, while the genres and markets connected to them can vary widely.

Early reader texts (also called *easy readers* or *beginning readers*) include simple stories with a limited number of words on a page and illustrations to support the story; more elaborately illustrated picture books intended to be read on their own by children (as opposed to read-alouds, shared with an adult reader); early chapter books; magazine stories and articles with limited vocabulary and sentence length; and even rebuses, in which concrete nouns take the the form of pictures.

Scholastic lists a number of early readers specifying ages 4 to 8, while others are directed at ages 7 to 10, by which time some children have become *independent readers* too. The consensus is that *early readers* usually cover the market up to middle grade. But Edward Wilson, Publisher of Absey & Co., defines early readers as encompassing the broader age range of 3 to 12. Some publishers even have specialty lines that support children and teens with reading difficulties, who are still at an early reader skill level. Marshall Cavendish's Benchmark Rockets are an example. These *hi-lo*, or high-interest/low reading level, books are written for students in grades 7 and up who are, in fact, still early in developing their reading skills.

Leveled Vocabulary: Working with Word Lists

Most traditionally, however, *early readers* refers to books for children in kindergarten to grade 2. Their content and style coincide directly with the process of reading acquisition. Early readers are often published in *leveled* series, by both by educational and trade publishers. Among the most established are HarperCollins's I Can Read Books and Random House's Step into Reading Books.

Marshall Cavendish Editor Michelle Bisson divides the category into *emergent, early*, and *fluent* readers. Houghton Mifflin Harcourt uses a "text level/grade conversion system" that divides its leveled readers into emergent (kindergarten), early emergent/early (early grade 1), early/transitional (middle of grade 1), transitional (end of grade 1 to the middle of grade 2), and extending readers (end of grade 2 to grade 6) (www.hmhschool.com/School/html/r_lr_chart.html).

Whichever specific level interests you as a writer, Wilson advises that it may be helpful for potential authors first to "get in touch with your inner child." The story interest and point of view must reflect those of the child reader, just as much if not more than word level and sentence structure. Bisson says the needs of the readership are paramount, and knowing what those are requires research. Writers of early readers are expected to know what young readers can and cannot yet read, and what they want to read.

As any parent or teacher knows, the difference between the working vocabulary of a child at, say, age four, is very different from any reading vocabulary. As any first grader knows, some words just do not play by the rules. Writers of early readers have to be very sensitive to words in every way—denotation, connotation, context, sound,

~ Writing Early Readers ~

Trade publishers like Scholastic, HarperCollins, Random House, and others publish lines of early readers, some of them among the most classic and widely known. Russell Hoban's Francis books, for example, are in the HarperCollins I Can Read line, and Random House's Step into Reading includes the Berenstain Bears and Marc Brown's Arthur books.

Many early readers are also published by educational publishers who use a regular set of writers for their series, which are at least in part developed in-house. To become part of these stables, writers may have to apply for under work-for-hire arrangements rather than querying with their own ideas. Individual publishers vary in requirements, but often want to see a résumé, a list of relevant writing credentials, and clips.

Some publishers target books to teachers for use in schools. Scholastic Professional is perhaps the only Scholastic division still open to unagented submissions. It creates instructor resources that include plays for children and titles like *25 Emergent Reader Mini Books.* It wants writers to submit a detailed proposal. (http://teacher.scholastic. com/products/scholasticprofessional/about/proposal.htm).

If you do not yet have many credentials or clips, work to build your résumé by writing early reader stories and articles for magazines like *Highlights for Children, Ladybug, Spider, Turtle,* and *Humpty Dumpty.* Their easy reader stories, poems, and articles have features similar to those in easy reader books, but you can send your writing as a freelancer who queries or submits, rather than applying for work-for-hire.

~ Reading Level Formulas ~

Early reader texts are graded on a number of factors, not limited to vocabulary. Renaissance Learning's Accelerated Reader (AR) system uses its ATOS formula to assign a reading level range keyed to grade levels. Renaissance Learning's AR program uses the ATOS formula for assigning a readability level. ATOS, the company says, includes statistics based in the reading of about a million books by more than 30,000 students.

For instance, *Goodnight Moon* has a grade level rating of 1.8, which correlates to the eighth month of first grade (regardless of the reader's actual age). For comparison, *Goodnight Moon* is designated on Amazon as being appropriate for babies (when Mom or Dad is reading it aloud) to preschool, when the child may read it on their own. The AR rating takes vocabulary into account, but also number of characters per word, and number of words per sentence.

Writers can upload portions of text or complete manuscripts to get the readability score instantly on Renaissance Learning's website (www.renlearn.com/ar/overview/atos). The company acknowledges an error variance because factors other than sentence length and vocabulary, including conceptual difficulty and punctuation, affect comprehension.

It also cautions that reading level does not measure content appropriateness. Still, the system also assigned an interest level rating: LG = lower grades (K-3); MG = middle grades (4-8); MG+ = middle grades plus (6 and up); and UG = upper grades (9-12).

homonyms. Educators and publishers have developed grade-level word lists that early reader writers must use well. (See the sidebar above on Reading Level Formulas.)

Familiarize yourself with the level of vocabulary, grammar, punctuation, and syntax of the early reader levels, and read widely in the genre. Nonfiction author Bridget Heos repeats the common advice to read a hundred books in the genre, and adds, "I would probably read

~ Reading Level Formulas ~

Lexile (www.lexile.com), a competitor of Renaissance Learning, assigns books a number from around 200L to upwards of 1700L, based on sentence length and word frequency. The measurements were developed based on the independent Common Core State Standards initiative (www.corestandards.org), which created learning norms for each grade from K-12. Lexiles rates *Goodnight Moon* at a readership of 1- to 3-years-old, but does not provide a Lexile rating for it because it is listed as NP or non-prose. This rating is used for any text comprised of more than half non-standard prose, such as poetry, songs, and prose without traditional punctuation.

Writers can also upload samples of text (standard prose, with a number of other constraints) to the Lexile Analyzer to get a Lexile number and statistics about the uploaded text, such as mean sentence length. Users must register to do this, and it is then free to upload up to 1,000 words. Access to the greater capacity of the Professional Lexile Analyzer can be requested by contacting the company.

A third reading level scale widely used is the Fountas & Pinnell system, or Guided Reading Level (GR or GRL), developed by literacy educators Irene C. Fountas and Gay Su Pinnell. It uses vocabulary, sentence structure, illustrations, page set-up, textual structure, concepts, and themes to divide books into emergent readers (levels A-E); early readers (levels F-J); early fluent readers (levels K-P); and fluent readers (levels Q-W).

several hundred children's books, from all areas, but zero in on different types of early readers." As you write your early reader book, check grade-leveled word lists to see when that word is introduced, or find a lower grade-level synonym. Because the diction of early readers is limited, you have to be flexible and prepared to give up your favorite word choice if it conflicts with the grade level you are trying to reach.Handy books like *The Children's Writer's Word Book*, by

Alijandra Mogliner (Writers Digest), provide lists of leveled vocabulary and a thesaurus section for replacing problematic words. Note that the second-grade word list, for instance, presupposes knowledge of the kindergarten and first-grade lists as well. But different versions of words come into play at different levels, sometimes surprisingly. While *music* is kindergarten-leveled vocabulary, *musical* is a fifth-grade word. *The Children's Writer's Word Book* notes that compound words are generally introduced in second grade, and also that a phrase might contain several words that are at the kindergarten level, but the concept behind the phrase might be better understood in first grade.

Theodor Geisel's famous *Cat in the Hat* and other books work as models for the success of books written with a set vocabulary list. If you want to feel like Dr. Seuss and have a fun writing challenge (and possible publication), create your own limited word list using leveled vocabulary. Remember that some degree of repetition is helpful to early readers.

Flow of Information

Publishers of early readers in every format have extremely specific requirements for word count, line length, topic, and style, and these are usually available in their guidelines.

Christianne Jones, Managing Editor of Capstone Fiction, says, "Although the books are short, they are not easy to write. It is important to research other reader programs and understand the levels and what makes a reader different from other types of books."

VS Grenier, founder of Stories for Children Publishing and Editor of *Stories for Children* online magazine, says, "You need to have a flow of information, be it fiction or nonfiction. Fiction needs to start with a hook or problem, build to a climax, and then wrap up the details at the end. Nonfiction needs to flow where the beginning ties into the end and the end wraps back up to the points stated in the beginning." *Stories for Children* word counts are 400 to 800 words for early readers (ages 7 to 9), for fiction and nonfiction. Her counsel applies equally to a 250-word rebus.

Capstone's Jones agrees. "It is also important to come up with a fun, unique story that has some action and a small twist to keep the reader interested, which is not easy using just 100 to 300 words."

The U.S Kids magazines offer material for early readers. They are *Turtle,* for preschoolers; *Humpty Dumpty,* for ages 5 to 7; and *Jack and Jill*, for ages 6 to 12. According to the guidelines, they look for material that is appropriate to and respectful of the age, and that is "simple, but not simple-minded."

Find a balance in early readers between simplicity and an interesting richness.

Finding a balance between simplicity and an interesting richness is one of the challenges of writing for early readers, and one of its strengths when it works. Jean Elders DeWaard, Managing Editor of Eerdman's Books for Young Readers, says, "Simple alone doesn't make it very interesting." She was referring to board books, the most condensed and spare textual form, but the statement is also true for early readers for preschoolers, kindergarteners, and early elementary children: "Simple yet lyrical" is a goal, along with "beauty [of] the language used," says DeWaard.

As is true in any art form, once you are a master of the rules, you can break them. Theodor Geisel not only demonstrated the range achievable by using limitations, but redefined the early reader genre. Author and illustrator Mo Willems has had extraordinarily humorous results with his early reader picture books, and has won the Theodor Seuss Geisel Award and two Caldecott awards. *Don't Let the Pigeon Drive the Bus!* has an AR rating of 0.9 (late kindergarten); his other Pigeon books range from 0.7 to 1.1 (kindergarten to early grade one). His Elephant and Piggie books have AR ratings within the same range, but Willems's books manage to extend the interest and range of the early readers beyond grade one.

Heos, author of *Do You Really Want a Dog?* and *Do You Really Want a Cat?* for Amicus Publishing, emphasizes the rigor of the early reader form: "With most stories, I revise and revise and revise. I also have to cut a lot of words. With early readers, I try to revise the idea before I write. Then I keep the word count low from the beginning. I want the early reader to have a voice. If I delete and delete, I'm afraid it will lose that voice. But if I write sparsely from the beginning, I can keep it." Heos also insists that the fun of it, for writer and reader alike, is just as important. "I like trying to make early readers laugh. I think early readers have a great sense of humor."

Similarly, Lisa Wade McCormick, author of 13 children's books that include five biographies in Scholastic's Rookie Readers line, speaks to both the challenges and rewards of the genre: "It's a great challenge to tell a story in a few simple and easy-to-read-and-understand words and sentences. It's also a challenge to hook young readers and keep their interest. Every word, every sentence counts. But what a joy to see the expression on a young reader's face when they like what you've written."

~ Early Reader Markets ~

~ **Abdo Publishing Company:** P.O. Box 398166, Minneapolis, MN 55439. www.abdopublishing.com. Attn: Submissions Committee.

~ **Absey & Company:** 23011 Northcrest Dr., Spring, Texas 77389. www.absey.biz. Edward Wilson, Editorin Chief.

~ **Action Publishing:** P.O. Box 391, Glendale, CA 91209 http://actionpublishing.com/submission_guidelines_for_writers.html. Attn: Submission Editor.

~ **Active Parenting Publishers:** 1955 Vaughn Road, Suite 108, Kennesaw, GA 30144. www.activeparenting.com. Molly Davis, Product Development Manager.

~ **Blue Dolphin Publishing:** P.O. Box 8, Nevada City, CA 95959. www.bluedolphinpublishing.com/msguide.htm. Paul M. Clemens, Editor.

~ **Blue Sky Press:** Scholastic Trade Book Division, 557 Broadway, 5th floor, New York, NY 10012. www.scholastic.com. Most authors are agented at Scholastic Trade imprints.

~ **Charlesbridge Publishing:** 85 Main St., Watertown, MA 02472. www.charlesbridge.com/client/client_pages/submissions.cfm. Attn: Submissions Editor. Charlesbridge remains open to unagented but *exclusive* (for three months) submissions of complete manuscripts; it responds only to those of interest.

~ **Chronicle Books:** 680 Second St., San Francisco, California 94107. www.chroniclebooks.com/our-company/submissions/childrens. Attn: Children's Division. The company publishes more than 150 titles a year and remains open to unagented submissions.

~ **Clarion Books:** Houghton Mifflin Harcourt Children's Books, 222 Berkeley St., Boston, MA 02116. www.houghtonmifflinbooks. com/clarion. Attn: Submissions.

~ **Critical Thinking Company:** 1991 Sherman Ave., Suite 200, North Bend, OR 97459. www.criticalthinking.com/company/author_guide-lines.jsp?code=p. Attn: Michael Baker.

~ Early Reader Markets ~

~ E & E Publishing: 1001 Bridgeway, Suite 227, Sausalito, CA 94965. http://eandegroup.com/publishing. Eve Bine-Stock, Submissions Editor.

~ Eerdmans Books for Young Readers: 2140 Oak Industrial Dr. NE, Grand Rapids, MI 49505. http://eerdmans.com/youngreaders/submit.htm. Attn: Acquisitions Editor.

~ Facts on File: Infobase Publishing, 132 West 31st St., 17th floor, New York, NY 10001. www.infobasepublishing.com/ContactUS.aspx? Page=AuthorSubmission. Attn: Editorial Director.

~ Finney Company: 8075 215th St. West, Lakeville, MN 55044. www.finneyco.com/authoring.html.

~ Free Spirit Publishing: 217 Fifth Ave. North, Suite 200, Minneapolis, MN 55401. www.freespirit.com/company/submissions.cfm. Attn: Acquisitions.

~ Holiday House: 425 Madison Ave., New York, NY 10017. www.holidayhouse.com/holiday_house.php Attn: Editorial Department.

~ Humanics Learning: 12 S. Dixie Hwy., Ste. 203, Lake Worth, FL 33460. www.humanicspub.com/Submit_Manuscript.php. W. Arthur Bligh, Acquisitions Editor.

~ Kaeden Books: P.O. Box 16190, Rocky River, OH 44116. www.kaeden.com/pages/ authors_illustrators. Attn: Editorial Department.

~ Little Tiger Press: 1 The Coda Center, 189 Munster Road, London SW6 6AW, United Kingdom. www.littletigerpress.com. Mara Alperin, Submissions Editor.

~ Mondo Publishing: 980 Ave. of the Americas, New York, NY 10018. http://www.mondopub.com/c/@Ho5ydjanoqTxg/Pages/index.html. Attn: Editorial Director.

~ Richard C. Owen Publishers: www.rcowen.com/indexabout.htm. P.O. Box 585, Katonah, NY 10536. Richard Owen, Publisher.

~ Peachtree Publishers: Peachtree Publishers, 1700 Chattahoochee Ave., Atlanta, GA 30318. http://peachtree-online.com/index.php/ resources/submission-guidelines/manuscript-guidelines.html. Helen Harris, Acquisitions Editor.

~ Early Reader Markets ~

~ Pipers' Ash: Church Road, Christian Malford, Chippenhan, Wiltshire SN15 4BW United Kindgdom. http://supamasu.co.uk/index.html. Attn: Manuscript Evaluation Desk.

~ Platypus Media: 725 8th St. SE, Washington DC 20003. www.platypus-media.com/node/85. Attn: Submissions Editor.

~ Mathew Price: http://mathewprice.com/contact. Submissions via email only, to submissions@mathewprice.com.

~ Reagent Press Books for Young Readers: P.O. Box 362, East Olympia, WA, 98540-0362. www.reagentpress.com/about.htm. Attn: Book Submissions

~ Running Press Kids: 2300 Chestnut St., Suite 200, Philadelphia, PA 19103, www.perseusbooksgroup.com/runningpress/sub_policies.jsp: Attn: Submissions Editor

~ Seedling Publications: 520 East Bainbridge St., Elizabethtown, PA 17022. www.continentalpress.com/company/careers.html. Attn: Managing Editor.

~ Soundprints: 353 Main Ave., Norwalk, CT 06851-1552. www.sound-prints.com/Contact_Us_s/18.htm. Jamie McCune, Editor.

~ Sterling Publishing: 387 Park Ave. South, 11th floor, New York, NY 10016-8810. www.sterlingpublishing.com/sterling/author-guidelines. Frances Gilbert, Editor.

~ Stone Arch Books: 151 Good Counsel Drive, P.O. Box 669, Mankato, MN 56002. www.capstonepub.com/content/CONTACTUS_SUBMISSIONS. Attn: Editorial Director.

~ Storytellers Ink: P.O. Box 33398, Seattle, WA 98133-0398. www.storytellers-ink.com/newAuthorIllustratorFAQ.php. Quinn Currie, Editor.

~ Tanglewood Press: P.O. Box 3009, Terre Haute, IN 47803. www.tanglewoodbooks.com/submissions.html. Kairi Hamlin, Acquisitions Editor.

~ Tradewind Books: 202-1807 Maritime Mews, Vancouver, BC, Canada V6H 3W7. www.tradewindbooks.com/submission-guidelines.html.

~ Early Reader Markets ~

~ Walker and Company: 175 Fifth Ave., New York, NY 10010. www.bloomsburykids.com/faq#submission-policy.

~ Windward Publishing: Finney Company, 8075 215th St. West, Lakeville, MN 55044. www.finneyco.com/authoring.html.

Screenwriting 101

Cents & Sensibility

By Christina Hamlett

I f you are an aspiring screenwriter, you will learn that sometimes the only thing standing between your script and a sale is a price tag. Between the cost of technology that allows Hollywood to digitally create entire realms and the squillions of dollars that A-list actors get paid, a myth has been fueled that the pockets of movie makers are bottomless. Is it any wonder, then, that writers assume no expense will be spared if someone really likes the way they tell a story?

At the same time that movie studios are being forced to dig deeper to fund upcoming releases, there has been a proliferation of shoe-string production companies that are hungry to discover the next *Blair Witch Project* or *Paranormal Activity*. If you are adept at writing economically, Hollywood's current tight grip on its purse strings may be exactly the opening you are seeking.

A Nice Backdrop

Location, location, location is the buzz phrase of real estate, and *budget, budget, budget* is what governs twenty-first century movie-making. While filmmaking has always been a mercurial industry, the

～ Rate Your Script ～

～ My film is (a) contemporary; (b) contemporary with historical flashbacks; or (c) historical or futuristic.

～ My film has (a) 0–10 special effects; (b) 11–30 special effects; or (c) more than 30 special effects.

～ My film has (a) fewer than 10 actors; (b) 11–50 actors; or (c) more than 50 actors.

～ My film has (a) no animals in it; (b) animals that are strictly for atmosphere (i.e., grazing cows, sleeping cats, etc.) or (c) animals that have a defined role or do special tricks.

～ My film has (a) 0–10 interior scenes; (b) 11–30 interior scenes; or (c) more than 30 interior scenes. (Note: If you have three scenes that take place in the same location (for instance, a kitchen), count it as only one interior no matter how many times it is used.)

～ My film has (a) 0–10 exterior scenes; (b) 11–30 exterior scenes; or (c) more than 30 exterior scenes. (Note: If you have three scenes that take place in the same location (such as a park), count it as only 1 exterior. If, however, you have a scene in a park, a scene at a beach, and a scene at an outdoor café, that would be 3 exteriors.)

margin for error and the willingness to take risks are far lower than they have ever been before. The advent of digital downloads and video-on-demand has been convenient for consumers, but it has not compensated studios for the loss of DVD revenue that they once relied on as a lucrative income stream. Not only are the studios seeing a steady decline in international distribution sales (a scenario fueled by piracy), but domestic investors who once had a reputation for generous underwriting have reduced their backing because of the impact of Wall Street and global politics.

In a perfect world, of course, writers should not have to don accountant caps and wear blinders against blockbuster visions. In reality, a script that is peppered with pricey elements invites close scrutiny and your pitching prospects will be reduced in inverse pro-

~ Rate Your Script ~

~ My film has (a) fewer than 10 night scenes; (b) 11–20 night scenes; or (c) more than 20 night scenes. (Note: Night scenes are those which take place outdoors and in the dark, not just evening scenes that are all shot inside a building.)

~ My film has (a) no car scenes or simply street scenes where cars are part of the background; (b) scenes in which my characters are traveling by car; or (c) car chases, crashes, or explosions.

~ My film primarily takes place (a) on a soundstage; (b) in an existing house or public structure; or (c) in a specially constructed set (i.e., a medieval castle built from scratch for the production).

~ My film would be most successful with (a) a cast of unknowns; (b) one name star; (c) three or more name stars.

~ Physical stunts in my film are (a) nonexistent; (b) computer-generated; or (c) performed by stunt people.

~ For scenes outside a soundstage, the majority of my film takes place (a) in a small town; (b) in a major American city; or (c) in a foreign country.

portion to your projected filming costs. Whether you are penning a new screenplay or are flummoxed as to why an existing one has not sold, it may be time to reconcile whether all those costly elements you ideally want in your plot are necessary to deliver an entertaining story with substance.

The easiest place to start is by looking at the size of the cast and determining who is necessary and who is expendable. One of my screenwriting mentoring clients, for instance, was writing a Western epic that included a scene in which 80 Indian warriors are seated outside a cluster of teepees as the women cook a bunch of elk over campfires. The scene, which lasted only 20 seconds, contained three lines of dialogue, one of which was a throwaway comment about when dinner would be ready.

"Why do you need all of these people in non-speaking parts?" I asked.

"I thought they'd make a nice backdrop," he replied. He was completely serious.

Suffice it to say, a producer with a modest budget will not be enamored with paying scale to 80+ actors, as well as procuring costumes, makeup, wigs, teepees, and a couple of hefty elk to round out the ambience—especially when those three lines could be dropped completely for not advancing the plot or being conveyed in a tight shot against a backdrop of trees. That none of these characters would ever reappear in the storyline would be as much a liability to

Cast a broad net in shopping a screenplay, and improve your odds of getting it made.

the makers of the movie as the requirement to provide meals, breaks, and workers' compensation. Adding to the zeroes in this already high-cost venture were death-defying canoe rides down the rapids, a stampede of wild horses, and the construction of more than 145 sets.

While I would never discourage someone from writing the big-budget blockbuster that they see so clearly in their mind's eye, a more conservative approach brings a twofold benefit: the ability to cast a broader net in shopping it and improved odds at actually getting it made. Accomplishing this calls for the ability to identify the most common red flags that set off a script reader's radar. Take the quiz that appears in the sidebar on pages 96–97.

Down with Costs, Up with Sales

Now, score your quiz. For each (a) answer, give yourself 1 point. For each (b) answer, give yourself 5 points. For each (c) answer, give yourself 10 points.

~ Budget Savvy ~

The more you know about film budgets, the better prepared you will be to look at your work through the eyes of potential funding sources. The following books on the subject are smart investments for your screenwriting library and provide expert tips on how to make ordinary resources look like extraordinary bling.

~ *Film & Video Budgets,* by Deke Simon
~ *How to Make a Hollywood Movie for Under $800!* by Ken Costanza
~ *How to Shoot a Feature Film for Under $10,000 (And Not Go to Jail),* by Bret Stern.
~ *The People and Process of Film and Video Production: From Low Budget to High Budget,* by Lorene Wales
~ *Master Shots: 100 Advanced Camera Techniques to Get an Expensive Look on Your Low-Budget Movie,* by Christopher Kenworthy
~ *Planning the Low-Budget Film,* by Robert Latham Brown
~ *Special Effects: How to Create a Hollywood Film Look on a Home Budget,* by Michael Slone

If your score is less than 40, you have a story that falls into the low-budget range and would be appealing to an independent producer with limited resources.

If your score is between 40 and 80, you are in the mid-range. This range gives you a lot of latitude to adjust up or down without extensive revisions.

If your score is between 80 and 120, your vision is definitely big-budget and, therefore, accessible to a much smaller pool of buyers. Risk-wary as these high-rollers are, it is your (c) answers that will attract their harshest looks. These are the elements to revisit for possible compromise.

As you begin the revision process, or start a new script from scratch, consider the following factors that impact a production's cost:

~ Contemporary plots are usually less pricey than period pieces. Can the story you want to tell be framed in a modern context or is the historical backdrop central to your characters' personalities and motivations? For futuristic tableaus, how do you intend to define the architecture, vehicles, planets, etc.?

~ Fires, floods, earthquakes, volcanoes, explosions: While many disasters can now be computer-generated or simulated with miniatures, those that cannot are going to cost money and plenty of it. The same thing applies to car chases and crashes and scenes involving dangerous stunts.

~ Anything involving animals calls for the presence of an ASPCA representative on the set to ensure humane treatment and safety for anything that swims, flies, or moves on four feet.

~ Exterior scenes leave the cast and crew at the mercy of light and weather, as opposed to interior shots that look exactly the same whether it is 3 AM in the dead of winter or 7:30 PM on a summer eve. The next time you watch a sitcom, make note of how the season and time of day are primarily dictated by what the characters are wearing.

~ Going on location is pricier than shooting on a soundstage, especially because of the logistics of getting everyone to the film site. It may be cheaper to shoot in a foreign country but in exchange for the host region's hospitality, there will be an expectation of staying in their hotels, frequenting their restaurants, and filling out the cast and crew with star-struck locals.

~ Every time the camera equipment gets moved, the cash register dings. Try to minimize your locations so multiple scenes can be shot in one place. Take into account, too, the expense of constructing and dressing a set versus the amount of time it is actually going to be seen through a lens.

~ Last but not least, specifying that "Johnny Depp has to be in this movie or it simply won't work" is not a compelling pitch in these days of belt-tightening. Bigger stars mean bigger salaries. There is no question that an award-winning actor can make a mediocre story shine but mediocrity is not what attracts star power. If a role is well written, any capable actor should be able to step into it and deliver a convincing performance.

At the end of the day, if a script can't stand on the strength of its message, plot and characters, no amount of superfluous glitz that is bolted on is going to save it. By respecting this rule from the outset, you are giving your screenplay a chance to truly be priceless in the eyes of a prospective producer.

~ Resources ~

Once you have a script you are convinced is budget-friendly as well as high-quality storytelling, you will need to find a production company, generally—though not always—through an agent. Here are some resources to help you.

> ~ *Hollywood Creative Directory:* www.hcdonline.com. An industry database from *The Hollywood Reporter* that includes a comprehensive list of production companies.
> ~ *Variety:* www.variety.com. Entertainment trade publication.
> ~ Writers' Guild of America: West. www.wga.org. A union that represents film, television, radio, and new media writers.
> ~ *Writer's Market:* www.writersmarket.com. Includes a section on screenwriting markets.

Children's Book Apps

A Bold, Exciting Market Beckons

By Judy Bradbury

Writing for children's book apps is all the buzz at publisher-populated meeting venues such as Bologna and BookExpo America (BEA), at day-long digital seminars, on myriad blogs, and at educators' conventions. Last year saw a ramping up of interest and excitement about creating and marketing book apps for children. Reviews of book apps began appearing in dedicated space in venerable publishing publications such as *Publishers Weekly* and *School Library Journal. Kirkus Reviews* launched Discovery Engine (www.kirkusreviews.com/childrens-book-apps), a children's app review source. New releases of children's book apps consistently swiped book-world headlines.

App-solutely Inviting

We are not talking games here, folks. We are talking book apps: books in an energized format that beckon a child to read, respond, react, and interact with characters in stories that literally come alive on a personal screen. "It's critical that we recognize the distinction among ebooks, book apps, and apps," notes Rubin Pfeffer, Partner and head of the east coast branch of East/West Literary Agency, and the agency's digital media strategist. "These often get clumped together and it's a disservice to the individual formats. I think of these three formats in this way: *ebooks* are largely digital displays of the printed book with varied, but limited, features and enhancements (page turns, audio, word highlighting). *Book apps* tend to have the same features as ebooks plus added functionalities. These include aspects of the story that may animate or respond to user interaction or that are a spin-off of the underlying [book's] story—games and music and activities that build on the *world* of the story. *Apps* are a different matter altogether—they may have little or no connection to any story (or adaptation of story) whatsoever. They are entities unto themselves that include as little or as many technological capabilities as necessary to create an experience or service for the user."

Reportedly, more than 80 percent of the top book apps for the iPad are children's book titles. Children seem to enjoy tapping, swiping, flipping, pressing, poking, tilting, and sliding their way through a story. Children's book apps range in price from free to around ten dollars, and run the gamut from adapted classics and bestsellers to original stories written for the market.

One example of the successful transformation of a beloved print book to a book app is *Freight Train,* by Donald Crews. The original book was published by Greenwillow in 1978 and was awarded a Caldecott Honor. It is a groundbreaking concept book that has sold more than a million copies in various formats. It vividly introduces preschoolers to colors, numbers, shapes, and simple train-related vocabulary. At the *School Library Journal*'s Day of Dialog at BEA, held at Fordham University in May 2011, Greenwillow Vice President and Publisher Virginia Duncan joined in a panel discussion, The Children's App Landscape. She noted the long time it took to successfully bring the classic *Freight Train* to the app format. A team consisting of the author, book editor, art director, developer, and digital publisher collaborated for more than a year and a half to achieve a satisfying product for use on the iPhone and iTouch (before the iPad was available).

~ Book App Markets ~

- **Atomic Antelope:** www.atomicantelope.com
- **Duck Duck Moose:** http://duckduckmoosedesign.com
- **FlickerLab:** www.flickerlab.com
- **Loud Crow Interactive:** http://loudcrow.com/news
- **Nosy Crow:** http://nosycrow.com/contact/submission-guidelines
- **Oceanhouse Media:** www.oceanhousemedia.com
- **Random House Digital:** www.randomhouse.com/kids/apps
- **Ruckus Media Group:** www.ruckusmediagroup.com
- **See Here Studios:** www.seeherestudios.com

Duncan listed the qualities *Freight Train* possesses that allowed it to translate well into an app format. "The book is award-winning and best-selling; has clean art and simple lines; the type is clear, easy to read, and relates directly to the art; the story is developmentally appropriate; and most important, *Freight Train* offers a linear experience making the book straightforward to adapt for the app format."

Think of that bold train track that courses through the book. According to Duncan, challenges included honoring the author/ illustrator's commitment to adding no new art for the project even though the developer begged for it. The goal was to maintain the magic of the original reading experience while merging the interactive qualities of the first half of the book app with the movie-like feeling of the latter half of the app, and seamlessly integrate five railroad songs into the app. Despite the challenges, Duncan found the project to be incredibly satisfying. She initially storyboarded the project before turning it over to Crews. "It was fun to imagine the interactions and the sounds, to put into the app one take on what the imagination supplies when an adult is reading *Freight Train* with a child."

Key Components

Rick Richter is founder and CEO of Ruckus Media Group, a global family entertainment company that specializes in developing children's book apps for a variety of popular mobile platforms, including Apple's iOS and Google's Android. Ruckus is the exclusive source in the mobile media of Rabbit Ears Library. It also develops apps with established children's brands. And it is partnering with Hasbro to develop original interactive storybook apps based on their Tonka, Chuck and Friends, My Little Pony, and Transformers brands that "deliver immersive reading experiences with interactive storytelling, including title-specific activities, coloring, and read-and-record functions."

Richter, who seems to be making news in the digital arena monthly, reflects on what makes a successful children's book app. "We can never forget we're still in the business of storytelling. Story comes first—you've just got to have a great story, but in the digital space, you need to marry that story with a high degree of interactivity to make a great app. At the end of the day, you want the child and family to have a sense of catharsis—that they've been really entertained. Anyone who forgets that is actually just in the gaming business."

Pfeffer agrees. "Like a print version of a book, a book app is all about a well-told story. The technology can offer additional sources of media to tell the story. These include sound, motion, and vast capabilities that technology can employ for the storyteller and the story reader. Key, though, is [that] any effect brought into the story must contribute to the reader's immersion in the story. And a caution to creators is to be mindful to avoid anything extraneous that may prove to be distracting, confusing, entirely unnecessary, or unnecessarily costly."

Emma D. Dryden, Founder and Principal of drydenbks (www.drydenbks.com) a children's editorial and creative consulting firm, identifies the key components of picture book apps as, "bold graphics, bright colors, a well-crafted storyline that can be supplemented by interactivity, and audio capabilities."

She continues, "Apps and print books are similar in that they rely on strong stories to be successful. The difference lies in the components in apps that allow swiping, linking, audio, layered visuals, and layered storylines. In addition, there are no limitations or rules as to pagination and size when it comes to apps. As print books move from page to page, so too do apps move from screen to screen for the most part. But the technology of apps also enables us to move around within each screen to uncover layers, reveal more story, go in close, pan out, and generally have more of a multisensory experience than a print book might afford."

Mike Austin, represented by Pfeffer, is creator of the stunningly successful book app, *A Present for Milo*, the first original app produced by Ruckus Media. Says Austin, "It's a fun, simple story that's easy for little fingers to tap, explore, and discover!"

Michel Kripalani, a veteran of the video gaming industry, is founder and president of Oceanhouse Media, a publisher of mobile apps for iOS (iPhone, iPad, iPod Touch) and Android devices that has licensing agreements with Dr. Seuss Enterprises, Hay House Publishers, Zondervan (a division of HarperCollins), Houghton Mifflin Harcourt, Mercer Mayer, Soundprints, Andersen Press, Character Arts, and Chronicle Books, among others. "The majority of children's book apps," says Kripalani, "contain a combination of various reading modes with professional narration and a custom soundtrack. Additionally, interactive features within the story are what truly set book apps apart from a traditional ebook. Interactivity is accomplished in a variety of ways, but typically includes tappable images on the screen that when touched display a fun animation or surprise sound effects. The interactive features in our omBooks (Oceanhouse Media digital books) focus on literacy, so we like to use picture/word association. For example, a child can tap the illustration of a hat and the word *hat* floats up on the screen. This is also reinforced by the narrator speaking the word. Tap a picture, see the word, and hear the word. This will help a child learn to read. Ultimately, the key to creating an enjoyable children's book app is simply to provide

~ Apps on Top of the Charts ~

~ *Alice for the iPad*, an *Alice in Wonderland* adaptation (Atomic Antelope).

~ *Elmer's Special Day*, by David McKee (Oceanhouse Media and Anderson Press).

~ *How Rocket Learned to Read*, by Tad Hills (Random House Digital)

~ *Jack and the Beanstalk, a Children's Interactive Storybook* (Ayars Animation)

~ *Pat the Bunny* (Random House Digital)

~ *Pop Out! The Tale of Peter Rabbit*, by Beatrix Potter (Loud Crow Interactive)

~ *Spot the Dot*, by David A. Carter (Ruckus Media)

~ *Wheels on the Bus* (Duck Duck Moose)

~ *Wild About Books*, by Judy Sierra (Random House Digital)

~ *The Wrong Side of the Bed in 3D*, by Wallace E. Keller (See Here Studios)

~ Several adaptations of *The Three Little Pigs* , including those developed by Nosy Crow, So Ouat!, Game Collage, and Coleco.

interactivity on the pages that is engaging and supports reading, playfulness, or both. The sky is the limit, really. We are only just now seeing the creative possibilities in this space."

Richter agrees. "There are so many opportunities presented by the interactivity with an iPad or a Smartphone."

Bright Future Ahead

"The fact that there are app-only publishers such as Ruckus Media Group, Callaway Digital Arts, Nosy Crow, and Oceanhouse Media popping up is very exciting news because it says to the children's publishing industry that apps are a viable and highly specific form of story publishing that requires teams of people who have an expertise in app creation, coding, production, design, and development," says Dryden, who consults with Ruckus Media Group and edited and executive produced its app, *Andrew Answers,* by Alan Katz. "Further, it sends a message to illustrators and authors that there is a potential new format and platform on which their visual and verbal stories can be expressed and shared. The fact that apps are being reviewed in traditional as well as nontraditional sources is exciting as well."

2011 was the year for great strides in children's book app development and marketing. Ruckus launched the news-grabbing, award-winning original app, *A Present for Milo.* Nosy Crow, an independent U.K. publisher of children's print books, ebooks, and original apps for iPad, iPhone, and iTouch, released its first app, *3-D Fairy Tales: The Three Little Pigs,* in February 2011 to rave reviews. More 3-D Fairy Tales followed, and the company has now launched an imprint in the U.S. in conjunction with Candlewick Press.

FlickerLab, an award-winning app developer who has worked with PBS Kids, was busy developing dozens of enhanced picture books for Barnes & Noble's Nook Color and the iPad. Magination Press, the children's imprint of the American Psychological Association, simultaneously released related books and iPad apps exploring moods, feelings, emotions, and interpersonal skills. In spring 2011, Random House purchased Seattle-based digital media agency Smashing Ideas, which produced apps for such books on Random's list as *Wild About Books* and *Pat the Bunny.* "I think it's going to be interesting to see whether other publishing houses who don't have staff to actually create or produce apps will go this same route—purchasing digitally-based companies in order to produce apps to supplement their traditional print publishing," notes Dryden.

"I'm excited by the new opportunities that the media offers," says Pfeffer. "By virtue of the emerging new digital publishers and the investments that traditional publishers are putting into digital publishing, more stories can reach more readers in more ways. So my exuberance is not so much in an explosion of apps just yet—it's that responsible publishers—new and legacy—are coming into the

~ Milo Comes Alive ~

Featuring more than 80 tap-interactive objects that prompt more than 125 randomized animations, the critical and popular sensation *A Present for Milo* has garnered notable awards, including the Parents' Choice Award, Mom's Choice Award, and About.com Reader's Choice Award, and has enjoyed an enviable length of stay on apps best-sellers' lists. Advertised as "just right for active young fingers and minds," this cat-chases-mouse story written specifically for the iPad targets pre-readers and young readers. Author and illustrator Mike Austin chronicles its path to success.

"I came up with the story of Milo about 15 years ago. One evening at bedtime, my daughter (who was around two years old at the time) and I were wondering what the heck our cat Milo was doing all day while we were out of the house. Why was he so sleepy when we got home and why was the house such a mess? Hmmmmm . . . I grabbed my sketch pad and started drawing Milo chasing Mouse around the house, causing all kinds of trouble. My daughter got such a kick out of it that I decided to make a book about Milo and his adventures.

"The finished dummy sat on my shelf for years before I was contacted by literary agent Rubin Pfeffer, who had seen my illustration portfolio. He asked if I was interested in collaborating on some projects, and I of course said yes! I spent about a month redrawing Milo in my current style and tweaking pages and copy before I sent a PDF to Rubin.

"*A Present for Milo* was introduced to a number of publishers, but it was Ruckus Media Group who thought it would make a great iPad app. I knew nothing about apps and thought this would be a great opportunity to learn about the process. I also thought how cool it would be to see Milo come to life in an animated, digital form.

"I worked with a great developer and art director at Sequel Digital (www.sequeldigital.com). The project took about three

~ Milo Comes Alive ~

months from concept to finished app. Once we had a storyboard of all the app pages, we decided what elements should be interactive. We figured out how many clickables we could have on each screen, and whether or not they enhanced or supported the story. We eventually narrowed the list to around five per page. I would send the developer layered Photoshop files, and he would then program and send me a working app that I could download and view on my iPad. It was very exciting to see the progression. The app was launched in early December 2010, and shortly thereafter I was offered a contract to create two new Milo books.

"Working with the right developer is the most important thing. I had never worked on an interactive book before, so I needed a lot of guidance—someone with the knowledge and expertise to take my ideas and turn them into an engaging interactive experience. If you have a story that you think would make a fun, engaging app, talk with a developer about your ideas. It's a lot more work than you might realize, so it's important to keep it simple and stay organized. It's a time-consuming process, too, and the development costs can be very high depending on the complexity of the project. For example, if you have 15 to 20 pages of story, and each page has backgrounds, lead-in animations, and five clickable elements that each do five random things, you end up with more than 500 illustrations! It's a lot of work, but if you have a strong story and a great developer, then go for it!"

business to create content, to preserve older content that might have prematurely gone out of print, and to leverage the mind-boggling number of devices in the hands of emerging, hesitant, and voracious readers of all ages. Some projections predict that there will be 250 million tablets in use within the next three years." Richter predicts, "You're going to see a collision of ebooks, enhanced ebooks and book apps, and I think all three will fold into one art form, which will become an industry entirely different from a book."

> **"Authors need to think more like illustrators in this arena, which will be daunting for some authors and thrilling and freeing for others."**

Into the Classroom

In the realm of educational publishing, Pfeffer believes, "Great textbook publishers will leverage the capability of digital publishing and tablets and apps to provide more successful learning outcomes for students. All the technologies that we are thrilled to see in apps will have much more profound impacts on learning and literacy. We've been stagnant for generations in graduating class after class with mediocre or poor results. Learning will be more engaging and more individualized. Technologies will help teachers teach more effectively. This will dovetail into more readers searching for more and more content in any form—printed book, ebook, and book apps."

Kripalani agrees. "The fact that the iPad2 can be connected to a large monitor is incredibly exciting, especially in the classroom setting. There is so much room for creativity and innovation in the area of integrated learning solutions both inside and outside of the classroom. The future for children's books apps includes a level of interactivity that will introduce significant awe, surprise, and ah-ha moments that no one has yet envisioned. The sheer number of mobile devices, both iOS and Android, is astounding and continues to grow. At the same time, the creativity and innovation with both devices and app development is exciting to follow and be a part of."

Words to the Wise

Dryden has spoken around the country on the subject of the digital landscape, advising authors, illustrators, and industry professionals on what they need to know and consider as the children's publishing industry reinvents itself in this digital age. "Authors are going to need to think as visually as possible in order to tell stories successfully through the app medium," she warns. "The technology of apps enables a lot of interactivity and flexibility for the child experiencing a story on an app, so it would behoove authors to think of their stories as mini-animations and to actually do some storyboarding as they write their stories in order to explore the possibilities and *extras* the technology can offer the story they want to tell. Yes, I am suggesting authors need to think a bit more like illustrators in this arena, which I know will be daunting for some authors, and thrilling and freeing for others. This is exciting territory for illustrators who already bring a form of visual pacing and visual cadence to their work; this is new territory for authors, but I think it can be fascinating for them. Above all, we need to remember the goal is to deliver excellent stories, whether the story is on an app or on pages."

Pfeffer agrees. "I'd offer the same advice I'd give to a writer seeking to be published in printed book form: imagine, experiment, innovate, and invent."

Kripalani suggests, "Take as much time and care choosing an app developer as you would choosing a publisher, and realize that the two are not one and the same. At Oceanhouse Media, we partner with great companies, we develop original ideas, we build exceptional apps, and we enjoy every minute of it. We are always looking for new children's book titles that would do well as a children's book app. Specifically, we'd like to speak with people who own the electronic or digital rights to books that have already been successful in print. The brand awareness that accompanies these books is key in making the apps stand out in this increasingly crowded market." (For a list of five questions Kripalani suggests children's authors ask book app developers with whom they are considering working, go to http://blog.bookmarket.com/2011/03/turn-your-book-into-app-5-questions-to.html.)

"If you're working in a native way, digitally, as an illustrator, you'll feel at home in this new market," states Richter. "I'd suggest authors think about their work in a way that's described as 3-D and become their own software engineer to some extent."

The world of children's book apps is bold and broad and rapidly evolving. Dryden offers a market picture. "Apps are a viable means of storytelling. We're at the very beginning of the app publishing revolution and so we're going to see a lot of apps that work, a lot of apps that don't work, a lot of app companies that succeed, and some app companies that fail. This is a heady time of experimentation and trial and error, but regardless of the outcome, apps for young readers and young adults are a means to reach readers where they live, in the digital space. It's well worth it for publishers, agents, illustrators, and authors to acquaint themselves with the possibilities the app technology has to offer and to try new forms of storytelling through the app medium."

Says Richter, "While it's hard to perfect or improve upon a great book, for those of us in this area, it's not our idea to improve upon the book. It's our intent to create an entirely new art form."

Let's Talk Nonfiction

Voice in Factual Writing

By Sue Bradford Edwards

L et's talk about voice. It seems as if talk about *voice* is everywhere. Speakers discuss it at writers' conferences. Magazines
and newsletters publish articles about it regularly. Search blogs
for posts on voice and you will find more than you can read in one
sitting. Voice is that important. One agent even says that by voice
alone she should be able to tell on page one if a story is a romance,
mystery, or historical fiction.

That is where the discussion often centers, on voice in fiction.
Fictional voice is tricky, shifting from story to story as an author
struggles to make each piece distinct and bring every point-of-view
character alive on the page.

Voice is no less vital for nonfiction writers because it helps pull
readers in, hooking them and not letting them go. Nonfiction voice
may be authoritative and scholarly, as in a literary journal; upbeat
and inspiring in a religious publication; objective and factual in a
news magazine; or humorous and personal for a general interest or
parenting publication. To understand how voice can be all of these
things, you must understand what it is.

Can You Hear Me?

At its simplest, voice is how you sound. It is what makes you sound like you. Not sure how you sound? Pay attention to your thoughts. Very few of us censor what scrolls through our heads, so our thoughts tend to reflect our true voice.

You create your voice by stringing words together. No two writers do it in quite the same way, and the voice that results begins with your own personal grammar. You may follow some rules of language slavishly and completely ignore others. Another component is word choice. Some writers tend toward threepenny words while others head straight for the ten-dollar variety. Then there is the rhythm of the sentences. Some writers rely mostly on short, choppy sentences. Others pen sentences that are longer, flowing, and possibly even serene. Mix these qualities together in various quantities and you have your voice.

No two writers sound quite alike even if they write in the same genre. Children's author Nicola Davies has a playful, humorous voice that is simultaneously smooth and elegant. Whether she is writing picture books or young adult novels, Jane Yolen's sophisticated voice is poetic and educated. These two wonderful voices would never be confused, although both generate the appeal that pulls young readers into their books.

Are You with Me?

Reader appeal is absolutely essential. To understand why it matters as much as it does, think back to memorable conferences, classes, or even sermons. You heard vibrant speakers who held your attention, and others who left you trying not to head-bob dozily.

"The author's voice, whether nonfiction or fiction, has to be one that the reader will not tire of," says author Richard Bank. "This is established early in the article or book, so it helps hook the reader in addition to the substance of the material. It's no different than hearing a speaker; you can usually tell in the first few minutes if you're going to be interested or find yourself drifting off to sleep."

~ Components of Voice ~

~ **Context:** formal or informal, factual or personal, depending on the market and audience

~ **Diction:** word choice, verbiage, level of vocabulary, formality or informality, regional words or dialect

~ **Point of view:** perspective from which information is presented; first, second or third person; authorial voice or a persona

~ **Rhythm:** movement of the language, timing, flow; tied to word choice and rhetorical devices like alliteration, assonance, repetition, and to sentence length and structure

~ **Syntax:** the arrangement of words and sentences, their length and structure, complexity of phrasing, grammar, punctuation, patterns, use of rhetorical devices (questions, repetition, etc.)

~ **Tone:** attitude, mood, feeling of the language

Essayist Dinty Moore agrees. "Your voice has to be appealing. We tend in real life to avoid people whose voices we find jarring, unpleasant, or unsettling," he says. "In the reverse, if we meet someone whose voice is friendly, comfortable, magnetic, we want to spend more time with that person. It is the same on the page."

If you want to draw in people with your voice, it helps if you write with enthusiasm. Perhaps you have a long-held passion for a topic, or you gained enthusiasm for it as you dove into the research. Either way, if your voice reflects this, it will engage the reader.

"I tell kids all the time, if I was forced to write a book about car engines, it would be a terrible book because I'm not interested in knowing how they work," says children's nonfiction author Kelly Millner Halls. "I love my book topics and that energy is obvious in my writer's voice. Those two things combined—preparedness and enthusiasm—lead to a strong nonfiction voice."

Whether your topic is a penguin colony or eco-friendly building products, whether your piece takes the form of creative nonfiction, personal experience, an essay, an industry article, or exposé, you will be more likely to hook readers if you write with enthusiasm. Think about the difference in how you sound when you discuss a favorite hobby versus when you are forced to recount a tedious meeting. Is it any surprise that the first engages your listener while the latter drives them away?

Disinterest in a subject is only one way to dull your voice and lose readers. Poor voice can also be the result of simply sounding false, mechanical, and flat; it can be clumsy, awkward, and hard to read. Problems with voice may come about when you try to write how you think an essayist, creative nonfiction author, or hard-hitting journalist *should* sound. You will sound phony, like you are trying too hard.

Whatever the reason for your poorly developed voice, any voice that cannot communicate with the reader is a problem. If an editor perceives a problem, you will be asked to do something about it. "A little more than 20 years ago, after I had been publishing nonfiction and some fiction for a number of years, the editor of my first book told me the following after reading my manuscript: 'This is good. Now, go and find your voice.' That's about the only good advice there is," says Bank. "It's a question of self-discovery. I followed his suggestion; I had no choice if I wanted the book to be published, and ultimately did find my voice. My writing was much different than it was before and once discovered, this voice has remained a constant in all my work whether nonfiction, creative nonfiction, or even fiction."

Even if you have never thought overtly about your distinctive writing voice, you probably have one even if you do not use it consistently. "Voice is a matter of sounding like one's self, not like one's English teacher in grade school. Often, to find her voice, a writer needs to loosen up some, not stiffen around the rules," says Moore. "There is no one-size-fits-all answer to this, so first of all the writer needs to be sensitive to tone and deliberate regarding the personality that comes through on the page."

At one point everything you wrote reflected you personally. You spoke in your own voice when you wrote notes to your friends in school, or in your diary entries, or in letters to family and friends. Along the way a well-meaning teacher may have critiqued what you wrote, trying to improve spelling and punctuation, but it may also have impeded your word choice and the rhythm of your writing. A teacher—or you yourself—may have struggled to shoe-horn your writing into a box of rules. While grammatical writing and clear communication are important, along the way you may have subverted style and stopped sounding like yourself.

If you have mislaid your voice, and write only within the rule box, your writing could sound clinical and dull. Perhaps an editor or writing buddy has told you to *develop* your voice. For Banks, that is not completely on point: "I don't think it's a matter of developing one's own voice but rather discovering or finding it."

Artist, find thyself? Paradoxically, realizing just how important voice is to your nonfiction can make it harder to find. But there are ways to bring it to the forefront.

Take a Deep Breath and Relax

The solution is to relax into your writing. Some authors transition into their writing by—writing. Not writing for publication, but journaling or free-writing. Author Julia Cameron, famous for her book *The Artist's Way* (Tarcher/Penguin), recommends writing morning pages, which consist of writing anything that comes to your mind for three pages. The process is intended as an exercise or a cleansing routine, like going for a jog or taking a shower.

Another option is to blog. Many writers view their blogs as conversations with their audience. They take a more relaxed approach to this kind of writing and it shows. "Your voice emerges when you blog because your voice emerges as you have this conversation," says author and writing coach Bobbi Linkemer. If you are struggling with a nonfiction writing project and cannot get the tone, the style, the voice right, write a blog post or two and then return to your current project. Does it sound any more like you?

Another way to relax into your writing is to tell your story. This technique is recommended by Tristine Rainer in *Your Life as Story* (Tarcher/Penguin). Pretend you are telling your story to a friend and record it. If you feel self-conscious while trying to tell your story to a recorder, you may stiffen up and the result will be no more naturally you than anything else. If this happens, invite a friend over to be your audience. Really tell your story to your friend with the recorder running in the background. Then transcribe your words and begin to rewrite. Working from an oral version can help weed out flowery or abstract language, or overly long or structured sentences. These are problematic because they create distance between you, the writer, and the reader. Your voice must let the reader in and make a connection.

Moore amplifies this idea: "Imagine you are telling the story to your very best friend. Let the words that reveal your personality shine through. Don't avoid colloquialisms or slang. Don't be a slave to correct usage. Be who you are, the friendly you. Eventually, in revision, you might want to tighten your prose and adjust the formality or informality of language up or down some, but choking your individual way of speaking on the page in the early drafts will only ensure lifeless prose. There is enough lifeless prose in the world. Don't add to it."

However you get the first draft down, read your piece aloud as you rewrite. "Trust your ear," says Moore. "Read your work out loud to yourself at every step of revision. Not in your head, but actually out loud. Listen for false notes, awkward phrasings, formalities and constructions that don't sound natural, and fix them. Your family will think you've lost your senses, but your writing will suddenly improve by leaps and bounds." You will find yourself telling your story to your reader like never before.

Voice & Persona

Once you have identified your own nonfiction voice and are comfortable in it, you will need to fit it to the market and a specific topic. Part of this is being aware of your personal style: Are you learned, balanced, and objective? Intense and personal? Humorous or chatty, like talking to a friend over coffee? How readers perceive you through any given piece of writing is your author's persona.

"Voice and persona are often so intertwined they cannot be separated, and persona often depends on the subject at hand. Do you need to sound authoritative, or do you want to befriend the reader by admitting your own vulnerabilities?" asks Moore. An inspirational piece would benefit from the latter while a political or social commentary would demand the former. Yet one author, with one voice, could write both, adopting two slightly different personas.

Compare this to someone in another creative medium: Rod Stewart was among the most successful of British rock stars in the 1970s and yet he reinvented his musical career in the last decade by singing American pop classics by composers like George Gershwin and Cole Porter. Stewart's voice did not change. He adapted it to the form and the market; it remains clearly recognizable as Stewart's very distinct vocals.

In much the same way, writers can shape their voice to suit a wide variety of markets and topics. A piece of creative nonfiction about a Civil War battle may have a tense, driving voice while the voice you present for an essay in a women's magazine can range from chatty to snarky. One writer can do both, and probably will have to do both to sell well.

Adapting is something writers must learn to do to sell their work widely, even if writing for only one niche, such as parenting magazines or children's magazines. "For ten years, I wrote for dozens of magazines and newspapers, prior to writing books. I learned how to adapt my writer's voice to meet each of those editors' specific needs," says Halls. "For example, the *Chicago Tribune KidNews* liked sass and slang. *Highlights for Children* did not. It was my job to adapt to their editorial purposes, and I think I did it well. Confidence and enthusiasm were still core, but my voice had to be more flexible. In books, it's more a matter of being age-appropriate. Younger kids need simplicity, where older kids allow for more detail. But my basic voice is now consistent, in developmental increments."

Halls did not abandon her voice, but altered her style, much as you do with personal correspondence. An email to your BFF sounds different from an email response to your editor, yet each reflect the voice that is you and you alone. In the same way, your style needs to vary with the writing project you have undertaken. A piece of creative nonfiction about honey bees will have a completely different style from a piece on how to build a sofa from upcycled doors. Different still will be an exposé on corruption in the local school district, yet each piece can and should reflect your author's voice.

Style and voice overlap, and some writers' voices make them more suitable for certain styles of writing than others. This may mean that your voice is perfect for an inspirational magazine but not ideal for investigative writing. Fine-tuning your voice for a publication is one thing, bending it out of shape to try to meet a publisher's needs is another.

"It's like how you dress when you go different places. Be authentic but be appropriate," says Linkemer. "Don't wear a suit to a farm. Don't wear jeans and loafers with no socks to a bank." Bring out the best that you have to suit a particular situation.

Rediscovering and refining your nonfiction voice sounds like work, and it is, but it is also a journey of self-discovery. "I just wrote a memoir about my career," Linkemer says. "I gave a copy to my oldest friend in St. Louis and she was reading it. She called and said, 'As I'm reading I'm hearing you speaking in my ear.'"

Do not be afraid to try a new type of nonfiction and modulate your voice. When you are done adapting your voice to the necessary style, set the piece aside. Then after some time has passed, read it out loud. Does it still sound true? If not, tinker with it and try it again.

Learn to whisper into the ear of an editor and his readers. Speak in a voice that is for him and him alone, and you will find your byline appearing in magazines and on bookshelves like never before.

The Wisdom of Scheherazade

Novel Structure

By Sharelle Byars Moranville

When King Shahryar drew Scheherazade into his incense redolent bedchamber, they both knew her fate. She would be beheaded at dawn. But with a clatter of castanets and a musical voice, Scheherazade surprised the sultan by drawing him into a bedtime story. With gentle rhythms, she led him in farther and farther until his affections for her characters grew, and the sultan settled back on his pillows, finding the storytelling very nice indeed.

Just when he was getting deeply comfortable, the rhythms of the story grew unpredictable and troublesome. The character Shahryar had come to love was in peril. The plot ensnared him. The complications grew and at midnight, wide-eyed, he sat up on the cushions, gazing at Scheherazade when the best story he had ever heard took an unexpected turn. He became so caught up in the rising complication, so curious about what would happen next, that he forgot to clap for his for his usual aphrodisiac. Just when the story reached its greatest intensity and King Shahryar had forgotten who he was—the sultan who had his brides beheaded at daybreak—Scheherazade drifted to the window where the melon of the moon had dropped from the sky and the hand of dawn opened her delicate fingers.

The king would have to wait for the rest of the story. Night after night, Scheherazade followed this basic pattern and King Shahryar never grew weary of her.

~

In his timeless classic on novel writing, *Aspects of the Novel,* E. M. Forster says that Scheherazade perfectly grasped the most fundamental aspect of the novel: a good story that holds and ultimately satisfies the reader's curiosity.

Authors may hold a reader's curiosity with a cast of fresh, unpredictable characters, a compelling fantasy world, or a plot that never lags. But what saved Scheherazade was structure. She hit her marks night after night. Quarter point, midpoint, build to climax, break for the business of the kingdom, dénouement.

These are the elements of the classic story arc. This arc is the fundamental structure of both the entirety of the modern novel and every scene within it. Tensions rise gradually from the beginning to the quarter point as the reader comes to care about the characters in their fictional world. At the quarter point, the protagonist is forced out of whatever level of comfort has existed until that moment and problems begin to build. At the midpoint is a jolt—a surprise, a reversal, or an astonishing revelation (something to make the sultan's eyes pop open at midnight with renewed interest). At the three-fourths point (the climax) pressures on the protagonist have accumulated to such intensity that they simply have to turn into resolution. The story ends with the satisfaction of a good dénouement as the reader enjoys a wiser, stronger, more empowered protagonist.

While the story arc is the structural backbone, the author has a thousand and one ways to build the narration and to pattern language to flesh it out. The simplest is a *linear story* told by one narrator, the conventional structure in novels for young readers especially.

The *hero's journey,* as explained by Joseph Campbell in *The Hero with a Thousand Faces*, is commonly represented by points on a circle—the call to adventure, events of separation, initiation into the unknown, and a point at which the hero makes a critical choice or

~ Mark the Arc ~

To learn more about story structure, try this experiment with a few novels.

Before you begin to read, eyeball the novel for the middle and put a sticky note there. Then estimate the quarter point and three-fourths point and place two more sticky notes. As you read, and after you have finished the novel, see if those three sticky notes mark (within a few pages):

(1) the point where the main character is forced irrevocably out of his or her old world,

(2) an unusually dramatic development, and

(3) where resolution begins.

performs a critical act before the returning. The journey is substantively the same as the classic story arc. In both story structure paradigms the protagonist arrives home (literally or metaphorically) the same, but different—having been rounded by the journey.

Complications

Young adult and adult novels offer more room for structural complexity in building the story arc. Jan Blazanin's *A & L Do Summer* (Egmont) is a funny and tender story of two girlfriends' romp through the summer between their junior and senior year in high school. Blazanin says of the novel's structure, "The plot is straightforward and linear, cause and effect, action and reaction. Laurel, the L in A & L, prefers to act first and think about it later, which keeps Aspen busy putting out fires. The plot moves quickly in chronological fashion from one event to the next."

But Blazanin does not have a purely linear structure. "I use flash-backs to show readers the consequences of some of Aspen and Laurel's impulsive actions. For example, the morning after the girls'

~ Linear, Circular ~

The structure of a children's novel is often linear, or like the hero's journey as described by Joseph Campbell in *The Hero with a Thousand Faces*, circular. An example is *Wasatch Summer* (Bonneville Books/Cedar Fort). Anola Pickett bases the story on the life of a real girl who lived in Utah in the late nineteenth century. In the first quarter of the novel, Pickett draws the reader deeply into the sensibility of 11-year-old Hannah so that when Hannah discovers she is being sent to the mountains of the Cache Valley by herself to graze the sheep for the summer, the reader, like King Shahryar, feels very unsettled.

At the quarter point, Hannah is alone in the darkness, gripping her doll baby in one hand and a rifle in the other, unable to sleep. The next morning, she sees Indians watching her. While the Blackfeet become her cherished friends, at first they are terrifying. As the days progress, a bear kills another shepherd on the mountain and is probably the predator that rips the throat out of Hannah's faithful herd dog, Shep. Hannah is frightened of the bear, but at the same time repelled at the notion of having to kill it.

At the midpoint, life becomes even more challenging when Hannah slips on the rocks and falls, hurting herself so badly that she must suffer the strange and frightening ministrations of a medicine woman. Meanwhile, the bear comes ever closer and finally crosses the stream into camp, cornering Hannah. Alone, Hannah faces the bear with a brave combination of chutzpah and noise—yielding a terrific *climactic moment* at exactly the three-quarters point:

> My feet burned. Hollering seared my throat. Smacking the pan numbed my hands. Worn out, I stopped to listen. No grunt. No roar. The bear had gone.
> Go!
> I jumped off the tub and scrambled into the camp. Bolted the door and crawled under the covers . . . boots, clothes, and all. I piled on more blankets to quiet my shivers and burrowed into the

~ Linear, Circular ~

farthest corner of the bunk. Thank you, Heavenly Father. When my trembles slowed, I dragged my charm string from under the pillow and fingered the black button from Grandma's coat. My bear's eye button. Liza Lou huddled with me as I stroked the smooth circle.

I spent the night awake, thinking about the danger I'd faced. I had sent the bear away without hurting her.

Without hurting me.

In discussing how the structure of the story changed as it went through revision, Pickett says, "At first I tried to stick to the real story as it had been told to me. In the original story, Hannah returns to her mountain post for eight summers until she marries. My first version opened as Hannah looks back at her summers in the mountains. I struggled with this structure and it became unwieldy. Not only unwieldy, but uninteresting and flat.

"Deciding to tell the story of her first summer made the structure much stronger—and easier to write. Then I did what many writers do. I started with a lot of backstory that slowed things down and became a sort of info dump. Once I made myself cut that and get to the story, things flowed."

The dénouement was revised in the editing process. Pickett explains, "The story originally ended with Hannah's brother telling her that she could stay on until summer's end and Hannah happily accepting that. The editor at Bonneville noted that the ending seemed unsatisfactory. She gave me no specific direction, so I took my time to figure out what made it was lacking.

"Luckily, a member of my critique group shared notes from a workshop about the [circular] hero's journey, and a week or two later it dawned on me that she had given me the answer. Hannah needed to complete her hero's journey by returning home, having been changed by her experiences and victories in the mountains. That did the trick!"

~ Study the Structure ~

disastrous barn party incident, Aspen reflects on the uproar when her parents arrive to collect her at the police station. The flashback provides the reader with necessary information about that ill-fated episode and Aspen's feelings about the event as she looks back on it."

Blazanin, like many writers, experimented with the structure of *A & L Do Summer* before it came right for her and her editor. "At first I considered shifting the first-person viewpoint between Aspen and Laurel. But that didn't seem the right way to show Laurel's cluelessness about all things country. When I decided to make Aspen the straight man to Laurel's antics, I knew I'd made the right choice." She continues, "One structural change I made during revisions was to flesh out those flashbacks. In the early drafts, Aspen's glimpses into the past were sketchy, more telling than showing. Ruth Katcher, my editor at Egmont Publishing, suggested that I build the flashbacks into scenes with action, emotion, and dialogue. Of course, she was right."

While Blazanin assesses the structure of her novel as "straight-forward," she cites A. S. King's *Please Ignore Vera Dietz* (Knopf) as a great example of a young adult novel with a more complicated structure. "King deals with the challenge of multiple viewpoints and numerous time shifts by using the heading of each section to tell the reader who is speaking, when the event takes place, and frequently the setting as well. King takes a complex structure, which could have been overwhelming, and makes it accessible to the reader."

Wendy Delsol's adult novel, *The McLoud Home for Wayward Girls* (Penguin), posed structural challenges because it covers multiple generations and has a twist that, like Scheherazade's tales, makes timing everything. Delsol says of her writing process: "Not only did I have three narrators, but I also had three distinct time periods: present-day, the mid-1990s, and the mid-1960s. In order to situate the reader, introduce the characters, and set up the central problem, the first few chapters were present-day. From there, I did find a somewhat natural unfolding of history. As information became necessary to the reader, I inserted flashback chapters. Nonetheless, as this novel contains a twist, there was a very important timing element to the narrative. The most difficult aspect of the structure was withholding certain informa-tion until the climax."

After the novel was acquired, Delsol says, her editor had helpful structural ideas. "Because there are timeline shifts and because two narrators have flashback chapters, my editor suggested that each character segue differently into their memories. For an older character there is virtually no transition; the setting, dialogue, context immedi-ately transitions the reader into the past, the 1960s in this case. For the main character, she begins in a present-day setting and something jars her memory. Though it wasn't a major structural change, it was the kind of finesse that kept the characters and voices distinct within the framework of the story."

Musicality

Delsol cites Anita Shreve's *The Weight of Water* (Back Bay) as an example of structural excellence. "It is the story of a photojournalist who travels to a remote island to research two century-old murders. In the first chapter, Shreve writes, 'When I look at the photographs, it is hard not to think: We had seventeen hours then, or twelve, or three.' This sentence—a warning, really—tells us so much about what is to come, about the structure. We know, for instance, that the narrator is telling the story with perspective. To phrase it as 'we had seventeen hours,' foreshadows some kind of loss. The chapters traveling back to the time of the murders are structured as testimony that the photographer discovers in her research: records from a survivor told 26 years after the events. There is a symmetry at work between the present day story—one of loss and betrayal—and the past murder mystery."

Another example of structural richness is Barbara Kingsolver's *The Lacuna* (HarperColllins). Protagonist Harrison Shepherd lives a precarious life as the son of a Mexican mother with a wandering eye and a flair for American slang. He works as a plaster mixer for revolutionary artist Diego Rivera, and is the intimate of Diego's artist wife Frida Khalo. Harrison works as a cook in the Mexican household where Leon Trotsky is murdered; becomes an art mover during World War II when the National Gallery is vulnerable, a successful and beloved novelist, and a victim of the times. The novel is about the memoir he never wrote. Frida tells him, "The most important thing about a person is always the thing you don't know." Harrison says of his own writing, "the most important part of any story is the missing piece."

As the title *The Lacuna*—meaning a missing piece, a gap—suggests, much of the power of the story comes from what is missing. Violet Brown, the archivist of Harrison's notebooks, functions as an important character in the story and as narrator as a structural element. She brings the novel full circle by describing her last trip with Harrison to the Mexican village of his boyhood. In the final chapter, Brown sits on the beach with her book as Shepherd swims out in search of the lacuna, an opening in the side of a cliff that is only accessible during the lowest of tides. As a boy, Harrison was fascinated by the lacuna after a servant told him that it was one of many holes "so deep they go to the center of the earth and you'll see the devil at the bottom. But some only go through the island to the other side."

The lacuna reflects the novel's signature structural pattern, as devouring mouth, passageway, and as something missing—notebooks, manuscripts, bits of memoir. But it is by no means the only pattern. Frida's hidden physical deformities have a rhythm throughout the novel. Other elements that repeat and contribute to the overall pattern include Harrison's mother's slang, her lovers, Violet's voice as an archivist, bits and pieces of manuscripts from Harrison's fiction. Even Trotsky's chickens, when used in subtle repetitive rhythms, contribute to the bones of this beautifully constructed book.

In *Aspects of the Novel*, Forster discusses pattern and rhythm as elements of structure. He says, "I doubt that it can be achieved by the writers who plan their books beforehand, it has to depend on a local impulse when the right interval is reached. But the effect can be exquisite. . . ." Forster analogizes writing to musical rhythms, both in their simplicity and complexity. "Rhythm is sometimes quite easy. Beethoven's Fifth Symphony, for instance, starts with the rhythm *did-didy dum*, which we can all hear and tap to. But the symphony as a whole has also a rhythm—due mainly to the relation between its movements—which some people can hear but no one can tap to."

These subtle rhythms and patterns can be found in novels with very simple structure. In *Wasatch Summer*, for example, Hannah's "charm string" is introduced in the opening pages, and appears periodically, each time in relation to Hannah's growth. The charm string is a collection of buttons and charms that is important because, her mother says, when she has collected and strung a thousand buttons and charms, she will meet her true love. The fragility of the charm string, and the rarity of buttons and charms in nineteenth-century Utah, makes it an important symbol of the passage to young womanhood. Its repeated presence in the story becomes one of the delightful structural rhythms—*leitmotifs*—"that some can hear, but no one can tap to."

Plotters & Pantsers

There are as many patterns and rhythms as there are novels, even with a universal story arc. Each writer has to find the way to incorporate the structural particulars. Delsol says, "For me, it works best to set out by establishing a few plot points; they can be as simple as three or four major events. I treat these as milestones among which I am free to narrate the course of action. Within the writing community, there is a *plotter versus pantser* debate. Plotters create detailed synopses before writing chapter one. A by-the-seat-of-his-or-her-pants type, on the other hand, has no set course or even an ending in mind. He or she writes scene by scene as the story dictates. Because I see advantages to both, I've found that a strategy somewhere between the two gives me both adequate direction as well as room to discover."

Studying successful or favorite novels can help hone your structural skills. But borrowing without discretion does not work. Blazanin points out, "Many young adult novels with nontraditional structures are being spotlighted with media buzz and awards. I think that kind of attention can put pressure on authors who want to be noticed. They try to write stories with complicated time shifts, multiple viewpoints, and secrets that don't really need to be kept from the reader."

She continues, "My suggestion for novelists is not to be so dazzled by the structures other writers use that they blindly mimic them. Each writer must study her story, consider several structures, and select the structure that works. If it's a tale best told through flashbacks, dream sequences, and multiple viewpoints, dig in! But don't fragment a linear storyline merely for the sake of novelty, or you'll be setting yourself up for disaster."

The backbone, the story arc, needs to be there by the definition of novel. But the other structural details—patterns of narration, shaping of timeline, organization into sections and chapters, repetitions with variations, cumulative patterns—will be unique. If the structure tells the tale the best way it can be told, then it is the right structure.

Sophisticated Show & Tell

Bring Your Story World to Life

By Chris Eboch

Surely every writer gets tired of the "show, don't tell." It may be good advice, but what exactly does it mean, and how do you do it? The phrase may have become cliché, but learning what it really means and polishing this skill will help your stories shine.

"As an author, reader, and editor, showing and not telling makes a world of difference in how I perceive a story," says Penny Lockwood Ehrenkranz, who is an editor at MuseItUp Publishing and Damnation Books. "It takes years of practice to craft a story with vivid action, dialogue, and scenes. Writing that tells instead of shows the reader what's happening is dull and boring and will be quickly tossed aside in favor of a story which brings the characters and world to life."

Ehrenkranz offers an example from "Ashley of Ashland," a short story in *A Past and A Future* (Sam's Dot Publishing), her collection of fantasy and science fiction short stories.

> A small group of musicians, gaily dressed in green and gold brocade, played a rollicking dance tune. Dancers of all ages bobbed, swayed, curtseyed, and bowed to each other as

their feet flashed through intricate dance steps. Serving girls wove among the dancers, tankards of ale and goblets of wine balanced on their huge trays. Ashley sighed and turned back to his fire; he had never managed to conquer those dance steps.

Ehrenkranz comments, "As you can see, I've shown the reader a vivid picture and involved the senses of hearing, sight, and taste, allowing the reader to become fully enmeshed in my story." This example also hints at Ashley's feelings about dancing, through his actions (sighing and turning away) and his specific thoughts.

Authors of historical fiction, fantasy, and science fiction should be especially careful to show life rather than tell about it. It is tempting to describe and explain everything you know about the time and place, either because you are afraid readers will not understand the culture or because of your own enthusiasm for this strange world. But resist the urge to explain it all, and instead show the place by showing people in action. In my Egyptian mystery for kids, *The Eyes of Pharaoh* (Pig River Press), I tried to weave in details without stopping the plot:

Seshta ran. Her feet pounded the hard-packed dirt street. She lengthened her stride and raised her face to Ra, the sun god. Her ba, the spirit of her soul, sang at the feel of her legs straining, her chest thumping, her breath racing.

She sped along the edge of the market, dodging shoppers. A noblewoman in a transparent white dress skipped out of the way and glared.

In just a few lines, readers learn the setting (dirt street, market), cultural details (noblewoman), and religious references (Ra, the ba). But they are all conveyed within the action, as the main character races toward her goal.

Janice Hardy, author of the middle-grade trilogy, The Healing Wars

(Balzer & Bray), says, "Showing allows the readers to lose themselves in the story. They can imagine what's going on based on the details and figure things out on their own, which is more rewarding than being told what things are. It's like the difference between being told about a new movie versus going to see it."

Vivid, Not Vague

To show, use clear and specific language. Look again at the example from "Ashley of Ashland." If Ehrenkranz had written simply that "people danced and girls served drinks," the setting could be a modern bar. Instead, note how the strong, specific nouns and verbs create a clearer picture to bring that time and place to life.

When you use adjectives, watch for vague words such as *big* or *small*, *young* or *old*. To me, the term *young girl* suggests a child no more than six years old. But I have heard the phrase used to describe a woman in her early 20s. Factual details or clear comparisons are less open to interpretation, so be precise: Instead of saying that a man is a big guy, you might say that he's 6'4" tall and 300 pounds, or he is built like a sumo wrestler. Specifics are especially important when writing for or about children, as a child may have a very different idea of what constitutes big or small, young or old. To a kindergartner, a 40-year-old teacher is ancient.

As for adverbs, some writers recommend avoiding them whenever possible. Adverbs may, on rare occasion, have their place, but often they are a lazy alternative to the harder work of showing with strong verbs. If someone *walked slowly*, did he stroll, stumble, shuffle, or limp? Those are all slow ways of walking, but each looks different to a viewer and has different connotations.

Hardy offers this suggestion for telling the difference between telling and showing: "One trick I use is to ask if I can act out whatever it is I'm describing. If the sentence is 'I hate you,' she said angrily,' I can actually say 'I hate you' but I can't act 'angrily.' Try to be *angrily*. You can't. But you can act out things that show anger. You can scream, you can yell, you can pound a fist on the table. But *angrily* isn't something you can physically do.".

Different people express their anger in different ways, from silent-
ly seething to screaming and throwing things, so showing the anger
through specific actions and words creates a clearer picture—and
one that shows much more about that character.

As Hardy's example demonstrates, *showing* uses sense data, information perceivable by one of the five senses. *Telling* interprets or
explains that data. If a character sees or hears something frightening,
the author is explaining that the character should be frightened. To
show, draw on the five senses—what the character can see, hear,
smell, feel, or taste—so that we sense the fear too. Physical sensa-
tions can include a pounding heart or sweating palms, as a character sees moving shadows and hears rustling in the bushes. You can
also include direct thoughts, such as "Just a few more seconds and
he'll find my hiding place!" or "What is that moving in the shadows
—human, animal, or monster?"

Specific thoughts can be used to show regardless of your point of
view. When writing in full third person, give the words the most
immediate kind of showing by avoiding phrases such as *he wondered, he thought about,* and *he knew,* which put the reader one step
away from the character. Instead of telling us, "He wondered what to
do next," show his thought: "What should he do next?"

Whose Views?

Point of view is one of the best tools for showing since it lets
readers see how the character experiences the world. A story told
from the outside, either as a too distant omniscient narrator or in
poorly written and *telling* first or third person, can make it difficult
for writers and readers alike to get to know and understand the
character well.

Hardy says that learning to show "allowed me to get deeper into
the heads of my characters, and thus craft a more immersive story. I
wasn't just describing events like I was covering a sport and explaining
the play by play. It made things more realistic, more unpredictable,

and more enjoyable for the reader. They got to live in my world, not just watch it from the outside."

There is no single correct point of view, and the correct choice depends on what the author is trying to accomplish. The distant omniscience of a strong authorial presence works in the novels of many of the Victorian masters, like Charles Dickens, George Eliot, and Thomas Hardy, or epics like the Lord of the Rings trilogy. A

Showing uses sense data, information perceivable by one of the senses. *Telling* interprets or explains that data.

second option is to have an omniscient narrator, as distinct from the author, as Hermann Melville did in *Bartleby, the Scrivener* and *Moby Dick*, Mark Twain in *Huckleberry Finn,* and J. D. Salinger in *Catcher in the Rye.* These viewpoints can be written in the first person or third, from the protagonist's perspective or another's narration.

Certainly, modern novels tend toward a more limited and intimate viewpoint that allows readers to feel close to a character, experiencing his or her life from the inside. This does not mean a novel has to have a single viewpoint. Many mystery novelists like to drop in brief third-person scenes from the villain's viewpoint. Romance novels may shift between the hero's and heroine's viewpoint, allowing the reader to understand how each one is feeling. Any viewpoint can work, so long as it is clearly established and used consistently.

Whatever viewpoint you choose, staying close to your characters can help you show their experiences. "One of the best tools for avoiding telling is to really understand point of view," Hardy says. "If you're solid in a character's head, everything you describe will be from their perspective, so it'll feel shown, even if it's not. You'll be able to see the story world through that character's eyes and show

~ Publishers & Authors ~

~ **Damnation Books:** www.damnationbooks.com. An epubisher of dark fiction created in 2009 to separate somewhat from the romance epublishers who also publish dark fiction. Its subgenres include AI (artficial intelligence), alien, fantasy, ghost, historical, horror, military, monster, paranormal, psychological, urban fantasy, vampire, and Western, among others. Open to unsolicited submissions of short stories, novellas, and novels.

~ **MuseItUp Publishing:** http://museituppublishing.com. An epublisher that opened two years ago. It is open to new and established writers. Genres of interest are romance, paranormal, fantasy, mystery, suspense, thrillers, horror, science fiction, and YA. Its MuseItYoung division publishes crossover chapter books for tweens. Open to submissions, though it closes for short periods; look also for the Editors Call for Submissions for specific needs. (http://museituppublishing. blogspot.com/p/editors-call-for-submissions.html)

~ **Sam's Dot Publishing:** http://samsdotpublishing.com. A small press that publishes a variety of magazines in speculative fiction genres, as well as ebooks. Guidelines are available on the website, and vary among the publications.

Authors

~ Chris Eboch: www.chriseboch.com

~ Penny Lockwood Ehrenkranz: http:pennylockwoodehrenkranz.yola-site.com

~ Janice Hardy: www.janicehardy.com

what they see and how they feel about it."

This means becoming your character and staying authentic to how the character views the world. In one novel I read, an undercover agent who grew up poor in a bad neighborhood is searching a woman's bedroom. He notices "petit-point pillows and romantic priscilla curtains." Really? Or would such a man simply notice "fancy embroidered pillows and ruffled curtains"?

The more unusual the world, the more important it is to show through viewpoint. "Point of view is the perfect tool for showing in a fantasy world," Hardy says. "A character will have opinions about what they see and the world they live in. Those opinions will influence how they describe the world around them, and allow the author to show how that world works by how the character interacts with it."

Often what you do not say is as important as what you do say. "A character who doesn't bat an eye while wizards fling spells around shows that magic is a natural part of that world and considered commonplace," Hardy notes. "Treating the sudden appearance of gods as normal occurrences shows that gods interfere and regularly make themselves known. The point-of-view character can make the fantasy world feel real to the reader by looking at it as they would see it. As soon as the author steps back and starts describing as [he or she] imagine[s] it, that told feeling can start slipping in."

When writing science fiction, fantasy, or historical fiction, you may occasionally want to break the rule about avoiding adjectives that are open to interpretation, to show an unfamiliar attitude. Still, to be true to your characters you have to trust your readers to notice and interpret shown details. For example, in my Mayan historical drama, *The Well of Sacrifice* (Clarion), the narrator describes her sister like this: "Feather was beautiful even as a child. . . . Her dark, slanting eyes were crossed, and her high forehead was flattened back in a straight line from her long nose." This uses the vague adjective *beautiful*, but then adds the details about the girl's eyes, forehead, and nose to show the different Mayan interpretation of beauty. To be true to your characters you have to trust your readers to notice and interpret shown details. In *The Well of Sacrifice*, I could not explain that the Maya did not have wheeled vehicles; I could only show them traveling by foot or canoe.

Once you get in the showing habit, it is great fun to create your story world through specific details, the five senses, and a close viewpoint. But do not get carried away and try to include every item in a scene or every nuance of gesture and voice. Too many details get in the way of the story, so focus on the information or mood you want to convey. One or two details, shown well, should be enough to bring your scene to vivid life so your readers feel like they are there, seeing for themselves.

Tension: Create a Magical Experience

By Leslie J. Wyatt

Tension. As readers, we know what it feels like: the worry lurking in the background, the growing intensity that keeps you turning page after page long after you told yourself to shut off the light and go to sleep. Whether it is the heart-thumping, chest-twisting, cannot-put-it-down suspense of a murder mystery, the emotional rollercoaster of a coming-of-age story for young adult readers, or a bedtime picture book, tension is a vital element in a compelling story.

For writers, tension is not so easily defined. "It is a reader's word, not a writer's word," says Jon Franklin. Best known for his pioneering work in New Journalism, Franklin's credits include two first-in-category Pulitzer Prizes, professorships at several universities, numerous articles and stories, and five books, including *The Wolf in the Parlor: How the Dog Came to Share Your Brain* (St. Martin's Griffin). Franklin states, "Tension is a combination of many technical things, but when they're all put together, they keep the reader hypnotized by what's going to come next."

Jeanne DuPrau concurs. She is the author of fiction and nonfiction for adults and children that includes the four Books of Ember (Random

143

House); *The City of Ember* has won numerous awards and appeared on the *New York Times* bestseller list. DuPrau says that while tension is not the only thing that makes readers turn the page, young readers usually want plot, as do most other age groups, and tension drives plot.

"Books are boring without tension," says Rene Gutteridge, award-winning author and screenwriter whose credits include 17 novels, including *Possession* and *Listen* (Tyndale House). "We like characters to say and do things we wouldn't in real life . . . or maybe we just might! We like to see them enduring the worst fate, and then we marvel at how they overcome it."

Author Lea Wait puts it this way: "Tension in the plot is what keeps the reader turning pages, keeps the protagonist focused on his or her goals, and keeps the writer up at night at night thinking up new twists and turns and problems for the protagonist to face. Tension is what changes a manuscript from *well-written* to *a great read!*" Wait is author of the five-book Shadows Antique Print Mystery series, which was nominated for the Agatha Award, as well as numerous middle grade and YA historical novels.

The Essential Element

If you have ever set up an elaborate pattern of dominoes, you know the task takes time and effort. Yet watching them fall, each triggering the next—around, across, over, through—the event seems almost magical. What we feel as we watch those dominoes go down is similar to what a reader feels as a story unfolds. In much the same way, components of the writing craft work together to create what the reader will ultimately experience as tension. If we have done our job well, our readers will be too caught up in the experience to see beyond the smoke and mirrors to the actual techniques.

Tension in a story is a factor of structure or plot, pacing, complication, and climax and resolution. "The reader has to trust that you're going someplace. That's the beginning of tension," says Franklin. Readers want to reach the destination the writer has launched them toward, and all the obstacles the story's characters encounter help create an *oh no!* response—tension—as the promised goal seems increasingly impossible to attain. In turn, the obstacles, difficulties, problems all boil down to one essential component of tension—conflict.

"I have to present a problem that needs to be solved (or a conflict that must be dealt with, or a question that must be answered)," DuPrau explains, "and I have to give this problem to my characters, make the characters interesting and/or likeable enough so that readers care about them and their fate, and then arrange events so

L ike the magic in watching an elaborate pattern of dominos fall, readers feel the pleasing tension as a story as a story unfolds.

that the characters have to struggle against increasingly difficult obstacles on their way to solving the problem. That struggle creates the story's tension."

Gutteridge agrees about the necessity of *plaguing* characters. "We really must make things hard for the poor souls. I read a lot of new manuscripts where the writer puts down a nice scene, but nothing happens. There's no inner or outer turmoil. It's a lot of dialogue about nothing. Maybe there's a little info fed in, but that's not what you want ruling your scene. You want tension, with info sprinkled in, not the other way around."

Not having any, or very little, tension is a problem for many writers. Wait points to internally focused character-driven adult fiction and books for children about everyday life as two types of books that may suffer in this way, and DuPrau agrees. Having a story meander along without any significant problems and without the characters getting into any big trouble is a common mistake writers make, as is having conflict completely exterior to the characters, which DuPrau describes as having the main characters "simply observe the trouble and not play an active part in causing it, suffering from it, and resolving it."

Planning for Tension

Many writers build tension into the planning process. "If my plot doesn't involve tension, then there's no story. So tension is built into every one of my books from the beginning," says Wait. The intended genre and audience should help the author determine the level of intensity, and plan from there. "In most genres, tension needs to be balanced with bit of humor, description, characterization. A satisfying book needs to be the whole day's experience at the county fair, not just the roller coaster ride."

Gutteridge also focuses on tension in the first draft. "Writing details (nice sentences, engrossing analogies) come later. But I've got to feel my way through the tension at the very beginning. It must be at the core of every scene for me."

Franklin keeps tension in mind as he outlines, rather than writing first and then going back and trying to fix it. "Which is usually almost impossible, even for the experts," he says. "You just don't do that. You have some kind of a plan."

Plan, then keep tension in mind as you revise. DuPrau says, "I've discovered that I tend to write much too tamely in my first drafts. Later I have to go back and ramp up the action. She relates that in the first version of The City of Ember, she didn't have nearly enough going on. "The characters thought and worried a lot, but didn't do much. I had to write the whole book again, making something interesting happen on every page, in every chapter—not just a nice description or a character's musings, but an action that complicated the plot and moved it forward."

"As I revise, the tension gets greater," Wait says, and she builds that tension "by reflecting it in sensory details, in weather, in character, in setting, and so forth."

Piece by Piece

To guide the reader through an experience, as opposed to shoveling information at him, writers must address three levels, Franklin explains. First, the story has to make sense. Second, it has to feel emotionally correct. And third, the rhythm, or pacing, must be right. "At one level, like programming, it is extremely technical, and on the extreme end, it's magic. But we mustn't forget that the rabbit didn't really come out of the hat."

Just like magicians, writers have certain tricks. The challenge as we build tension into the story structure is to use various techniques (tricks) without creating a technically correct yet strangely generic work. Author Philip Reeve says, "I'm always very wary of the idea that there are rules to good writing. Hollywood screenwriters are great believers in rules, and look what's happened to movie scripts over the past 20 or 30 years—they've become bland, homogenized, almost indistinguishable, partly, I suspect, because everyone is following the same golden rules about 'what makes stories work.'" Reeve is author of the Mortal Engines series, the Larklight trilogy and other novels, and is winner of the Blue Peter Prize, Smarties Gold Award, Guardian Prize for Children's Fiction, *LA Times* Children's Fiction prize, and the Carnegie Medal.

While avoiding a by-the-rules, mechanical feel in a manuscript, writers must build tension by weaving certain elements into the fiber of their stories. See the sidebar on page 148 for some classic techniques that can help.

Regarding characters, Gutteridge says, "I dig their hole deeper (physically, emotionally, mentally, or spiritually) and then I hope they can get out of it." Bad things need to be happening and getting worse all the time.

Ultimately, every book needs conflict of some sort that is appropriate for the genre. Wait elaborates: "An adult thriller may start with the serial killer finishing off his most recent victim, or making plans for his next. The next scene is that very victim living a normal life, not knowing that he or she is about to be stalked and perhaps, if the

~ Tension Tricks ~

Here are some writing techniques to help you build tension in your fiction.

~ Change the characters' lives so they have to do something in order to survive, and grow in the process.

~ Create characters that seem trustworthy and reliable, but are not.

~ Add plot twists. The unexpected helps ramp up tension.

~ Write tense dialogue. Fragments. Short sentences. Lots of white space.

~ Expose characters' flaws, strengths, self-concepts, desires, secrets, and backstory.

~ Include red herrings that misdirect, or alternatively, subtly use elements that are not immediately recognized as important.

~ Raise suspicions about other characters, causing unnecessary fear and concern.

~ Follow an ebb and flow of tension, allowing the reader to breathe and brace for the next scene.

~ Set scenes in storms, bad weather, and other uncontrollable physical phenomenon or unexplainable and scary happenings.

~ Present a new challenge in every chapter, with new troubles cropping up throughout.

~ Use cliffhanger chapter endings.

~ Foreshadow effectively.

~ Establish high stakes for your characters.

murderer is successful, killed." But for a children's chapter book, she suggests appropriate conflict might be a girl discovering she is the only one in her new fifth-grade class with her hair in braids and wearing a dress.

Personalized Journey

Some people seem to be able to nail tension without much forethought or planning. Reeve says he has very few opinions about the writing process. "I pretty much write from instinct. Either a story works for me or it doesn't, and if it doesn't, I rewrite it until it does."

But if injecting tension into a manuscript is not your strong point, do not stress. You can enhance whatever skill you possess. "It comes naturally for me, but only because I've read for so long and studied writing," Gutteridge says. Wait concurs: "Building tension is something I've learned from reading other authors and studying their techniques. For me, the best way to learn to write is to read. Analyze what you're reading: What works? What doesn't? And why?"

DuPrau suggests watching some good thrillers, observing how tension is injected into the story right from the start, and noting the kinds of events that intensify it as the story progresses. "Sometimes this is easier to see in movies because a movie tells its story in only a couple of hours." Her first attempts at fiction were so mild and inward, she says that even she was not interested in them. "Conflict doesn't come naturally to me. In real life, I like to avoid it."

Indeed, it is one of life's paradoxes that the very thing most humans strive to avoid in personal and professional circles is the very feature they enjoy when they read a story. As long as readers desire to feel tension, writers will work to create it. Planning and revising, using various techniques with all the precision and placement of dominoes, they build their stories. Then, disbelief suspended, readers rush breathless through the pages, having one emotional experience after another as authors take them around, across, over, through; bringing them at last, safe and secure—though perhaps still slightly tense!—to the promised destination.

~ Got Tension? ~
Recommended Reading

If you're looking for books that teach or model tension at its most tense, pick up one of these recommended reads:

Novels
- ~ Suzanne Collins, *Hunger Games* (Scholastic).
- ~ Jeanne DuPrau, *The City of Ember* (Yearling).
- ~ Jon Franklin, *A Wolf in the Parlor* (St. Martin's Griffin).
- ~ Lisa Gardner, *Alone* (Bantam).
- ~ Rene Gutteridge, *Listen* and *Listen* (Tyndale House).
- ~ Philip Reeve, *Mortal Engines* (HarperTeen).
- ~ Lea Wait, *Shadows of a Down East Summer* (Perseverance Press).

Writing Technique
- ~ James Scott Bell, *Plot and Structure* (Writers' Digest).
- ~ Don Maass, *The Fire in Fiction: Passion, Purpose and Techniques to Make Your Novel Great* (Writers' Digest).
- ~ Christopher Vogler, *The Writer's Journey: Mythic Structure for Writers* (Michael Wiese Productions).

In Fantasy's Grip

By Lynda Durrant

My introduction to fantasy came in college, with Edmund Spenser's sixteenth-century epic poem, *The Faerie Queene*. *The Faerie Queene* was written in six *cantos* in which Spenser's hero, the Knight of the Red Cross, engages in quests. He battles evil sorcerers, Saracens, giants, lions, weary pilgrims, and creatures that are half-man, half-beast. Some antagonists only appear to the evil, some antagonists only appear to be good, but everyone has much to say about the nature of evil, the nature of good, and the nature of man.

Each of the six cantos represents a quest in which the Knight, with his loyal dwarf sidekick, must find the virtues of Holiness, Temperance, Chastity, Friendship, Justice, and Courtesy. The Faerie Queene herself appears in the Knight's dreams to give him cryptic advice that only makes sense once the danger is obvious.

I learned to read *The Faerie Queene* standing up because if I sat in the library, or lay down on my dorm bed to read it, I would fall asleep in 15 minutes flat, even if it was 10 in the morning. It is an excruciatingly dull read.

Thank you, Edmund Spenser. I have since learned how valuable

~ Fantasy Publishers ~

~ Ace Science Fiction and Fantasy: 375 Hudson St., New York, NY 10014. http://us.penguingroup.com. Open to manuscripts.

~ Baen Publishing: P.O. Box 1188, Wake Forest, NC 27588. www.baen.com. Open to manuscripts.

~ DAW Books: 375 Hudson St., New York, NY 10014. www.daw-books.com. Open to manuscripts.

~ Del Rey Spectra: 1745 Broadway, New York, NY 10019. http://sf-fantasy.suvudu.com. Random House/Bantam speculative fiction imprints. Agented submissions.

~ Edge Science Fiction & Fantasy: P.O. Box 1714, Calgary, AB T2P 2L7 Canada. www.edgewebsite.com.

~ Firebird: Penguin, 375 Hudson St., New York, NY 10014. www.fire-birdbooks.com. Reprints of science fiction and fantasy for teens. Editor Sharyn November also edits the genres in hardcover for the Viking list, which takes agented submissions.

~ HarperCollins Voyager: 10 E 53rd St., New York, NY 10022. www.harpercollins.com/imprints/index. aspx?imprintid=518005. Imprint formerly called Eos. Dedicated to science fiction and fantasy. Agented submissions only.

~ Orbit Books: 237 Park Ave., 16th floor, New York, NY10017. www.orbitbooks.net. British science fiction and fantasy publisher with U.S. and Australian imprints. Orbit US is part of the Hachette Book Group. Agented submissions only.

~ Pyr Books: 9 John Glenn Dr., Amherst, NY 14288. www.pyrsf.com. In addition to the adult line of speculative fiction, Pyr launched a YA line in 2011.

~ Tor/Forge Books: 175 Fifth Ave., New York, NY 10010. www.tor-forge.com. Science fiction and fantasy publisher. It has a middle-grade imprint, Starscape, and a young adult imprint, Tor Teen.

your cantos are, as a cautionary tale of how *not* to write fantasy. Spenser's epic poem has no suspense. The predictable aimless wandering, a bad guy, an epic battle, and triumphant victory—never changes. There are no surprises.

The Faerie Queene suffers from a fatal lack of grip. I never had a sense of the Knight's motivations and could not identify with him as a character. I could not even see his face in my mind's eye. His six quests seem more like aimless jaunts, full of hoping against hope that the good guys will come running to the rescue at opportune moments.

Is it a surprise that no one but English majors read *The Faerie Queene* anymore, probably standing up?

To be fair, *The Faerie Queene* is not truly a fantasy as we would define it today. It is an epic poem that refers back to Virgil's *Aeneid* and to the medieval chivalric romances. It is also an allegory about Tudor politics—Elizabeth I is the model for the Faerie Queene, Gloriana—including a serious but allegorical discussion in the final canto of the politics of English domination of Ireland. (Spenser recommended a scorched earth policy in Ireland.) It is also strongly in the tradition of Arthurian epic, which is very much alive today in fantasy fiction.

An Exemplar

Nonetheless, let us take *The Faerie Queene* as an exemplar of what contemporary fantasy should not do, and in turn, what it should.

Fantasy is a touchstone in children's literature, and for many readers endures as a pleasure and interest well into adult reading. Children are fantasy's natural audience because their sense of wonder is so easily elevated. Their magical thinking has not yet been thwarted by the cold, stark realities of life. In a child's world, toys talk, the wind whispers secrets, animals are best friends, and fairies and sprites are as real as Uncle Steve and Aunt Sally.

Fantasy helps young readers recognize in a striking way that the world holds good and evil—and that the most unlikely gang of heroes can conquer evil. Think of C. S. Lewis's the Chronicles of Narnia. If a ragtag bunch of kids and sidekicks can conquer the kingdom's most sinister foe, young readers feel they can gain a sense of control in their own lives. They too can conquer hardships, even if their hardships are nothing more than schoolyard bullies, shyness around girls, or diagramming sentences. Or when they are grown, paying bills, facing illness, or struggling with relationships.

Good fantasy is timeless. So why is it so hard to write well? Why does so much fantasy have a sameness to it: The same fair youths enter on the same epic quests, with the same false friends/evil warlocks/wicked queens thwarting the fair youth's chances until the very nick of time?

Edmund Spenser's manuscript, as admired as it was in its time, would be swiftly rejected by an editor today. If you do not want your reader to fall asleep 15 minutes into your first chapter, here are the "mistakes" he made that you should correct.

~ *Create a readable, engaging style; watch your tone and language choices.* Spenser purposefully chose to write in an archaic language, even for Elizabethan England. He was creating an epic, fantasy poem that referred back to the medieval romances and Arthurian legend, and his poetry used diction and word choices that were dated to create atmosphere and reference, and to amplify the allegory. For a fantasy novel today? All wrong, just like this sample:

> "My name is Glynneth, known as Glynneth the Good Witch in this, the Forest Deep." The beautiful young woman's bright green eyes gleamed in the sunset.
>
> The fair youth enquired, "Where may I find the dragon's lair? For the sorcerer has given me my quest, to slay said dragon and return the Jeweled Sepulture to King Blackheart."
>
> "The dragon's name is Smite-Mirth, and his lair is on the very top of Doom Mountain." Her green eyes gleamed brighter. "'Tis a fair distance, fair youth, and the day is growing short.

Perchance you should spend the night under yon tree."

Perched on the prince's shoulder, his parrot whispered in his ear: "Dear sir, forbear! Prince Avingnoth, this witch is not all she seems."

Avoid a self-important tone to your language. Your hero's quest is not the retelling of Arthurian legends, or of *Beowulf.* Your story, and not your tone, should propel the reader forward.

Use contemporary speech patterns. True, you will want the flavor of fantasy, but understand that a little "Dear sir, forbear!" goes a long, long way.

~ *Lighten up.* Why is so much fantasy so serious? Sure, the main characters fight evil, but there is no reason why they cannot have fun too. If brevity is the soul of wit, then levity should be the soul of fantasy. Crack a few jokes. Put your characters in humorous situations. Use running gags to push the plot forward.

The Faerie Queene is a long, grim slog. The Knight of the Red Cross takes himself so seriously that he is unintentionally funny to modern readers. We laugh at him, not with him. He is also one-dimensional, which is a quality acceptable and common in allegory but all wrong for modern storytelling. Like any other main character, your fantasy protagonist needs to grow or he or she will be dull and unsympathetic. Whenever the Knight of the Red Cross gets into a jam, something unbelievably fantastic happens to save him. A talking tree lets him use his branches to climb out of the Well of Despair. His own walking stick glows suddenly, magically, and lights the Knight's way out of the Cave of Desolation. The Knight blunders into the Black Mist of Despondency, and the Faerie Queene's bright minions appear to light his escape. Or a section ends, and the Knight wakes up and realizes it was all a dream after all. In an allegorical interpretation, that tree may refer to the tree of life and faith that leads one from despair; the walking stick, inward knowledge, and so on. But allegorical interpretation is not the way we read fantasy now.

Fantastical resolutions are a huge problem in modern storytelling. When the Knight of the Red Cross is saved by external forces, he does not use his own intellect, his own wits, resources, cleverness, his own strengths to get out of predicaments. It can seem as if, because his strengths are never tested, he thus never learns to draw

Fantastical resolutions are a huge problem in modern fantasy. Protagonists must stumble, but rely on their own strengths.

on them. The reader never sees those strengths develop, or the Knight grow in a human way, as he continues on his quest. The reader never gains a chance to identify with him. This is why I never *saw* the Knight's face in my mind's eye. The reader never has a chance to wonder if the Knight's own weaknesses will trip him up because we never see the weaknesses either.

Character development is plot development. The Knight of the Red Cross never grows as a character.

~ *Make the protagonist's purpose, struggle, or goal worthwhile.* Whatever the main character is looking for, make sure it is worth his time. Let us say your main character needs to find the Golden Harp of Sovereignty so that the one true king can overcome his evil brother's pretensions to the throne. Well, why can't the one true king and his loyal minions just put the evil pretender in the dungeon? Why can't the one true king call on the forces of good and put this brother in his place? What makes it necessary for your protagonist to get involved?

In other words, what is in it for your main protagonist? If your answer is just truth and beauty, that is not enough of a motivation to keep your main character (and your reader) moving forward. Give your main character a stake in your plot's climax. Give him a tangible reward for his hard work. Does he need the king's help in return to save his parents from losing their land? Does he have a long lost sister under the influence of the evil brother?

~ Fantasy it may be, but do not let fantasy take over the story. We have all read about them in books, seen them on film: talking rocks, giant flying insects used as air transportation, color-coordinated kingdoms, mental telepathy used for dialogue, and all manner of feisty and opinionated birds, mice, cats, and unicorns that help the main character in his quest.

It is fun to create these creatures and fantastical elements—it is one of the charming aspects of fantasy—but be careful. Do not give sassy critters all the punch lines. Do not let fantastical elements steal the great scenes. Do not create gimmicks that absorb all the cool, magical qualities, while your hero is just another character blindly bouncing or slogging through a magical kingdom. Give your main character some magical qualities too, or the fantasy will take over the story and overpower the protagonist.

Harry Potter's wand does not always do what Harry wants it to do. His best friend Ron's broken wand sets his spells askew. Hermione's book sense fails her at times, when she neglects life sense. Harry, Ron, and Hermione have to draw on their own strengths to win the day. They cannot depend on mere magic. Let your main character try and fail, and try and fail again and again. It is the only way to grow as a character.

~ Give your main characters a rich, real backstory. In the Harry Potter books, He-Who-Must-Not-Be-Named is always in pursuit, but Harry has much more than an evil wizard making up his life. He has a dysfunctional foster family, faces schoolyard bullies, experiences schoolboy crushes, has burned-out teachers, and confronts the deaths of his parents and mentors, the loss of innocence, and his own identity in an ever-changing world. Harry Potter's quest takes him well beyond just Hogwarts' dining hall. Ron and Hermione have

their own issues. Ron's family is poor and Hermione's parents are Muggles. Slowly but surely we see Ron and Hermione fall in love, but not without a whole set of complications.

It is the realistic problems that keep fans reading. Yes, the magic and the fantasy are exciting and page-turning, but Harry, Ron, and Hermione are characters with whom readers identify because their lives mimic their own.

The fantasy elements in fantasy fiction, whether for children or adults, have to make sense within the context of the story. Readers should not scratching their heads over parts of the story that do not make sense. Head-scratching will lift your reader right out of the page to reach for the universal remote.

While obstacles, complications, tension, and conflict are essential in any good fiction, they must also add to the story and have a clarity. Remember the Knight of the Red Cross's sidekick, the dwarf? In the allegory as it was meant to be understood in the 1590s, the dwarf represented common sense, and Spenser's meaning was likely that it was in short supply. But in a modern retelling of *The Faerie Queen* we might ask, why a dwarf? What does his stature add to the story, or is it just an unnecessary complication? It is the dwarf's job to carry the Knight's weapons and treasure, just in case the Knight needs to challenge a villain or pay for a night on the town. How can a dwarf carry an 18-foot lance, a 6-foot sword, a bristling assortment of cudgels, knives, and maces, and a chest full of gold?

Even in fantasy, it is what is similar, and not what is different, that keeps a reader involved. Ground your characters in reality, even as you include all the most appealing qualities of fantasy. Give your characters a fast-moving plot with plenty of conflict and do not rely on the fantasy to support your story. The fantasy is the icing on the cake, the lemon slice in your tea, the glimmer in the Faerie Queene's wings.

If your fantasy story is bogged down in the Word File of Despair, Languor, and Rejection Slips, boot it up and consider how to add energy and grip to your story. Even if you have to read it standing up.

A Penguin Walks into a Bowling Alley

What's So Funny?

By Christina Hamlett

"Man is the only animal that laughs and weeps," wrote English essayist William Hazlitt, "for he is the only animal that is struck with the difference between what things are and what they ought to be."

Pain and loss are the common denominators that produce tears; identifying the elements that trigger giggles, chuckles, and knee-slapping guffaws is much harder. Humor is not only predicated on whether we are a victim, participant, or observer in the hilarity but also on age, gender, education, ethnicity, social status, and even where we live. A penguin that walks into a bowling alley in a *New Yorker* cartoon generates adult mirth from an incongruous caption that mixes sophistication with silliness. In a children's show, the same penguin is not funny until he gets hit in the face with a cream pie or tries to evade an oncoming rush of bowling balls. If someone trips over a penguin in *America's Funniest Home Videos* and smacks his head against a block of ice, we laugh at the man's clumsiness and disregard the realities of potentially knocking out his teeth or getting a concussion that causes a blot clot and subsequently kills him.

Humor sits at a complex intersection between context and audience. A comedic villain who engages in pranks is not perceived at the same level of threat as a sadistic one who uses jokes to humiliate. A class clown who is the life of the party either makes a predictable fool of himself or has the sensitivity to recognize when his flippant antics would be inappropriate.

Humor sits at a complex intersection between context and audience.

Infusing a story with the right level and kind of humor invites readers to take life less seriously—and your characters more so. The humor adds to the sense that they are willing to show that they are only human. The challenge is in understanding what type of levity best sets the tone and delivers your message.

Slapstick

Pratfalls, chases, mimicry, exaggerated facial expressions, sight gags, and fisticuffs over minor kerfuffles are the signature traits of slapstick humor and can trace their origins not just to vaudeville, but well back through Shakespeare and beyond, to the ancient classics. The buffoon, or *bomolochos*, was one of the stock characters of ancient Greek comedy.

In the modern era, the broad brushstrokes of physical comedy were wielded with finesse in film by notables such as Buster Keaton, Charlie Chaplin, Abbott and Costello, the Three Stooges, and Red Skelton. Because of its heavy reliance on a visual context and a snappy pace, slapstick lends itself best to film and theatrical projects. It does not call for maturity or a particularly deep intellect to follow any of the story lines or to understand what is driving characters' motivations.

Conflicts in this genre typically arise from innocent accidents; mistaken identities; escalated arguments over trivial events; or fish-out-of-water personalities attempting to navigate social mores that are foreign to them, and who attempt to avoid detection and exposure as frauds.

Satire & Parody

At the opposite end of the humor spectrum are satire and parody, both of which poke fun at existing social orders, political institutions, and pop culture by imitating their most recognizable characteristics and placing them in thinly veiled spoofs and lampoons. Characters are given names similar to their real life counterparts—Okrah Winfrid, Arnold Shortsnogger, Angelina Gelée, Justin Tumblecake—and also imitate their physical appearance. In the American paradigm, *Saturday Night Live* has been a hotbed of such humor for more than 35 years.

To understand the jokes and subtext in satire and parody the audience, whether reading or observing, must have an awareness of the references, coupled with the ability to interpret concepts abstractly. Today, the references could be to anything from historical events, classic literature, art, fairy tales, 1960s television shows, political personalities, or current events. If, for example, a character in your contemporary short story says, "Would you stop following me? It's just a piece of bread," the set-up has more meaning to a reader familiar with *Les Miserables* than to the person who has never heard of Jean Valjean and Inspector Javert.

Not all satirical fare translates flawlessly to those outside the target audience. If the audience is not *in the know*, the humor fails. Think of skits you may have done in high school or college, replete with insider jokes about students and faculty. Would anyone outside the school univerise have laughed? It is not hard to imagine why some American sitcoms exported to another country would fail to gain a following, if the references are insularly specific to the American lifestyle and pop culture. What is hilarious to those in the know generates head-scratching from those who do not share the same frame of reference.

As an illustration of this disconnect, my husband and I had decided on a trip to Edinburgh to observe a session of Scottish Parliament. Our expectation of a serious-minded government forum unraveled with the introduction of the first order of business: a discussion of super-market shopping carts. Given the ribald laughter, elbow jabs, and anecdotes that filled the next 20 minutes, one can only assume that there was quite an amusing backstory we were not privy to.

We can read *Gulliver's Travels* today and still appreciate some of its literary qualities, but few readers now have the same context to understand the political and cultural satire and irony that Jonathan Swift mastered. Readers are somewhat closer in time and so understand Orwellian satire, and Kurt Vonnegut's.

The Element of Surprise

Readers and audiences of all ages enjoy being caught off-guard by the funny and random. Whether it is the elegantly dressed matron who emerges from the restroom trailing toilet paper on the heel of her shoe, the revelers who show up with noisemakers at the wrong address, or a volleyball lobbed over a fence that lands in the middle of a birthday cake, it is usually easier to laugh when such glitches of fate happen to someone other than us. The ease with which a *good* character can extricate himself from an embarrassing event through the use of witty comebacks or self-deprecating humor endears him to us and provides inspiration should we find ourselves in similarly uncomfortable circumstances.

Our funny bones are also tickled when *bad* characters get their just desserts. The haughty starlet whose designer gown is accidentally shrunk by the maid, the school bully who steals a lunch bag only to discover it contains underwear, or the maniacal manager who belittles a customer unaware she is actually the company's new owner: We take whimsical solace in scenes of comedic comeuppance that may not happen often in real life, but probably should.

For surprises and random humor to work well in a story, they need to be believable and in balance with the realistic situations in which the characters find themselves. Otherwise, they become little more than a succession of contrivances stitched together for a forced laugh, and having nothing to do with the plot.

Hurling Insults

In the 1987 comedy *Roxanne*, Steve Martin is a modern-day Cyrano De Bergerac who has endured a lifetime of insults about his prominent nose. In a deft turnabout, in one scene he challenges one of his critics with artful zingers of his own about his nose:

"Obvious: 'scuse me, is that your nose or did a bus park on your face?

Meteorological: Everybody take cover, she's going to blow!

Fashionable: You know, you could de-emphasize your nose if you wore something larger, like . . . Wyoming.

Punctual: All right, Delbman, your nose was on time but you were fifteen minutes late!

Humorous: Laugh and the world laughs with you. Sneeze, and it's goodbye, Seattle!

Polite: Uh, would you mind not bobbing your head? The, uh, orchestra keeps changing tempo.

Complimentary: You must love the little birdies to give them this to perch on.

Obscure: Whoa! I'd hate to see the grindstone.

Inquiring: When you stop to smell the flowers, are they afraid?

Religious: The Lord giveth . . . and He just kept on giving, didn't He?

Aromatic: It must wonderful to wake up in the morning and smell the coffee. . . in Brazil."

Sarcasm and a rapier wit have long been the weapons of choice by sophisticates seeking to knock their opponents down a few pegs without inflicting bodily harm. Consider these miscellaneous examples as well:

~ "I've had a perfectly wonderful evening. But this wasn't it." *Groucho Marx*

~ "I am enclosing two tickets to the first night of my new play; bring a friend . . . if you have one." *George Bernard Shaw to Winston Churchill*

"Cannot possibly attend first night; will attend second, if there is one." *Winston Churchill, in response to George Bernard Shaw*

~ "He is not only dull himself; he is the cause of dullness in others." *Samuel Johnson*

~ "Why do you sit there looking like an envelope without any address on it?" *Mark Twain*

~ "Some cause happiness wherever they go; others, whenever they go." *Oscar Wilde*

~ "This is not a novel to be tossed aside lightly. It should be thrown with great force." *Dorothy Parker*

The younger or less sophisticated the person casting the insult, however, the faster the humor context can go from class to crass. This is helpful to keep in mind if you are penning stories for YA readers and attempting to capture the snarky mindsets of some so-called *popular* kids and self-absorbed fashionistas versus campus newcomers and misfits.

Notwithstanding the attention paid to political correctness, note that many of the insults that choose meanness over cleverness stem from racial and sexual stereotyping. Although completely frowned upon by today's children's and YA publishers, humor that belittles others for their ethnicity, gender, or physical imperfections still appears in novels, plays, and films as a way to reflect cultural and generational insensitivity.

Irony & Understatement

In *Pirates of the Caribbean: The Curse of the Black Pearl*, it is revealed that the former first mate of the pirate ship was sent to a watery grave before anyone realized his blood was needed to lift the ship's curse. "I guess that's what you'd call *ironic*," remarks Ragetti, a member of the villainous crew. That line is made that much funnier because of the person saying it—a clueless, ragtag rube whom we would never suspect would have such a word in his vocabulary. Ragetti further amuses and baffles us with his knowledge of Greek mythology, his observations about the dichotomy of good and evil, and his scholarly correction of best friend Pintel that the much feared Kraken is actually a *cephalopod* and not a *stupid fish.*

The contrast between intellect and appearance is one of many ways that irony is an effective, and sometimes subtle, device for creating and sustaining humor. The incongruity of seeing something that does not quite fit its environment—whether physically, mentally, or socially—tweaks our curiosity, especially when it appears that no one is even reacting to it. Much of the goofiness in the Naked Gun films, for instance, features luminaries in absurd scenarios (i.e., Queen Elizabeth at a baseball game) or someone au natural strolling past the background of a suburban mall.

Whether in the form of snappy repartee or droll wit, understatement also plays a key role in comedy. A popular staple of BBC series like *As Time Goes By*, understatement takes something that is clearly obvious and reduces it to a simplistic observation. If, for example, a family on a camping trip comes back from a hike and discovers that bears have destroyed their tent and are currently eating the tires off their Volvo, the husband might remark, "Well, this is certainly awkward." It is more than awkward; it is disastrous. But it is also comic relief.

Masters of humorous (and sometimes serious) irony include Oscar Wilde; P. G. Wodehouse; Ken Kesey in *One Flew Over the Cuckoo's Nest;* in a rather harsher vein, H. L. Mencken and Christopher Hitchens; and more classically, Jane Austen's fans know the humorous sting of her subtle ironies. Of course, irony becomes big with teens, so it is not uncommon in some YA books. What would Holden Caulfield be without irony?

Like irony, understatement often needs a visual or other context or it lacks meaning. Consider the comment: "Not a look for everyone." I recall a company fire drill where our office scurried outside and awaited instruction from the attorney who was our designated floor warden. Although we all knew he had this role, we had never actually seen him in his fluorescent orange vest and matching plastic helmet. It was clear, though, when he joined us in the park across the street that the ensemble he had donned over his pinstripe suit had last been worn by a much tinier predecessor. "Not a look for everyone," one of my associates murmured. Had I been drinking coffee at the time, it would have come out my nose.

The interpretation of humor in the arts has suffered no shortage of analysis throughout history. The following quote by Victor Borge, however, perhaps sums it up best: "Humor is something that thrives between man's aspirations and his limitations. There is more logic in humor than in anything else. Because, you see, humor is truth."

~ Agents & Humor ~

The following agencies or agents are open to submissions of humor.

~ **The Bent Agency:** 204 Park Place, Number Two, Brooklyn, NY 11238. www.thebentagency.com. Jenny Bent represents humorous fiction and nonfiction.

~ **DeFiore and Company:** 47 East 19th St., 3rd floor, New York, NY 10003. www.defioreandco.com. Agents Brian DeFiore and Laurie Abkemeier are open to humorous nonfiction.

~ **Dystel & Goderich Literary Management:** One Union Square West, Suite 904, New York, NY 10003. www.dystel.com. Jim McCarthy and John Rudolph look at fiction and nonfiction humor.

~ **Foundry Literary + Media:** 33 West 17th St., PH, New York, NY 10011. www.foundrymedia.com. Peter McGuigan represents humorous fiction and nonfiction.

~ **Writers House:** 21 West 26th St., New York, NY 10010. www.writershouse.com. Agent Daniel Lazar is open to humor submissions.

~ **Nancy Yost Literary Agency:** 350 Seventh Ave., Suite 2003, New York, NY 10001. www.nyliterary.com. Nonfiction humor is accepted.

Keeping the Promise

Leads that Work

By Patricia Curtis Pfitsch

A good lead, says Tom Wolf, co-author with Patricia Bryan of true crime novel *Midnight Assassin: A Murder in America's Heartland* (University of Iowa Press), "is like meeting one's prospective in-laws for the first time. Comb your hair, Brush your teeth. Don't wear a shirt with frayed cuffs. Be direct and make eye contact. A good lead is important to create that first impression."

The obvious person to impress upfront is an editor. "The number of submissions we receive increases," says Susan Van Metre, Senior Vice President and Publisher of Abrams Books For Young Readers, Amulet Books, and Abrams Comicarts, "and the time we have to read them seems to decrease. Editors don't have time to read a whole manuscript if they don't see any potential. It's a very competitive publishing environment."

How much time an editor can spend to find that potential varies. "It might be 10 pages or it might be 50 pages," although Van Metre admits that might seem unfair. "But in a way it is fair because the beginning is so important. If you're not bringing your very best game to your opening pages, then you're not bringing your best game to the project."

It is not just editors who have to manage their reading time. Ann Angel, whose latest book, *Janis Joplin: Rise up Singing* (Amulet) won the YALSA Award for Excellence in Nonfiction for Young Adults and an SCBWI Crystal Kite Award, is an example of today's busy readers. "I'm one of those people who stands in bookstores and libraries reading first pages," she says. "If I like the first page, the book has won me over and I'll read it. If not, it goes right back on the shelf."

Of course when a reader is already familiar with a writer, the beginning might not matter so much. "I don't really care what hap-

> **"For me, the lead is the heart of the story. It sets the tone, it sets the voice, it establishes the setting. It's key to have that opening down pat."**

pens in the first couple of paragraphs of a short story by Alice Munro," admits Wolf, who also writes short stories, book reviews, and essays. "I've read enough of her work to trust her. But if I'm reading a short story by a writer I don't know, the writing had better appeal to me, or else I'll put it down and look for something else."

"For me, the lead is the heart of the story," says picture book writer Lisa Moser. "It sets the tone, it sets the voice, it establishes the setting. It's key to have that opening down pat." Moser's latest book, *Perfect Soup* (Random House Books for Young Readers) was chosen by Bank Street College for their Best Children's Books of the Year in the *under five* category.

"I think the opening line has to be one of the very best lines in the book," says Angel. "Whether fiction or nonfiction, that first line has to introduce the work's tone, engage the reader, speak in a clear voice and hint what this book is going to be about."

Whew! That seems heavy to hang on one line. Others say that the lead may not be make-or-break. "The lead is just one of many parts," says creative writing professor Don Knefel, who is also a columnist and author of three books on writing, including *Writing and Life: An Introduction to Nonfiction* (Harcourt School) and *Aims of the Essay: A Reader and Guide.* "The lead has an important function, but so does the body, and even more so the conclusion. All the parts of a work are vital to its success."

"I'd argue," says Wolf, "that the content—movement, development, examples, analysis, conclusion, resolution—is more important to the completed work." He does not deny one fact, however. "If the lead isn't any good, the reader may not continue reading."

Organic Growth

Writers may struggle with methods for coming up with a lead that keeps the reader reading. "There is no formula," says Knefel. "It emerges organically from the material and signals that the piece will be interesting, useful, entertaining, personally expressive. One of the challenges of writing is that it's different every time."

Add to that the fact that fiction leads are different than nonfiction. Length of the writing—article, short story, early reader, novella, novel— make a difference, and so will audience, whether children or adults. Nevertheless, it is possible to pinpoint some characteristics that good leads share, characteristics you can use to strengthen your writing and keep your readers reading.

"If there's one guideline," says Knefel, "I think it's to keep the language concrete."

"In a picture book," says Moser, "especially because we have to do things so quickly in a limited amount of words, the lead can establish the character's personality." Her easy reader *Squirrel's World* (Candlewick) begins like this:

> Squirrel was busy, busy, busy.
> He had to help his tree. "Grow, grow, grow!" cheered Squirrel.
> He had to help the river. "Flow, flow, flow!" said Squirrel.

Note the specificity of the language. Moser sets the tone of the story directly, using dialogue to show us squirrel's hyperactive personality. "The river doesn't need his help to flow," she explains, "and yet his perception is that he is making the river flow and the tree grow. It shows him in all his misconceptional glory. And he's so overly excited he talks in triplicate." We get a first hint of the problem as well—this effervescent, frenetic character thinks he is helping his friends when he is really not helping much at all.

In *Perfect Soup,* Moser again begins by setting up Murray Mouse's personality foibles.

> Murray shined the teapot. "Perfect," he said.
> Murray set the table. "Perfect."
> Murray looked out the window. "Soup is perfect on a
> snowy day."

"It was so important to establish Murray's perfectionism because that's what he has to overcome," Moser explains. "Everything is absolutely *just so* in his world that it becomes a hindrance to him. He has to learn to accept that things aren't perfect and they may be better."

In a longer work for teens or adults, the lead can set the tone of the story more indirectly, keeping the language concrete, and yet preparing the reader for what is coming. Van Metre points to the first scene in Nancy Farmer's novel set in Zimbabwe, *The Ear, the Eye and the Arm* (Firebird). "The opening is very sensual. It prepares you for the fact that you're going to have to rely on all your five senses throughout the course of the mystery to figure out what's going on. It's not just going to be about listening or seeing."

The beginning of *Jellicoe Road* (HarperTeen), by Melina Marchetta, takes an even more indirect approach, but the language is almost painfully immediate and vivid. "She starts with a scene that takes place 20 years before the rest of the events of the novel," Van Metre explains. "The characters you're meeting in the opening aren't going to be the main characters in the novel but they are going to be important to the main character. You're thrust into the middle of a car accident but you don't understand its relationship to the rest of the story for about a hundred pages. This lead works because it communicates that the author is going to be playing around with time and with perspective and that the past is going to impact the present."

A Sense of Purpose

"I think good leads come from a writer's clear sense of purpose and audience," says Knefel, "what he or she is trying to accomplish, and for whom."

"Once the opening changed, I could feel it. It's like a door. Until you hit it, the story is pretty much a locked door. But when you get that opening right, you can step through it into the story."

When Moser, who had been a fifth-grade teacher, was writing *Kisses on the Wind* (Candlewick), her picture book about the Oregon Trail, she first set it in contemporary times. "It was pretty bland," she admits. Then she remembered teaching the westward expansion to her students. "I thought, what if I start it on the Oregon Trail? And that opened everything out." The story came to life because Moser more clearly understood her audience and her purpose. "Once the opening changed," Moser said, "I could feel it. It's like a door. Until you hit it, the story is pretty much a locked door. But when you get that opening right you can step through it into the story."

When Van Metre edited *Janis Joplin: Rise up Singing*, she and Angel found the best lead for the book when they focused on the audience.

Van Metre explains that the original manuscript of the biography began with Janis at the 1967 Monterey Pop Festival, when Joplin literally became a star. "That was a very big moment in her life, but it was plunking the reader too far into the middle of her story." Teen readers in 2011 might not understand what had been going on in the 1960s, 35 years before they were born. "That's when we came up with the idea of starting instead with Janis as a teenager," Van Metre says. "Her experience was so universal it didn't need as much context or explanation."

"When writing for young adults," explains Angel, "I want to grab their attention through my subject's voice. I want to get inside my subject's head in a way that will engage someone who's between 12 and 30." So the biography begins like this:

> The popular girls wore their hair short and perfectly curled, with tiny bows fastened at their temples. Their skirts swung demurely as they walked down the school halls. The round Peter Pan collars of their blouses were buttoned neatly and decorated with tasteful circle pins and pearl necklaces. The girls were pretty and petite, their soft, jingling southern laughs drawing smiles from teachers and from the boys who jostled for their attention.
>
> Janis Joplin had only to look in the mirror to see frizzy brown waves of hair that refused to be tamed and a plump face spotted with acne. She was heavier than the other girls. Louder too. When she laughed, it came out as a cackle or a raspy, flat "hah!"

"You know from the very first lines that *Janis Joplin, Rise Up Singing* is going to be about an outsider, someone who was picked on and bullied for being different than the popular girls," says Angel. "The biography reveals how Janis, who always remained vulnerable to wanting love, stepped out of Port Arthur, Texas, into the spotlight and used her voice to rise above it all."

In her biography, *Robert Cormier: Author of the Chocolate War* (Enslow), Angel again focuses on her young adult audience. "I realized [Cormier] had been the stay-at-home writing dad and so I wrote his story through the eyes of his teenaged girls, who grew up coming home to Dad at his typewriter. That biography answered the questions what is it like to grow up with a dad who is a writer and outspoken activist against censorship. That was the hook I hoped would intrigue teens."

Wolf found the lead for his article, "Homecoming: Family, Place, and Community in Sara Vogan's *In Shelley's Leg* and Thomas Oliphant's *Praying for Gill Hodges*" by knowing the audience. "My thesis was that families and groups of people bond through baseball," says Wolf. "I knew my audience would be well-read, intelligent people who were sympathetic to this idea. I wanted the lead to be personal, and I knew I wanted to end with an anecdote about my relationship with my mother and how we shared a moment that reflected a common interest in baseball. So my lead took the form of another family anecdote—an event that happened years ago, when my parents were alive and I was a young boy." As with Angel's books, Wolf's intended audience, as well as the structure and tone of the article, dictated the lead. "Homecoming" was published in *The Cooperstown Symposium on Baseball and American Culture, 2007–2008,* (McFarland & Company).

The Beginning at the End

Angel describes the first lines of a piece of writing as "a promise of story that the writer has made to me." But if the lead suggests in a meaningful way what the readers will experience if they keep reading, then perhaps the best time to write the lead is after the first draft is finished.

Knefel agrees. "It's been my experience that openings are often revised after the body of the work gains clear shape and focus. Then you can go back and find the most logical and pointed lead." He suggests that writers can start with a provisional lead. "But be open to

~ Form Makes the Difference ~

Since nonfiction takes so many different forms," says author and creative writing professor Don Knefel, "to me it's a different animal. Some nonfiction takes a narrative form, and openings there might share elements with fiction—concreteness, description, portrayed action, dialog between real life characters, etc.

"But other kinds of nonfiction take the form of essays, articles, personal reflection, or autobiography, etc. Leads there might be more abstract or speculative—posing questions, stating problems—or they might be concrete illustrations of something specific that embodies the material. So the nonfiction writer faces a whole host of different content and structure issues, plus the imposed limits of form and genre." A travel piece, an interview, a book review, an article on advice have different opening needs.

"In fiction," explains Susan Van Metre, Senior Vice President and Publisher of Abrams Books For Young Readers, Amulet Books, and

revision later."

Wolf and his wife Patricia Bryan had just this experience when they were working on *Midnight Assassin*, the story of an unsolved murder of an Iowa farmer in 1900. "Our original opening described the morning that was to be John Hossack's last day before he was murdered in his sleep. As we wrote, we decided that the last sentence, in fact the last image in the book, would be of John Hossack lying in his grave, side by side with his wife of 32 years, Margaret, who was also the woman accused of killing him. So we revised the opening by writing a prologue—a description of John Hossack as a young man, full of energy and dreams, as he looks over the land on which he plans to build his future."

Wolf also ended up rewriting the lead and the ending of his award-winning story "Boundaries," which will be published in the *North Carolina Literary Review* in the coming year. Originally, the story began with a middle-aged man looking back on a murder that

~ Form Makes the Difference ~

Abrams Comicarts, "often the strategy is to start with a really exciting theme no matter where it actually falls in the chronology of the story. I'm thinking of mystery novels where you might start with the murder and then go back and seed in from the backstory of the victim."

What is more, she continues, "I think really good nonfiction steals from fiction in the way you might choose to open." *Janis Joplin: Rise up Singing* begins with Janis as a teenager and then, in chapter two, backtracks and lets the reader see her as a young child in the same way that a mystery might start with the murder and then flash back to earlier in the victim's life.

"Looking for the best way to start something is never easy," admits Knefel, "but it's easier if writers understand the basic nature of the form they're working in, and the elements that define it. As always, I think that means doing plenty of reading and observing closely what other writers have done that seems successful or appealing."

occurred in his hometown when he was a boy. "But because the story is about the past, and about the power that the past has to seep into our lives in the present," says Wolf, "I created a new opening and a new ending that gave this man an unnamed wife who knows nothing at all about this incident from the man's past that has so powerfully impacted him. I try to suggest that there are boundaries that are not to be crossed in their relationship, namely disclosing too much about their own past."

Angel usually finds the best lead after revising too. "The first sentence and first paragraph, that first page and that first chapter, are the ones I go back to again and again to tweak and mess with."

Moser's experience is different. "I can't progress unless that first line is perfect," she admits. "Some people can jump past it and get into the heart of the story, but I can't, because it is voice, it is tone, it is everything."

Don't Make This Mistake

On the other hand, as Moser points out, "you can fall so in love with the beginning sentence that it can hinder you too. You have to be able to toss out a really fabulous opening sentence if it's just not the right one. You work a long time, but then, when you toss it, it frees you up."

Another classic mistake writers make in writing the leads is including too much information. Van Metre says, "Don't frontload a lot of background information that would be better delivered gradually over the course of the story. Trust the reader to get it."

Yet Moser attests, "I really believe in the big jump in. If you're going to have a monster in the backpack, just have the monster in the backpack." She's referring to her picture book, *The Monster in the Backpack* (Candlewick), which begins like this:

> Annie's new backpack came with pink and blue flowers.
> Annie's new backpack came with a zipper.
> Annie's new backpack came with a monster.

"You're leading the reader," Moser says, "And if you do it well, you can say, 'this is the way it is. Follow me.' You're telling them what the world is, and as long as you're consistent and true to it, they'll follow you. I don't think you have to add a long explanation about why the monster is there."

Finally, says Knefel, "I think writers often make a mistake in assuming that there's a set of tricks they can learn that will make writing easier." The truth, he points out, is both more difficult and more liberating. "A lot of the decisions writers make are ultimately based on instinct and intuition. Maybe the best way to look at an given lead is to ask: What is the lead that would make me want to keep reading?"

Something New Under the Sun

Breathing Life into Archetypes

By Sue Bradford Edwards

With editors and publishers seeking character-driven manuscripts, the importance of creating characters with whom readers can connect is greater than ever before. Do this by tapping into the energy of character archetypes.

Archetypes are traditional character types that we already know. We have met them in our daily lives. They are a part of the literary tradition we grew up with. These archetypes have occurred repeatedly throughout history, beginning with the stories told around the campfire and continuing into written literature, theater, and film. It is their familiarity that creates an almost instantaneous connection between character and reader and did so even before psychologist Carl Jung first called them *archetypes*.

"Characters based on archetypes work effectively in literature and film because they tap into primal human psychology," says author and psychologist Marilyn Peake. "In writing about the role of archetypes, Carl Jung posited that humanity, through its collective experience, has developed a collective unconscious, meaning an unconscious shared by all people. For example, all human beings have a mother and father, people who mean so much to an infant's survival. *Mother* and *father* are symbolic, meaningful archetypes capable of stirring up strong emotions in all people. Likewise, heroes and villains have been part of the human experience for all of human existence."

When the hero strides across the screen, the audience sits up and takes notice. When the heroine confronts her rival, we hold our breath, waiting to see how she will win. "Most of us are raised listening to fairy tales and watching Disney adventures and all of those bodies of work include deliciously wonderful examples of traditional archetypes," says writing mentor and professor Laurie Scheer. Use them to strengthen your work by first learning what some of the common archetypes are and how they function within a story.

Eight Archetypes

The labels used to discuss archetypes vary somewhat, often depending on the background of the person leading the discussion. Psychologists use one set of terms and mythologists another. While the terminology may vary, here are eight archetypes you are sure to recognize.

~ *Hero.* Usually the main character, the Hero is the one called upon to make a sacrifice for the good of others. Readers want to see the Hero succeed. Contemporary heroes include Rowling's Harry Potter and Riordan's Percy Jackson.

~ *Shadow characters.* Every good hero needs someone standing against them. Shadow characters represent the dark and undesirable. We often call them villains or antagonists. Shadows challenge and threaten to destroy the hero. At their best, they possess some good quality, such as the beauty of the White Witch in C. S. Lewis's the Chronicles of Narnia.

~ *Herald.* Villains are often essential, but usually not the ones that get the story rolling. Often this role is filled by the Herald, the bearer of change. This character may be the one to let the hero know what his task will be. When R2-D2 brings Luke the message from Princess Leia, he is a Herald. Anyone who delivers a message can fill this role.

~ *Mentor.* Simply knowing what the task is may not be enough. The Hero often needs someone to prep him for the adventure, a role performed by a wise Mentor. The Mentor shares knowledge or gives a gift. Many mentors, such as Merlin, are separated in some way from the everyday world in which your story begins. In Sarah Addison Allen's *The Peach Keeper* (Bantam), Grandma Osgood lives in a nursing home.

~ *Shapeshifter.* As the name implies, Shapeshifters first seem to be one thing and then another. Shapeshifters are often, but not always, villains. They introduce tension into the story. They change sides. In Sarah Rees Brennan's *The Demon's Lexicon* (Margaret K. McElderry Books), Nick is both dark hero and Shapeshifter, not human as he initially appears, seeming to change form before the reader's eyes. Sebastian shifts from unattainable friend to love interest in *The Peach Keeper.*

~ *Threshold Guardian.* Threshold Guardians are minor villains that get in the Hero's way. They must be overcome. Sometimes this function is performed not by a character but by some kind of barrier. Charon and the River Styx are Threshold Guardians of the Underworld.

~ *Tricksters.* Tricksters are mischievous agents of change. They often act as comic relief but also act as catalysts, getting things moving. Dobby in Harry Potter is a typical Trickster, as is Coyote in Native American myth.

~ *Child.* The Child archetype portrays innocence and potential. Sometimes they are actual children. At other times, they are child-like adults. They are often a bit naive. Tolkien's hobbits are child characters.

From Hero to Trickster, you know these character types. You have encountered them since you were a child. Just do not let this familiarity lull you, as a writer, into a false sense of security about them.

Making Them Work Within the Story

Just as familiarity is in many ways the saving grace of archetypes, it can also be their greatest liability. Largely because they are part of the collective experience, editors have seen them all before, whether you are talking Heros and Shadows or Mentors and Tricksters. Because of this, your job is to harness the power of the archetype in a way that is unique to your individual character and your story.

First and foremost, do all of the work that goes into creating a strong character. Do not try to use the archetype as a short cut. "It is often that the characters within a story are not developed enough and the result is often worse than a two-dimensional stereotype," says Scheer, who refers to these flat attempts as paper doll characters. Her solution? Spend time on your character development. "Developing characters—giving them a complete background, creating a biography for each of your main characters and getting into their shoes and clothes—is what is necessary to create strong, solid characters that audiences will resonate to. Additionally, the author must give these characters a soul, of course, and their own motivation and interior and exterior wants and needs."

In doing all of this for the variety of characters that people your story, you will in turn develop a strong story. "The story is what is most important. The writer's most important responsibility is to create a new and meaningful story," says Peake. "In the process of creating a brand new story, a writer must also add depth to the characters, including those who are archetypal symbols."

As you develop your story, make sure that your archetypal characters each have a serious role to play within the story itself. "Gandalf in the Lord of the Rings is a wise old man [or mentor] archetype, but he does a lot more than sit in a rocking chair, spouting advice. Likewise, in many ways the hobbits meet the criteria of the child archetype, but they accomplish so much more than acting like playful children. Galadriel is a mother archetype, but one who is a very powerful, spiritual protector," says Peake. If you think your character may be a bit flat, give her something else to do. Don't add an archetype just to try to create familiarity.

You can also strengthen your archetypal characters by setting them up in contrast to each other. Peake says of the Lord of the

~ Who Am I? ~

Still not sure you can identify some of the archetypes? Consider these popular characters matched with the archetypes they embody.

- ~ Maude in *Harold and Maude:* Mentor
- ~ The grandfather in *Little Miss Sunshine:* Mentor and Trickster
- ~ The Dude in *The Big Lebowski:* Hero and Shapeshifter
- ~ Rooster Cogburn in *True Grit:* Hero and Threshold Guardian
- ~ Captain Jack Sparrow in *Pirates of the Carribean:* Trickster, Shapeshifter, Shadow, and Hero.

Author and psychologist Marilyn Peake reminds us that you can sometimes use inanimate objects in the place of certain archetypes. "The house itself is a character. In human psychology, a house often symbolizes the self," she says. "And that house frequently portrayed the "shadow" archetype, or "dark side" of the ego." An example is the house in *House of Leaves,* by Mark Z. Danielewski.

Rings, "Saruman is perhaps an evil, dark father archetype, and he is a wizard much like Gandalf, but turns to evil—a dichotomy that creates powerful emotions in the person reading the books or viewing the films." Giving characters complex roles to play not only makes them more interesting, it helps you use the archetypes to their full effect and power, especially when you play one off the other as Tolkein did with Gandalf and Saruman or Rowling did with her Hero, Harry Potter, and her Shadow, Voldemort.

Another way to make your archetypal characters unique is to play around with the forms. Go beyond the typical person to fill that particular archetypal role. After all, you are starting with a clean slate even when you seek to use archetypes. "The test of a lazy writer is the one who utilizes the same old tired types to embody the classic energy, i.e. magicians and elderly aunties as Mentors or animated birds and small beings as Tricksters. Do you see what I mean? Those are the predictable Merlins of the world," says Scheer. "Why not make your Mentor the five-year-old daughter of your main character, who is attempting to find balance in their life? Again, switch things up. We would not expect a down-on-his-luck homeless person to be a Mentor, at least at first. Think Fisher King. But he could be, and that surprise usually produces what I call *wonderment*, or the grace

Make your archetypal characters unique by unpredictable combinations that produce *wonderment.*

one feels when there is a moment of real tangible wonder in a story. So don't be lazy; use the archetypes to your advantage and create, and create, and create some more."

Remember that a character does not have to fit into one and only one role. As you play with your scenes, see how you can mix and match the roles of various archetypal characters. "Throw the Shadow or Hero energy into a character within a paragraph or scene and then change it. Now write the same scenario with the character as a Trickster (this is fun, actually) and see how the character stretches and grows. Sometimes I advise my students to do this exercise while developing their characters," says Scheer. "It helps to take that new character out of their comfort zone, [away from] what you might think that character would do, and, as a result, the writer sees the character's strengths and weaknesses and can adjust appropriately."

Let your story guide you as you create new combinations. "Often a writer needs a way to get information distributed within a story-line. Well, then have a character embody Herald or Mentor energy. If the writer needs villainous energy, then give Shapeshifter traits to a

~ Readings on Archetypes ~

~ *45 Master Characters,* by Victoria Schmidt (Writer's Digest Books)
~ *The Complete Writer's Guide to Heroes and Heroines: 16 Master Archetypes,* by Tami D. Cowden (Lone Eagle Publishing Co.)
~ *Fallen Heroes: Sixteen Master Villain Archetypes,* by Tami Cowden (Amazon Digital Services)
~ *The Hero with a Thousand Faces,* by Joseph Campbell (New World Library)
~ *The Writer's Journey: Mythic Structures for Writers,* by Christopher Vogler (Michael Weise Productions, 2007)

major player in your plot," says Scheer. "Remember that often the most loved characters are those that are complicated and can move from archetype to archetype."

This ability to mix and match and use unexpected people to fill archetypical roles does not mean that just anything goes when using character archetypes. Part of knowing what will work is understanding the archetype and how it functions. Peake explains, "Monsters are shadow archetypes, and much great art includes monsters." They tap into our fear of the unknown, the thing that goes bump in the night. "However, if the monster is silly and not really a monster, the psychological effect won't be profound," says Peake. This does not mean that you cannot write a humorous vampire character, but if you do, do not expect this character to click automatically with your readers the way that a traditional vampire would. You might have to write your vampire into the role of Hero or Trickster.

Speaking of vampires as monsters or even in other roles, the popularity of certain character types creates problems for the writer trying to tap into their energy as an archetype. "Vampires have been powerful Shadow archetypes for a very long time," says Peake. "But after these types of characters become a fad, the next book or film about vampires needs to have a new angle in order to avoid a story based on routine stereotypes. A new twist that develops the archetypal nature of vampires is quite likely to find a fascinated audience."

Use archetypes and you will be tapping into cultural familiarity to help your reader connect with your character, but do so with the understanding that you still need to create a character that is as unique as the story he or she is driving. Once you learn to piece together this puzzle of what is traditional and what is uniquely your own, you will find readers wanting to find out what happens to this new Hero, Trickster, or Shapeshifter.

Build Your Writing Career

By Veda Boyd Jones

A s I write this, my hometown of Joplin, Missouri, is recovering from the deadly F5 tornado. Businesses are rebuilding, and it occurred to me that the process by which the stores are starting to rebuild are not unlike our efforts to make careers in writing. Our blown-away Walmart, which carries the most products known to man—from TVs to strawberries to duct tape—is across town from the flattened Dude's Donuts, which specializes in magnificent glazed confections. The Walmart approach to rebuilding is the way I have approached my writing career, not concentrating on any one area, but writing whatever comes my way. I have friends who have used the Dude's Donut approach and built a platform in one specific area. They are different ways to the same end, a successful writing career.

The Walmart Way

If you like the variety of writing for different audiences, you might like my Walmart approach. The first piece I ever sold was an article about Andy Rooney to *The Encyclopedia of American Humorists,* and that was because I knew the editor from our local university. In the book's contributors' list, other writers' names were followed by the universities where they taught. Since I wasn't teaching anywhere, *independent scholar* followed my name. My family had a good laugh over that, but independent is how I would describe my writing.

Writing that one article got me a gig with another encyclopedia, but then I took a turn down a whole different aisle of my Walmart store: romance novels. While writing those, I also slipped into the magazine aisle and sold a few children's articles and stories, and some to adult magazines. Then I turned to the children's fiction aisle and wandered over into children's nonfiction books as well.

I've always written fillers, like the stuff that beckons as you stand waiting at the checkout—a little of this and a little of that, small things. While writing a few fillers for teacher magazines, I stumbled into educational materials. I've written ancillary activities for history textbooks and workbooks for studying novels for teachers and students. I've even written testing materials for an Internet reading program, which is another, but not distant, aisle of my serendipitous business.

Over in yet another department is the corporate aisle where I've written copy for construction companies entering safety contests, and interviewed kids in a children's hospital and put their words on a wall by their portraits to decorate a new wing and entice donors to give. Recently, I walked down the reviewing aisle and now write for *Publishers Weekly*. I'm sent advanced copies of books and get paid to read. Wow!

The Dude's Donut Way

Author Jen Singer has not only homed in on a platform, she has copyrighted it. She taught herself HTML and created an award-winning website, MommaSaid.net, "The Back Fence of the Internet," in 2003. It featured one of the first blogs for mothers who needed a laugh, advice, or just companionship from someone who is also guiding children to adulthood. Singer thought her blog might grow into a book, and it has grown into five, including the Stop Second-Guessing Yourself series (HCI Books) for different stages of kids' lives.

As a pioneer of mommy blogs, Singer confesses that at first only her mother followed her blog, but her readership grew as local newspapers wrote about it and then magazines picked up her story. "I had to use old school media to promote something new. And somehow it worked." She's been quoted as an expert source in the *New York Times*, *USA Today*, and the *Washington Post*, to name a few, and she has appeared on national TV including on the *Today Show*, the *Early Show*, and the *CBS Evening News*.

Another writer who has taken the Dude's Donuts approach is Jane Boursaw, who several years ago felt burned out with her freelance life of writing articles for consumer magazines. "The querying-waiting-following-up process was getting old fast. I thought hard about what I'd like to write day in and day out, and that was movie and TV content." Her website, Reel Life with Jane (www.reellifewithjane. com), reflects her love of writing entertainment news and reviews.

"Brainstorm ways you can build a business that isn't dependent on editorial regimens and advertising dollars."

Create Your Own Business

Both Singer and Boursaw have created their own businesses, and they work hard to keep them going. Boursaw advises, "Writers are entrepreneurs at heart, but take it a step further. Brainstorm ways you can build a business that is not dependent on editorial regimens and advertising dollars. One revenue stream is my syndicated family movie and TV columns, Reel Life With Jane, which are published in some 300 print and online publications and read by 20 million readers monthly. I'm constantly in build mode, and if I lose a publication here and there, it's not going to send me into a panic."

Boursaw has sent out oodles of letters of introduction to potential subscribers to her syndicated columns. Getting the word out about her service is imperative.

Singer believes in *coopetition*. That means meeting other bloggers, commenting on their blogs, and sharing information. "It comes back to you in good things." By linking to other sites, she has increased her readership. More readers means more exposure for her books.

Network & Diversify

Both entrepreneurs give the same advice as a critical factor in anyone's writing career: Network! "Keep evolving and changing with the times," Boursaw says, "and make networking a priority."

"Learn and use social media because you have to for survival these days," Singer says. Both writers have developed a presence on Facebook and Twitter and have built up followings.

Network with others in the writing world, and you will meet those writers, editors, and agents face-to-face at conferences. I met my first book editor at a quarterly meeting of the regional Ozark Writers' League. I set a goal to attend two well-chosen conferences each year.

Even using the big-platform approach of becoming an expert in one wide subject, Boursaw advises writers, "Don't put all your proverbial eggs in one basket. In addition to my syndication business, I teach online classes and tutor folks one-on-one in blogging, social media, syndication, writing, and time management," which stretch the areas she already works. "Teaching others has the added bonus of keeping me turned in to new ideas."

Singer added public speaking to her business. She recently gave the keynote address at the American Society of Journalists and Authors (ASJA) annual conference in New York City, has spoken to parenting groups, and become a spokesperson for some parenting products.

A few years ago, when Singer learned she had cancer, she searched the web for advice on being a mom with cancer and how much of her illness to share with her kids. She found little information, and when she achieved remission, she launched another site,

Parenting with Cancer (www.parentingwithcancer.com). This opened up more aisles in her business, yet all relate to her original brand of parenting.

Diversity is my middle name, not because I have thought consciously about it, but because one writing project calls to me and then another market, or editor, is dropped in my lap by a friend (and I reciprocate, of course).

Writer/Editor Relationships

My writing life has been shaped by contacts and none as much as Stephen Reginald, the editor who bought my second through ninth romance novels, pushed me into historical fiction for kids, and then took me with him to one nonfiction publishing house and then another. Although we have never met, I can identify his Eastern

> "One thing an editor can do for a writer is encourage him or her to try writing in new genres that, at first, might not seem safe."

accent with the first hello, and within hours of the tornado, he called. In our professional relationship, he has never hesitated to call me on the carpet if needed (rarely, I must add), and he sent flowers to us on the day my husband got out of the hospital after a stroke. I treasure him.

I asked him for his thoughts, which he shared. "One of the things an editor can do for a writer is encourage him or her to try writing in new genres that, at first, might not seem safe. A writer who can tackle both fiction and nonfiction projects is doubling his or her income potential. If I can get personal, for a moment, Veda is a wonderful fiction writer. I loved her storytelling skills with her adult novels and thought she had the ability to write fiction for young adults and encouraged her to do so. She mastered that genre with very little effort (easy for me to say!) and now has a handful of young adult novels on her résumé. One thing I haven't gotten Veda to do is tackle an adult historical fiction novel. With her master's in history and her great fiction-writing skills, she could open another door in an already successful freelance career."

Marti Attoun, who formerly was a general-assignment newspaper reporter and naturally falls into my Joplin Walmart freelancer category, has written about everything from apron collecting to atomic clocks. She advises writers "to focus on building relationships with editors and magazines you admire and hope to work with long-term. After delivering your first A-plus article, suggest a second perfectly targeted idea. If you can consistently come up with good ideas and turn in topnotch work, then you'll be at the top of the editor's list for assignments. The key to a steady writing income then isn't so much breaking in, as staying in, decent-paying markets where you click with the editor and publication."

Stuart Englert, Attoun's editor at *American Profile,* panicked when he failed to reach her via phone and email just after the Joplin tornado hit. He plotted the path of the tornado based on sketchy news reports and her familiar address, and did not like what he found. The next morning in the Tennessee office, when co-workers asked if he had heard from Marti, he answered "no" in a tight voice. "I emailed Marti again, and fortunately got a "I'm okay" reply about an hour later. My sense of relief was tremendous," Englert says. "Marti and I have worked together as a writer/editor team for more than 10 years, researching, developing and painstakingly (Marti will affirm) editing more than 100 stories since 2001. She is a great, capable, and dependable writer. I appreciate her quality work and I cherish her as a person I've come to know."

This writer/editor team form a mutual admiration society, and Attoun says, "Wrestling with a lede or a transition with Stuart can be painful, for sure, but the beauty of working regularly with the same editor is you get to know his and the publication's likes and dislikes, style quirks, mission, and readership. The whole process from pitching an article idea to shaping the final piece becomes faster and smoother. The happy result? One more assignment."

Boursaw has a wonderful relationship with her syndication partners because "once I send columns and images to them, they're free to edit for their space and needs. I'm not picky about how they use content, and I deliver quality content on deadline. I also throw in extra stuff—bonus reviews, posts spotlighting their publications on my blog, and mentions of them on Twitter and Facebook. They're also free to swipe whatever they want off my blog, including images, as long as they give me a byline and link back to my site. Be generous with your time and connections, and people will be generous to you in return."

Persistence

In her keynote speech at ASJA, Singer told the story of a writer who called and asked about websites since she was preparing to launch one: When the writer typed *Jen Singer* in Google, the first thing to pop up was the blog followed by thousands of results. How did she do that? Singer answered flippantly, "Oh, there's a switch on the back of your computer. You get the flashlight and then you go behind the computer, and ooph, like that, [she pretended to flip a switch] and that's how easy it is."

The crowd of ASJA writers laughed because they know how much work goes into building a solid writing reputation. Writers must build their own careers. They may use social media to build a following. They may use connections made at conferences and connections with editors they've cultivated by turning in first-rate work ahead of deadline.

All of this takes time. I'm reminded of an old *Tonight Show* where Johnny Carson asked singer Willie Nelson how it felt to be an overnight success. Nelson said he'd played every honky-tonk and two-bit bar for 25 years to become an overnight success with a number one record. He had built his following.

You start building, day by day, laying the foundations of your writing career, putting up the frame, mortaring brick or hammering clap-board siding. Every freelance career is different. Our experiences are different; our opportunities are different; our decisions are different.

But one thing is the same. You keep building, just like Joplin will rebuild from the horrible tornado that wiped out a third of our town. Walmart will come back. Dude's Donuts will return. They are building now, and you must do the same. Whether you are making contacts for the variety of things you want to write or laying the planks of your platform on one grand topic, keep going. Don't give up. Keep building.

Résumés for Writers

By Casie Hermansson

Whether you are a writer of fiction or nonfiction, write for adults or for children, you will need to become a technical or business writer too, at least temporarily. Résumé writing is taught in technical and professional writing programs, and for the rest of us there are enticing résumé samples to download online. But if ever there were a case of *caveat scriptor*, it pertains to these samples. Some might work if you are a superhero and like ono-matopoeia and lightning bolts sprinkled throughout your résumé.

Since that is not likely, here are some practical considerations and suggestions for a strong writing résumé.

Audience and Purpose

All professional writing communicates most effectively when the audience and purpose are clearly defined and targeted. The purpose for your résumé is to get a job or prove your credentials. A résumé has a persuasive function. As a writer, your publications are extremely important to include, and the résumé should not include a single error. Any formal education and experience that contributes to your credibility in your field are also crucial. Beyond that, keep the specific purpose of every résumé you design in mind as you create it, because there is no such thing as one-size-fits-all. The résumé you put together for a children's book editor will not be the same as for the editor of the local newspaper or a a general interest magazine, or for human resources at that publishing company that has an editor's job available.

Make educated assumptions about the projected reader of your résumé, starting with how busy they are, how inundated with paper, and how grateful they will be for an easily navigable résumé to peruse. To make it easily navigable, two things are required: (1) the purpose you share—finding someone with your skills, experience, and publications—should be evident in the manner in which you have composed your résumé, and (2) it should fit résumé conventions. Just as editors decry glitter, chocolates, or cat fur sent with manuscript submissions in a misguided attempt to catch their attention, résumés are also not the place to proclaim your radical uniqueness.

Conventions

There are more myths about résumés than mythical beasts in a bestiary. Everyone has stories of an employer who "never reads the cover letter" or "skips the objective statement." That is as may be. But just as you cannot send a manuscript without a cover letter, so you cannot apply for a job without one either, and for every employer who skips the objective there are nine more who expect to see it.

The following are conventions reflected in current teaching of the genre in university programs, and matched to industry expectations.

~ A résumé is as long as it needs to be, no longer or shorter, unless your audience has a length restriction. If a one-page résumé is requested, then that is what you will provide (and at no less than 12-point font, one-inch margins, either—no cheating here). Otherwise, if you have three pages of clips to list, then your résumé will exceed a page.

All documents longer than one page should be paginated. Include a header or footer on all subsequent pages that includes your name. Page one of your résumé begins with your name and contact information prominently set out. Page one is unmistakeable. The second and subsequent pages should not imitate the layout and format at the top of the first résumé page. Similarly, the cover letter is a different document and forms no part of the page count of your résumé.

~ Print your résumé on good quality paper stock. Avoid paper that has strong color connotations (pink); makes legibility difficult (artisanal or "bark and twigs" papers); or uses graphics (bubbles, globes, etc; unless you are a graphic artist and graphics are relevant to employment). Cover letters are never printed on résumé paper.

~ Know your fonts. All fonts are either *serif* (they have flourishes, like the type you are reading now) or *sans serif* (without flourishes, as in this book's sidebars). A page of *sans serif* type has more white space and appears easier to read than an all-serif page. Pick one font for your body text and, at most, one other font for headings and subheadings. More than this and you risk a chaotic design. Avoid difficult-to-read fonts, such as floral or cursive type. Use all capitals for headings, but not otherwise; all capitals decrease legibility. Use only one style for emphasis—underlining, italics, or bold.

~ When printing using colored inks, avoid using more than two colors on the résumé. Choose colors that enhance legibility. Dark text on a light background is best.

The Big Picture

Standard headings on a résumé should include: Objective, Education, Experience (or similar heading), References. Objective should always come first. The references heading is the equivalent of saying *the end,* even if you only say "available on request." Beyond that, there is no prescription for a set list of headings or their order. In all cases headings should be relevant to your experience, target the audience and purpose, and tell your story. The order should convey some internal logic. If you have won writing competitions, a heading such as Writing Prizes would work fine.

For a writer's résumé, Publications is an expected heading and may stand in lieu of Experience. You can use subheadings to distinguish

~ Sample Résumé ~

Dale-Marie Bryan
Address: 123 Main Street, Anytown, CT
Email: dmariebryan@gmail.com
Web: www.dalemariebryan.com

OBJECTIVE: Seeking work-for-hire writing educational materials where I can contribute my skills and experience as an award-winning author of children's writing and educational materials, and as a certified K–12 educator.

SUMMARY OF QUALIFICATIONS AND SKILLS
 - Bachelor of Science in (Elementary) Education
 - Elementary and junior high teaching experience, current certification
 - A published educational writer
 - Meticulous researcher
 - Creative and award-winning fiction author
 - Strong backgrounds in critical and creative thinking, education, language arts, and children's literature
 - Operating Systems: Macintosh, Windows XP, Windows 7
 - Software: Microsoft Office, InDesign, Photoshop
 - Photography

EDUCATION
 - Bachelor of Science in Education, Fort Hays State University
 - Elementary education, recertified 2009
 - Post-graduate course work, Pittsburg State University, KS

WORK EXPERIENCE
Evaluator of Teaching Effectiveness, Educational Testing Service (September–October 2011)
 - Analyzed ELA and math videos at the 4–9 grade levels
 - Assessed, commented, and submitted scores based on eight effectiveness scales for a pilot teacher evaluation project

Curriculum Specialist, Pitsco Education, Pittsburg, Kansas (2007–2010)
 - Led a team of editors, quality assurance personnel, graphic artists, and multimedia specialists in maintaining 100+ K–6 curriculum titles
 - Supervised content and multimedia updates
 - Edited materials and trained fellow curriculum specialists and teachers
 - Created an online training program for current and future employees
 - Assessed and correlated curriculum materials to state and national standards

~ Sample Résumé ~

Teacher, Kansas School Districts 316, 317, 294, 234 (1974–2006)
- Taught academic, social, and critical thinking skills to elementary and junior high students in self-contained, team teaching, combination, and special classes, and as an extracurricular activity sponsor
- Supervised student teachers
- Prepared and presented statewide professional development materials - Prepared objectives and outlines for courses of study and assisted in curriculum development and textbook adoption
- Prepared and administered assessment materials
- Designed and initiated innovative instructional materials and resources
- Wrote technical instructions for nationally distributed materials
- Organized conferences, workshop, and support groups

Freelance Writer (1987–Present)
- Write and publish award-winning fiction and nonfiction for children and adults
- Write technical instructions for nationally distributed educational materials

Books
- *Top 10 Tips for Building Friendships* (forthcoming, Rosen Publishing)
- *Living With Celiac Disease* (forthcoming, ABDO Publishing, 2011-12)
- *Experiments with Magnets* (True Book/ Scholastic, 2011)
- *Obesity Discrimination* (Rosen Publishing, 2008)
- *About Geography, South Dakota* (Children's Press/Scholastic, 2007)
- *About Geography, The Colorado River* (Children's Press/Scholastic, 2006)

Articles and Stories
- "CD Rainbow," *Highlights for Children* (2009)
- "Puppy Love," *Highlights for Children* (2007)
- "From Trash to Treasure," *Country Woman* (2007)
- "Resistance," *Blue Cubicle Press Anthology* (2006)
  [Editor's Note: Continue with a full list of credits, or attach a separate list.]

Awards in Writing and Publishing
- *Highlights for Kids* Author of the Month (February 2007)
- Highlights Foundation Scholarship (2003)

REFERENCES
    Available on request.

between different types of publications, as needed. If you are aiming for an editing position, you need to have editing experience, references, and possibly also a section dedicated to your computer skills.

Your résumé is a selection of details documented with your audience and purpose in mind. You should be able to fit anything relevant to these into the résumé format. Headings should clearly tie the experience you have to the purpose; there is no single right way to label something. For instance, if you have worked as a science teacher substitute and you are applying for a teaching job, you might use the heading Teaching Experience. But if you are applying for a position writing science experiments for an education publisher, you could instead use a heading such as: Science Experience or Science-Teaching Experience.

A plethora of other secondary headings are suggested in templates and résumé samples: Honors and Awards, Military Service, Professional Memberships, Volunteer Activities, and so on. Only use what is relevant to the audience and purpose at hand. The résumé is not a keepsake list of your life history (which distinguishes it from a *curriculum vita*—a life list), but it is a list of thoughtfully selected facts that support your application. You can use the adjective Select in your headings to make it clear when you have used a culling principle: Select Experience or Select Publications.

As long as you do not try to mislead, what you put on a résumé and what you leave off is up to you. An employer looking for a record of employment will see red flags when there are holes in dates or lack of specifics. They are looking for a consistent story in your résumé: two years of community college, followed by two years of employment, a year volunteering overseas, and another job. The overseas volunteering position may not appear chronologically under Employment, nor is it required on a résumé. But in this example, leaving a full year unaccounted for may be problematic and leave an employer assuming the worst.

Do not underestimate the value of independent work. If you are self-employed, you freelance, or work as an independent contractor and so on, you have more skills to offer, not less. You can descriptively sell this to a prospective employer (editor) by noting that you work well to deadlines; that you multitask with ease; that you are an effective manager of time and resources. You would not be a successful freelancer without these skills! If your experience has included freelance editing, do not use a vague phrase like "editing work." Instead, specify the exact nature of services performed.

Beware TMI, too much information. No editor or prospective employer needs to know that gaps in your résumé were related to divorces, custody issues, and so on. Stay strictly professional.

Basic Layout:

~ *Name and Contact.* Your contact information should be professional. Your email address ideally contains your name (it is another way to have your name in front of the prospective employer). Include all contact information both in your cover letter and on your résumé. They are separate documents, even though they are sent as a packet.

~ *Objective.* The Objective statement is notoriously hard to pin down. It is easy to strike the wrong tone in your objective and put your reader off. One online Sample Author Résumé (www.bestsamplerésumé.com/sample-communication-résumé/author-résumé.html) gives this example of an objective: "To get more experience in authoring books and magazines and become well-renowned in this field." Granted, the site authors indicate that you are free to customize to your own needs. But look at this objective from an editor or employer's point of view. First, it is writer-centered, not reader-centered. You are applying for a position or a contract based on what skills and experience you already have to offer. It is not a paid training exercise. Of course, by getting the contract you will gain more experience. But that is an expected by-product and not your stated objective. Second, "authoring books and magazines" is so broad and generalized that it is not helpful. Third, fame (to "become well-renowned") is another hoped-for by-product but not what the editor is aiming to bestow upon you. They have a job, you have skills/experience/credentials, and you are aiming to persuade them of a match.

Aim for clear, concise, and relevant: "A position as a writer-for-hire writing fiction and nonfiction leveled readers for K-6" is a clear announcement of what you are looking for now, and what the résumé can support. Note the prevalence of keywords: *writer-for-hire; fiction and nonfiction; leveled readers; K-6.* Go through your objective statement and note the keywords. Have you covered the necessary bases? Six months from now, will the database select your résumé if the editor searches using keywords?

~ *Education.* Education should come after the objective statement if any of the following are true: It is significant (a degree or higher degree); it is relevant to the writing situation for which you are applying with this résumé; it is recent education, even if not relevant to the writing situation (all education is good!). If not, or if for instance your degree is older and you have since parlayed your education into other relevant experience, such as employment or publications, then education can drop in the hierarchy below the more recent and relevant headings. If you employ reverse chronology (most recent on top), then be consistent throughout the résumé and do the same for publications. State the name of the school, its location, dates attended, or the date you were awarded a degree or diploma.

Beware the story your résumé will tell if you have had many shifts of location, changed degree programs, or half-completed programs without explanation.

~ *Publications.* All clips, like employment, should be verifiable. Give enough information and specifics to make it clear that your claims of publications can be supported: dates, names of magazines, URLs for ezines, and so on. Indicate *forthcoming* or a scheduled future date if the work is not yet out.

~ *References.* For contract writing, references may not be as relevant as clips. But for other work, they are important. Provide between three and six references. At least one should be from a previous employer. Avoid character references from family members, guidance counselors, pastors, coaches, or high school English teachers. Choose references who can speak to your ability to do this job.

Who Is Going to Read This?

Profiling Your Audience

By Katherine Swarts

Books without identifiable potential readers do not sell. Neither do articles and stories for which editors cannot visualize readers. To avoid creating a manuscript no one wants, successful writers consider who will read the results of their efforts.

How thoroughly they consider their audience runs a wide gamut. One writer may create an essay-length description of her *typical* reader, find a magazine photograph to match it, and hang them by the computer for frequent reference. Another writer may proceed almost entirely by instinct.

Those near the latter end of the spectrum are, whether they realize it or not, writing for people like themselves. This is a sufficient formula for success for them. "I don't do reader profiles, at least not consciously," says YA author and playwright Sandy Asher. But "I tend to write for the young person inside me. I am my own reader profile, I guess! If I'm not deeply interested in the characters and their story, or in the nonfiction topic I'm working on, I can't expect anyone else to be interested, either. When I'm not deeply involved in the material, I'm not likely to do a very good job. A passion for the material, and the young me inside eagerly waiting to see what I say

203

next, keep the creative flame burning."

For fiction writers, the story's protagonist may also function as the reader profile. "I rarely even think about my reader," says children's author Marion Dane Bauer. "I focus on connecting with my character and getting that character right on every level. The character creates a window into the story for appropriate readers."

Fits All, Fits None

Not all writers, however, can home in on those appropriate readers by instinct. The writer who is new to a genre may especially need to research a market's typical customers, lest submissions be judged good, but too mature/formal/feminine/high-end for a publisher's readers.

One of the most frequent mistakes made by novice writers—barely a step above the writer who does not even look at the guidelines—is to assume that *everyone* will enjoy a work. "If you try to please everyone you will end up pleasing no one," says fantasy author and screenwriter Teel James Glenn. "To try and make every story everything to everyone is like diluting soup with water."

Thinking in terms of everybody means "writing to a middle audience at best," says author Bill Nolan. "Everybody cannot and will not relate to how you sculpt your ideas, your intent, and the basis of your writing. I'm glad I don't write for everybody; it's far too much responsibility."

"If you hold the view that there is an *everyreader* out there, take a step back and look around," says Moira Allen, Editor of Writing-World.com. "Within your own circle of friends and family, would you say that everyone is the same, or has the same interests? Are you even the same person you were 10 or 20 years ago? If you walk into a bookstore, you won't find a section for *everybody*. You'll find sections for readers of mysteries, romance, and literature; you'll find nonfiction sections for a wide range of interests. Not even every, say, computer book is going to appeal to every computer user. Claiming you have an idea that will appeal to everyone instantly broadcasts that you do not understand the basics of identifying your audience. Editors recognize this assumption as the rankest of amateur mistakes."

That is not to say there are not published works that appeal to a huge range of ages, ethnicities, or economic backgrounds. Glenn points out, "I think there is no typical reader of any type of story these days. Sitting on the train, I see men reading romance, women reading spy books, and every strata of society reading Harry Potter." But a writer should start with some idea about where the largest portion of an audience will come from, and trust that extra markets will open on their own.

"A writer trying to speak to all readers runs the risk of not speaking to anyone," says Evelyn M. Fazio, Publisher of WestSide Books. "The writer shouldn't be trying to write a crossover" between YA and adult, between religious and secular, or between male and female. "They should focus on the audience at hand and if their book is great and they're very lucky, it'll cross over on its own. Otherwise, it may not even succeed with the original target audience."

It may not even succeed with the writer. "If the motivation comes from outside," says Asher, "if the imagined reader is everybody rather than the crucial somebody within, the writing tends to be forced and flat. I quickly run out of steam, and tend not to finish those pieces."

Speak to Your Strengths

A good first step toward knowing your readers is learning what they already like. "The way to *see* the readers you want to reach," says Glenn, "is to read what they are reading. Reviews help, but you really need to know the books yourself to understand the needs they fill: who the main characters are, what emotions are dealt with. Then you can find the parts that appeal to your strengths as a writer and your likes as a person, to make sure that the book you write is not just a carbon copy of some successful series, but rather a new and vital piece. Like the old wedding phrase, 'something borrowed, something new.'"

Nor is textual content the sole way to learn about the reader, especially in graphically oriented media. "Look at a magazine visually," advises Allen. "As writers, we tend to focus on what we read; to learn more about a publication's readers, pay attention to what you see. Take a look at the pictures, particularly the ads: Do they show high-end antiques or inexpensive collectibles? Food displayed on

> "**P**ay attention to what you see in a publication, particularly the ads: Do they show high-end antiques or inexpensive collectibles? Young or old models? Visual nuggets can tell you far more about the audience than guidelines alone."

fine china or crystal, or on plastic plates? Young or old models, casually or elegantly dressed? Visual nuggets like these can tell you far more about a publication's demographics than guidelines alone. After all, guidelines are often generic and politically correct—but advertisers know who buys through a venue and will target their images accordingly."

Allen continues, "Gather as much information as you possibly can about a potential audience or market. For example, if you know that your audience will consist primarily of single parents, your article can avoid references to how to work with a partner or spouse. If you know that a magazine's readership prefers expensive vacations in exotic locales, you won't waste time pitching the ten best hikes in your backyard. The more you know about your readers, the more you can tailor your work to their needs and interests—and that will impress your editor."

Consider also your intended readers' everyday language; you

don't want to sound either pompous or ignorant. "I'd suggest novelists read their work and record it, then listen to it," says Fazio. "That would be a good way to judge if the writing is right for the intended audience."

Finally, consider the level of knowledge the reader already has on a given topic. "One key question to ask is, "Who does not know this?' A common amateur mistake is to send beginner information to a magazine widely read by people who already know a great deal," says Allen. "For example, if you've just taken your first hike, you might think a lot of people would like to know some of the lessons you learned through that experience. However, people who subscribe to, say, *Hiking Monthly* probably made their beginner mistakes years ago; you have nothing to teach them. So look for a market that would attract people who can learn from what you have to say, rather than those from whom you would be learning."

A Bit Too Narrow

All that said, it is possible to be too thorough with a reader profile. The average writer tends to find an approach of "define your reader like you would a character, down to the last freckle" more of a hindrance than a help. The same may be said of the notion of a visual aid such as hanging up a photo to represent the reader.

"Trying to identify your entire audience with a single image," says Allen, "is like trying to apply a one-size-fits-all approach" to the text itself. "There is no one reader who adequately represents the potential range of your readership. Say your photo is of a tall, blonde woman in her mid-thirties, tanned, wearing upscale casual clothes and sunglasses and striding along a beach. Just this word-picture alone conjures an image of a particular type of person—and in so doing, it prevents you from imagining the short, dark-haired Latino woman reading a newspaper over her latte, or the slightly overweight brunette who just entered the gym. When your article is about savings strategies for working women between the ages of 20 and 40, how can you capture your audience with an image of one woman? Accept

~ Circulation, Demographics ~

Knowing something about how magazines use demographics to sell subscriptions and advertising can help writers identify more about their targeted magazine markets. Here are some basics about magazine circulation and demographics.

The Audit Bureau of Circulations (ABC, www.accessabc.com) is an organization that gathers and reports information on magazine and circulation and distribution. It verifies the data so that advertisers can be sure when they purchase ad space in a publication they know who it is going to, and how many people will see it. Magazines often provide this information in their media kits.

ABC distinguishes between circulation and audience. *Circulation* means the number of copies of a magazine published and distributed, whether paid or unpaid, newsstand or subscription. *Audience* or *readership* means how many readers of the magazine—including the many people in a household, a doctor's office, and so on. The latter is typically gathered through surveys.

Audiences are studied by geography—where is a magazine sold— and by demographics. ABC provides Reader Profiles to magazines based on the demographic data it gathers, and this information too may be included in magazines' media kits. Reader Profiles include gender, age, education, household income, marital status, household composition (children, their ages, etc.) race/ethnicity, employment status, working women, occupation, and primary residence type.

As a writer targeting potential markets, it is useful to know: Is a given publication directed at 18- to 34-year-old males? 18- to 34-year-old females pursuing careers, or beginning to raise a family? Is it a general interest magazine for the more educated, with a mean age of 40? Or a small, niche publication targeted at families trying to save money? Combine this with a study of the content of several issues of a magazine, and your submissions are likely to be on point.

the diversity of your audience."

Defining the reader profile too strictly can also limit a writer's long-term opportunities: "If you write for too narrow a demographic," says Glenn, "you will never break into a wider and more profitable market." That does not mean every writer must do both children's and adult books, or both men's and women's fiction, although there are certainly enough successful writers who create material for widely different audiences. It does mean that writers are well-

> **"If you write for too narrow a demographic, you will never break into a wider and more profitable market."**

advised to take a basic profile concept and consider how many, rather than how few, people it can encompass. For example, defining *traditional families,* as one survey did, as "married heterosexual couples and whoever happens to share their households," rather than more broadly as "mom and dad with two kids at home—no more, no less, and all kids under 18."

Using a fairly broad profile can save writers from overanalyzing to see if every word or term they use in their writing is comprehensible. Although writing over readers' heads is a danger, condescension is perhaps an even greater one. If a piece as a whole is well-written and the context is clear, readers will forgive an occasional strange word. They may even appreciate the chance to learn something new. "It's okay to use harder vocabulary when writing for kids," says Fazio. "It's good for them to stretch a bit." Readers will not be interested at all if you tell them only what they already know.

Where It All Begins

Probably the most important rule in all writing is to know your readers, but do not become so obsessed with them that they interfere with your writing what you love.

"In reality," says Allen, "I think most of us start with ideas, not readers. We have an idea for an article, and then we start looking around to see where we might create a fit with a magazine—and by definition, an audience. Sometimes an idea may fit with several different audiences. So perhaps the best way to start creating your reader profile is to start with your idea, and then ask, 'Who will this interest? Who will this help? Who needs to know this? Who wants to know this?' You might even start by asking why this idea interested you, and by identifying the aspects that appeal to you. Then you can start to identify the type of reader who will benefit."

"I think our basic feeling," says Susan Burmeister-Brown, Co-Editor of *Glimmer Train Stories*, "is that rather than having an awareness of your readers shaping your literary fiction, it is smart to read fine literary work and let that be what has a gentle influence on your writing."

"'Become the readers in your mind," says Glenn, and then "forget it and write the best darn book you can!"

Website Creation & Design

By S. M. Ford

O nce upon a time a professional had a résumé, and a business business card that provided basic means of contact, like a phone number and postal address. Today, businesses and professionals are at risk of being virtually invisible if they do not have an online presence. So now, in addition to refining our craft, keeping abreast of markets that change with the speed of a mouse click, and managing professional finances, writers should have a website or we are not optimizing our careers.

Plan Content First

Writers are creative people, but most are amateurs at website creation. Even if we pay a technological professional to do the job for us, we need to have visual and verbal input and some under-standing of how to optimize our author website if it is to represent us well and have an impact on our career.

Step one is to decide the website's purpose and use. It can promote or sell our work, help attract and arrange speaking engagements, answer fan questions, assist or interact with other writers, function as a forum to talk about our passions, or be a unique combination of

~ Content Ideas ~

~ administrative details for writers, such as copyright information

~ articles or essays, or a subscription newsletter about writing

~ blog with RSS feed

~ other services you offer, such as critiquing or book editing

~ book trailers

~ contact information, which could include publisher or publicity contact information

~ discussion forums

~ downloadable press releases

~ ebooks

~ excerpts of books, stories, articles

~ FAQs (frequently asked questions and answers)

~ interviews

~ links to other related sites or blogs

~ maps for a created fictional world related to your writing

~ behind-the-scenes information about your work or research

~ photos of you working, speaking, or your office or writing location

~ playlists related to your writing; no music should auto-start

~ podcasts

~ polls

~ publication credits

~ quotes

~ reading group discussion questions

~ recommended books

~ search box for finding content on website

~ shopping—direct book purchase or link to Amazon or other sites

~ social networking connections to Facebook, Twitter, Linkedin

~ speaking events calendar, and how to book you

~ testimonials to author's writing or illustrating

~ upcoming projects

~ writer résumé or biography

~ writing prompts or activities for kids or adults

all of these. Be prepared to answer visitors' questions about you and your work, and to assist them in resolving some of their own questions or problems. Your website needs to give its visitors something, graciously and productively. That will increase interactions with readers, other writers, and maybe editors.

"Provide value," says Thomas Umstattd, an author and a developer of websites for small businesses. "An effective website is a site with information so valuable visitors would be willing to pay for it and are pleasantly surprised to find it for free. This surprise turns into sharing, which turns into traffic." (See the article on building Search Engine Optimization and building traffic on page 223.)

Most fundamentally, your author site should have information on your publications and perhaps your work-in-progress. Include lists of your credits, book cover images and blurbs, an appealing author biography, a picture, and contact information. Include awards you have won, and a calendar of upcoming author appearances. Offer sample articles, stories, or book chapters to entice readers.

Beyond these basics, consider including the backstory about how a topic intrigued you or why you were drawn to write a certain book. Your personal passions will pull people in. A historical novelist might share fascinating details learned while doing research, or tell what in the story was true and what was imagined. A fantasy writer might include character histories, or the governmental structure of the story's make-believe world. (Imagine J. R. R. Tolkien creating a website with the elvish language revealed.) If you write American historical fiction, put up a recipe for a seventeenth-century New England recipe or an Alabama family recipe too old to trace. If you write science fiction, create interactive games or activities your audience will appreciate. If you specialize in inspirational or advice articles, offer self-help quizzes for teens, mothers, fathers, singles—your audience.

"Nonfiction authors should pack their sites with so many tips and info related to their books that visitors are compelled to share it with their friends," says Umstattd, but the advice is applicable to fiction writers as well. Each website should uniquely show the author, and reveal a professional identity.

Be aware of the balance of static and dynamic information you choose to include. Static information stays the same for the most part, such as your contact information. A blog is an easy way to add dynamic content on a regular basis. Some author's blogs are their website. New content is important to bring visitors back.

Edit and proof your website copy carefully. No matter how beautiful a site looks, if the content is unreadable; has typos or poor grammar and punctuation; or is inaccurate, visitors will not stay or come back. "Your website design is like the frame around a picture," Umstattd says. Do not make the mistake many website amateurs do and overdo the design and underwhelm with information. Umstattd continues, "Many authors spend more time on the wrapping paper than they do on the present."

You will need to develop a nice wrapping—the layout—but first, find the place and means to create the site.

Do It Yourself

Once you know what you want to include in your author website, and have an idea what you want it to look like and how to organize it, you will need to take several steps to create the site.

- *Purchase* a domain name from a Domain Registrar. The domain name can be as simple as www.yourname.com.
- *Decide who will host your site.* Your Internet Service Provider (ISP) may already provide website hosting. If not, find one among many other possible hosts. The cost for website hosting ranges from free to monthly or annual fees, depending on storage provided, data transfer limits, number of email addresses provided, and other services. When reviewing website plans, check how many web pages are allowed. A basic plan is appropriate for a first website.

Some authors use blogging software such as WordPress, TypePad, or Blogger to create a website. You should still purchase a domain name, and then redirect the domain name to the site.

⁓ Website Hosting Services ⁓

Comparisons and reviews of different platforms can be found at sites such as Find My Hosting, www.findmyhosting.com, and Web Hosting Stuff, www.webhostingstuff.com. Check out award winners at Award Winning Hosts, www.awardwinninghosts.com.

Below are specific hosting and building sites, listed in order by price. This is not an extensive list by any means—just a sampling. Mac users should also check out what is available at www.apple.com. Look at iLife, which includes iWeb and much more, and Pages.

- **Weeby:** www.weebly.com. Free hosting. No ads. Extra features for a fee. Uses drag and drop.
- **Wix:** www.wix.com. Free, with ads. Premium features start at $4.95/month, with no ads. This is a Flash site.
- **Snap Pages:** www.snappages.com. Free for 5 pages. $8 a month after a free trial for more space and many more features, including the domain name.
- **Yola:** www.yola.com. Free, including hosting, with no ads, but you cannot customize your domain name. For a custom domain name and other features, $99.95 a year. Good ease of use.
- **Homestead:** www.homestead.com. One month free, but must give credit card to sign up for trial. $4.99/month and up, depending on features.
- **Moogo:** www.moogo.com. 14-day free trial. Starts at $4.99 a month. Free domain name with a year's payment.
- **Living Dot:** www.livingdot.com. $8.95 a month and up. Offers domain name registration. Supports Movable Type and WordPress platforms.
- **Square Space:** www.squarespace.com. 14-day free trial. $12 a month.
- **Site2you:** www.site2you.com. 7-day free trial. $19.95 a month. Free domain name.

~ *Look at the advertising.* Some hosting sites include ads and the author has little, if any, control over which ads appear. Often free or trial website hosting will include ads, but paid sites will not. Take this into consideration when selecting a host.

~ *Create the page.* Hosting sites often provide software for site-building that includes layout options, formatting options for text and pictures, color choices, widgets for special applications, etc. Many provide templates, so the user does not have to decide on every individual element. Commonly, these programs offer drag-and-drop or cut-and-paste techniques for dropping information into the available space. (See below for pointers on creating an appealing visual layout and optimizing visitor ease of use.)

If even reading this article pushes the limits of your understanding, do online research to understand the terms. Read up on the basics of how a website works. Attend classes or workshops on website building. When you are ready and willing to jump in, the hosting sites usually provide product assistance; check the resources and help menus. Forums or discussion boards for users of the web hosting software may also provide answers.

~ *Test the site.* When you have established your domain and created your new site, testing is a must. Does it work how you expected? Does it work when viewed in different browsers (Internet Explorer, Firefox, Chrome, others)? Do all the links work?

~ *Do not design an entire website using Adobe Flash.* It makes for slower loading and is less flexible. Tessa Elwood, who writes speculative YA fiction and does Web coding for her day job explains, "Search engines can't read Flash. Most mobile devices can't display flash. RSS readers can't read Flash. It's slow except on high-speed Internet connections. Inside pages in a site can't be bookmarked." Flash sites can be difficult to access in general.

~ *Be aware of photo and image copyright.* An author should not just snag pictures from the Internet and put them in a website or blog. Of course, public domain images, or those with a Creative Commons license (http://creativecommons.org), are usable without permission. Public domain images are available on some government websites, listed at www.usa.gov/Topics/Graphics.shtml. Always read the disclaimers on individual websites that appear to allow use of images.

Stock.xchng (www.sxc.hu) and morgueFile (www.morguefile.com) both offer free images. Often, the photographer only wants to know where the image was used. Bigfoto (www.bigfoto.com) images are free if users provide a link or reference with their use. Flickr (www.flickr.com) photos are not free, but the creator of an image

> O ften hosting sites include ads and the author has little, if any, control over which ads appear. Take this into consideration when selecting a host.

may grant permission for use. Stock photo sites such as Getty Images, Dreamstime, Shutterstock, iStockphoto (www.istockphoto.com), and others provide images for a fee.

~ *Look for help when needed.* If creating your author website is more than you want to take on yourself, find someone with expertise to help. Mike Smith, a WordPress blog designer for Guerilla, says, "If you come across something you need help with, it's ok to ask. . . . Sometimes you'll find people who are willing to help for free (openly ask on Twitter or Facebook), but if you want someone to really spend time working on something with you, you should always be prepared to pay a fee. And keep pushing forward, you never know how much you can learn until you dive right in."

If a professional designer is too expensive, talk to local college professors. They may have students who can take on a project. But one caveat: These students probably will not be around to maintain and change your site for you later. Make sure they teach you how to make changes yourself.

Looking Good in Layout

In this age of instant gratification, web surfers are not patient. If a website takes too long to load, visitors will move on. Many are annoyed by a gatekeeper screen where they must click to enter your site. If they cannot find what they are looking for, visitors are more likely to try another site than to keep searching yours. "Do not make the viewer spend ten minutes searching for the basics, like contact information. Actually, it's a good policy not to make the viewer search too hard for anything," says Elwood.

How well your site is used, and how often visitors return, is a factor of both the content and your layout. The layout of each page and structure of the entire site needs to be clear and easy to follow. Layout includes headers, a navigation bar or menu, content areas, images, footers for administrative material, and the number of pages. "The best layouts show off the content to the best advantage and reflect the style of what the site is about," says Elwood.

~ *Navigation.* The navigation choices are customarily at the top of each page of the site, or on the left in a sidebar. Page headers and navigation should have a consistent style and location from page to page within the website.

Use your sidebar well. "A big mistake I see many authors make is that they put content in their sidebar," says Umstattd. "People tend to be *banner blind* to sidebars. Sidebars are for less important information and navigation, not core content and photos."

~ *Scrolling.* Consider how the pages will appear on the screen. Visitors should not have to scroll left and right to see the full page. Scrolling down for more information or clicking on links is common usage.

~ *Search box.* A search box is especially useful for return visitors. When they remember an author's post on a topic, they can enter the subject in the search box and find it quickly. Make the box immediately accessible to users. Do not put it in some out-of-the-way place on the page. Most search boxes are at the top near the navigation bar or in the sidebar.

~ *Links.* Link directly from body text to other areas on the website.

~ Hiring a Professional ~

It takes research to find a really good web designer. Get testimonials from other authors, and get estimates not only on cost, but on length of time to finished development.

Go into a meeting with a designer prepared to explain the purpose of your website and the content, including high-quality images. Give your ideas, but also listen to the professional's suggestions. If a web designer is resisting something you want, ask why.

Usually, web designers will provide some basic mock-up ideas. That is the time to discuss changes of layout, structure, color, etc., and not once the design is finished and the website is ready to go.

The web designers interviewed for this article were:

~ Tessa Elwood: http://ipopcolor.com/
~ Lee Munroe: www.leemunroe.com
~ Mike Smith: www.madebyguerrilla.com. WordPress blog designer.
~ Thomas Umstattd: www.umstattdmedia.com

In addition to a navigation bar, this helps users find their way around without having to figure out where to go. Linking to sites outside of your own can make it more friendly to search engines. However, when a link goes outside the author site, it should open in a new window so that the original site is still on the visitor's screen.

Do not include too many links, or make them difficult to locate on the page. Elwood recommends that navigation "links should be no more than three deep." That is, do not make visitors need to select more than three links to get where they want to go.

~ *Picture size.* A picture may be worth a thousand words, especially in such a visual medium as the internet, but that image better not be so large it takes too long to load or does not fit in the page layout. A website designer knows to resize images; a do-it-yourselfer needs to learn to make appropriate web-sized images.

~ Visual Mistakes to Avoid ~

"The biggest visual faux pas I see are lame author photos," says Thomas Umstattd, an author and website developer. "Invest in an expensive portrait artist and publishers and readers will take you more seriously."

Mike Smith, a WordPress blog designer for Guerilla, says, "An on-running joke in the design community is that a lot of clients ask to 'make the logo bigger.' They want logos bigger, fonts larger and ads that are more 'in your face.'" He also says, "Pop-ups and excessive advertisements are my top pet peeve. They scream *spam* and usually don't get my full attention. Ads and pop ups have their place, but they don't need to be overused in order to be effective."

Web designer Lee Munroe steers his clients away from animations. YA author and web coder Tessa Elwood agrees and adds the recommendation to avoid "light text on a dark background." It is difficult to read.

~ *Text.* The home page should not include everything you want on the site, and certainly should not be text-heavy. Achieve a happy balance between very little text and an overwhelming amount. Think of the home page as a focal point. Links from it to other pages, plus an unambiguous navigation menu, should make it clear that there is more information and indicate how to get to it easily. We read web pages differently than we read print on paper.

Too much on a page can be confusing or off-putting, and then you lose your visitor. Break up your text. Use subheadings, bullet points, images. Keep the paragraphs brief. Most recommendations are to use between 250 and 1,500 words on one web page.

Be sure visitors can cut and paste your text. If you make it into inaccessible artwork or images, you are bound to frustrate users you want your information.

~ *Visuals.* Colors, background, images, and fonts all contribute to visual feel. Observe other sites and take note of the ones with most appeal; they probably have a limited palette of colors and fonts. The backgrounds add, not detract from the site. Textures and gradients can give a website depth and help focus the eye.

~ *Maintenance.* A related point about website creation is maintenance. Have you ever gone to what appears to be a great website only to discovered out-of-date information? Maintaining current content on a website takes commitment. If a website is easy to change, update, add to, it is more likely that those changes will be made. If you used the services of a web designer, a maintenance schedule and cost agreement for updates should be made or included in your arrangement.

Visual and Verbal Tone

When you have put together your site, review its personality. What impression do you want it to give? Is it successful?

Think about a book jacket and the flap copy. The words and images or colors fit well together. The visual and verbal tone of a website should do the same. A romance writer's website colors and background may imply candlelit dinners or hot sultry nights in the bedroom. Excerpts from books will be about relationships and love. A space opera author's website might give the feel of being inside a spaceship. His language will fit. A Western writer's website should make visitors at home on the range and ready to tip their hats to the ladies.

"Tone," according to Elwood, "should reflect you and your audience. If your target audience is older, small font, bright colors, and busy graphics won't make your viewers feel comfortable. Simple is best. If your audience is younger, too plain with no edge will come across as unprofessional or boring."

This website is, after all, one portrait of you. And you want to put your best face forward to your reading world.

Double Your Website Traffic: Learn SEO

By Darcy Pattison

The year before last, I doubled the traffic on my website from 125,000 to more than 250,000 page views. I did it by paying attention to simple principles of search engine optimization, or SEO. The online world is negotiated, by and large, by searching for information on a search engine. What that means for authors is that your webpage is worthless unless it can be found in a search engine. Making sure a site is optimized for search engines is now a field unto itself.

SEO usually begins with a look at how a search engine (usually Google) sorts through pages to find and display information. It is admittedly tricky in some ways: The mathematical formulas, or algorithms, used to do the sorting change constantly and, on top of that, Google guards its algorithms carefully to keep its search results untainted by commercial concerns, or worse. But some constants remain, even if the relative weight and nuances of each element might shift. You can use these to optimize access to your website.

Content: The Most Important Way to Get Found is Header Tags

Search engines look for information that answers specific needs of the searcher. Content was declared *king* early in the development of the World Wide Web, and it remains king. Your website needs solid information on the topics you cover; let us assume you have included that.

How do search engines know what information is present on your site? They *spider* it. A spider is a robot visitor to your site. It arrives, downloads, catalogues and analyzes your information.

What is important here is how the spider actually looks at the data. It does so through hypertext markup language, or HTML. It is the language or coding on websites that tells browsers how to display the information. An HTML *tag* is enclosed in bracket symbols: < >. The tags almost always appear in pairs, an opening and a closing tag, with the closing tags preceded by a back-slash (/). For example, the title of a page might be marked up like this, and the browser will show this text in its title bar:

<title>Fiction Notes by Darcy Pattison</title>

Search engines make use of this information originally meant only for browsers. Of importance for this discussion are a series of tags for headers in our text (coded from <H1> to <H6>), and the title tag (<title>). These header tags tell search engines to stop and pay attention because these headlines mark key pieces of information on the site.

Each web page has one set of <title> tags, but can contain any number of header tags. When you choose software to create a website or blog, make sure the software uses header tags. I often see a webpage or blog where important information contained in the headlines and sub-headlines of a page are instead marked by <strong> or <bold> tags. These will provide a weak return in SEO. Also note that websites that are based on frames (a means of having multiple HTML documents on the same page), or Adobe Flash may have no header tags, rendering them almost invisible to search engines.

How to Check your Page's Header Tags

~ *Step one.* Surf to your website page. Right click (Control-click on a Mac) on the page and click View Page Source. This pulls up the html for your website. If you've never looked at this before, it is likely to be confusing. You can spot your content in there somewhere but there is confusing code surrounding your text.

~ *Step two.* Not to worry. You only want to check your header tags. Control-F (Apple-F on a Mac) will bring up a search box. (This search box works on any web page, by the way; if you are researching on a long web page, it is invaluable.) Type H1 in the search box and hit enter. If your page has tagged information as H1, the cursor should move forward to highlight it. Repeat (or arrow down, depending on your browser) to see how many times this tag is used. It should only be used twice on a page, once at the beginning of the page's title text as <h1> and once at the end of that text as </h1>. H1 is usually reserved for the name of the blog or website. Depending on your software, it might also be a title tag.

~ *Step three.* Repeat the search for H2, H3, H4, H5 and H6. H2 should be the title of the current blog post or name of the particular page of the website. There should be both an opening and closing H2 tag. H3 through H6 are used at your discretion to indicate subheadings on your site or post. Each might occur multiple times.

A potential weakness in terms of SEO is to use generic categories in these tags. Subheadings like *books, resources,* or *recent posts* add little unique value to your website's content and do nothing to differentiate you from dozens of other sites. Sometimes it is unavoidable, but consider the advantage of these: Darcy Pattison's Books, How-to-Write Resources, Fiction Notes. They are much better subheadings for SEO because they are more specific and different from those likely to be used on countless other websites.

Notice also that the header tags are hierarchical, to show the level of importance of information. Often a site will only use H1 to H3 tags and that is fine. But consider using a deeper level of tags for longer or more complex information.

~ WordPress Blog Tags ~

If you use a WordPress blog and you do not know HTML, then you are using the Visual Editor when you edit a post. Do not be tempted to put headlines and subheadings in a boldface font and then adjust the font size. It may look the same to you, but it looks very different to a search engine. You need those header tags for great SEO.

To find them, hover over the icons on the Visual Editor until you find Hide/Show Kitchen Sink (or just use the keyboard shortcut of Alt+Shift+Z). This will reveal more options for formatting: There should be a dropdown menu to tell you if the text is regular paragraph text or header text. Highlight the text needed and click on the header of choice. Remember, H1 tags are for the title of the page, so begin blog postings with H2 and add subheadings as needed.

For software other than Wordpress's, look for tutorials on how to use the header tags.

If you are surprised at so much time spent discussing on header tags, do not be. They are that important. Get them right and you are halfway there with SEO.

Keywords

Another key to SEO is deliberately choosing great keywords. These are words or phrases that you will highlight in header tags and repeat often on a page. To make keywords work well, you need to know what people are searching for. Google makes it easy with their Google Keyword Tool, at https://adwords.google.com/select/KeywordToolExternal.

Simply put several keywords into Google Keyword Tool and you will get a list of the various ways people search for your information. For example, if you have written a book on World War II history, specifically about D-Day, you might consider the following keywords. But note the difference in the number of searches done for them on Google.

Keyword	Monthly global searches
WWII	4,090,000
D-Day	1,500,000
d day wwii	5,400

Obviously, you should use *WWII* and *D-Day* as your main keywords. Note that *d day* and *D-Day* are not interchangeable.

Before you decide on keywords, scan the Google list for any potential unwanted traffic. For example, the keywords *little girls* might get hits from those looking for pornography. Try to anticipate the audience searching for the keywords you have chosen and make sure they are the right audience for your purposes.

Once you have great keywords, then use them well. Of course, put them in headings and subheadings, but also include them in your text. Some experts suggest that keywords should take up from 3 to 7 percent of the text on a page. You can check keyword density on a page at David Naylor, an SEO marketing firm (http://tools. davidnaylor.co.uk/keyworddensity), or with Live Keyword Analysis (www.live-keyword-analysis.com).

Links

Links from one site to another—the interconnections inherent to the web—can demonstrate the relative importance of a website and its information. National Public Radio (npr.org), for instance, has many, many links because it is a major news organization. Information on NPR's site will always be ranked higher on search engines than on your individual site, just by virtue of size and volume.

You want people to link to your site not just because you are on a blogroll or as some automatic listing. Instead, you want them to link to your page because it has great information, and to text that is specific, not generic. Someone might link to my site, www.darcypattison. com, with link text, *Darcy Pattison says.* That is great, but the SEO would be better if the link text said, *30 Days to a Stronger Picture Book and* linked to this specific page www.darcypattison.com/pic-

~ SEO for Content ~

*For each of these categories that might appear on your website, think
about what information or content would be most useful to visitors,
and about keywords and links.*

~ **Author biography:** Think about the information a reporter
might look for or a kid doing a book report might need. *Keywords:*
name, city of birth or residence, book titles. *Links:* website of schools
attended, online stores, family website, Facebook Fan Page.

~ **FAQs:** Frequently Asked Questions answer questions you often
receive as an author. Where do you get your ideas? Where did you
grow up? What is your favorite book? *Keywords:* genres, book titles,
topics of books. *Link:* To appropriate topics related to your writing.

~ **Bibliography:** Include titles, ISBNs, reviews, synopses. *Keywords:*
Look for keywords to use from reviews. *Links:* online stores, reviews.

~ **Calendar of events:** If you have frequent public appearances,
include a calendar with contact information for each event. *Keywords:*
names of places, events. *Links:* associations or organizations sponsor-
ing your appearances.

~ **Contact:** One of the most neglected pieces of content is how to

ture-books/ 30-days-to-a-stronger-picture-book. The specific information in my series of posts about writing picture books is better
than just a link to my name.

Some bloggers and webmasters go to great lengths to acquire
incoming links. You can do much just by being a part of the online
community. Comment on posts, offer to write guest posts (with links
back to your site, when appropriate), and write great content that
makes people want to link to you. One strategy is to write *link bait,*
or an article that makes people want to link to you. In a 14-month
period, about 30,000 people visited this webpage on my site: 43 Book
Trailers Sites to Inspire, Instruct, and Share (http://www.darcypattison.
com/marketing/book-trailers/). About 25,000 people visited this

~ SEO for Content ~

contact an author. Sometimes, very popular authors leave it off deliberately because of the potential volume of emails they might receive. But most authors should have a contact form or list an email. *Keywords:* contact, email, your name. *Links:* to your other web pages, like a blog on Wordpress.

~ **Links to Sell Your Book:** Readers of your website or blog are interested in you and may want to buy one of your books or maga-zines with your articles or stories. Provide links to an online or local bookstore, or provide a way for readers to buy from you directly. *Keywords:* Buy, discount, titles, your name.

~ **News:** Regularly updated news about your books, your career, or related issues. *Links:* titles, names, places, topics. *Links:* press releases, photos, new books, promos for your career.

~ **Posts:** Posts related to your books or other writing can be the trickiest type of content to optimize. Think about what extra informa-tion you can give your readers: Maybe it is a book club guide, or perhaps information you researched but could not include in the book. *Keywords:* research appropriate keywords. *Links:* Website of current publisher, resource sites.

page: Checklist of 17 Character Qualities (http://www.darcypatti-son.com/characters/character-checklist).

Yes, I knew these pages might be strong pages when I wrote them, so I took time to make them interesting, comprehensive, and useful. Remember, content is king.

Test Your SEO

You have taken care of your tags, you are using strong keywords, you are seeking out strong links, and writing great content. How do you know if the SEO is working?

When you put a keyword or phrase into Google, what you really want is for your page or site to be the first one listed. Depending on the study, researchers report about 60 percent of people click on the first site listed and the percentages drop drastically after that. Rarely do people go through more than three pages, the top 30 sites listed, on a search engine results page (SERP). At the time of this writing, a search for *book trailers* lists my webpage, "43 Book Trailers Sites to Inspire, Instruct, and Share" seventh on the SERP page. Not bad. At least it is on the first page.

Electronic Earnings

From Tree Books to Ebooks

By Mark Haverstock

T o paraphrase Mark Twain, rumors of the death of print books have been greatly exaggerated. Hardcovers and paperbacks still make up 85 percent of total publisher sales in the U.S. Retailers like Amazon, however, say their customers now buy more ebooks than print books. Since April 2011, Amazon sold more than 105 Kindle ebook titles for every 100 hardcover and paperback books; that included books not available on the Kindle and excluded free ebooks.

Even if ebooks overall do not outsell print books across book-sellers as a whole, the numbers are strong indicators of a growing trend in publishing. In September 2011, the Association of American Publishers (AAP) figures showed that ebook sales were up 161 pecent for the year, while print trade books were down 10 percent.

Ebooks have also become vastly more accessible to consumers in the last year, thanks in part to the growing number of inexpensive electronic reader devices, including Amazon's Kindle Fire, which at the end of 2011 was, well, on fire. Barnes & Noble's Nook also had solid sales since its debut in November 2010.

Publishers have been rapidly digitizing their catalogues, making older titles available in ebook form for the first time. Even small independent houses have adopted electronic media to sell their backlist books, traditionally a large part of many publishers' revenues.

Publishers have never had a substantial conflict of interest to push one format over another until now, says Paul Aiken, Executive Director of the Author's Guild. "Royalty rates are the issue—they've shifted from 50 percent of net proceeds for hardcovers to 25 percent for ebooks with no good reason. The publisher has an incentive to favor ebook sales over hardcover sales, so there's going to be a natural tendency to shift sales toward digital over print."

Book Evolution

Before the electronic age of books, you went to a local bookstore and bought either a hardcover or a paperback. You owned it (at least the physical book, with the cover and pages) as a piece of property. You could give it away, lend it, read it to your toddler, but you could not copy it.

Ebooks redefined the sale of print. Downloads of books are like software or music downloads from iTunes: You are licensed to use them, but technically do not own them. "This is a hot topic right now, because it's a big change from traditional publishing," says Rose Auslander, an attorney in the intellectual property group of Carter, Leyard & Milburn. "The e-vendors are doing their best to structure [the sale] and say that these ebooks are licenses, so they can restrict what you do." The law is still being written on ebooks and their status is still being debated.

While the publishers, retailers, and legal minds are sorting out ebook issues, another technology is poised to deploy. The *cloud*, which consists of remote servers on the Internet, is allowing readers to stream or access content on demand. Whether you have a Kindle, smart phone, or a tablet computer, regardless of your equipment or operating system, you will be able to access books, magazines, music, and other media via the cloud. And you will not take up valuable memory space since your device won't need to store it.

E-vendors are lining up to profit from the new technology. "It seems like Amazon is looking to develop a successful business model based on access to content, not ownership," says attorney Lloyd J. Jassin, whose firm specializes in copyright and intellectual property law. "Streaming to one or multiple devices, the ability to sell ancillary services, and social networking features, make cloud-based publishing a very exciting prospect."

Sales Models

Authors should be familiar with sales models and how they affect their bottom line, as well as their publishers'. Ebook royalty rates are generally uniform among the major trade publishers. Pricing and discounting fall into two distinct camps, however: the *reseller model* and the *agency model*.

In the reseller model, the publisher sells ebooks to the reseller at a discount that is usually about 50 percent of retail. The reseller can sell the books at any price; the only real limits are antitrust laws and the seller's ability to absorb losses. From the launch of the Kindle, "Amazon has been taking huge losses on ebooks so it can sell them for $9.99 or less," says Salley Shannon, President of American Society of Journalists and Authors (ASJA.) "It was a stroke of genius on their part—trading money for market share."

Under the agency model, the online bookseller pays 70 percent of the retail price. Acting as the publisher's agent, the bookseller sells the ebook at the price established by the publisher. But the publisher, by agreement with resellers (such as Barnes & Noble), sets the price significantly below the hardcover version of the book.

For authors and publishers, the agency model is the best option. "Publishers should be able to set the price of the their works—they know how much went in and the market value," says attorney Anthony Elia, whose boutique law firm specializes in intellectual property litigation. "Allowing online retailers to engage in a race to the bottom with prices doesn't help anyone. Using the reseller model would mean the domination of the ebook market, probably by a single player. Ultimately, the public is going to get better books from more sources with the agency model."

Keeping Amazon in Check

It is dangerous to have any single aggregator in control of the market. Amazon's market dominance as a reseller was nearly complete two years ago, but this situation was changed by two events: (1) the introduction of Apple's iPad and Barnes & Noble's Nook, and (2) the adoption of the agency model by publishers. "When publishers adopted it, they said there would be a fixed price for each ebook title sold by vendor," says Aiken.

The strategy was effective at leveling the playing field and kept Barnes & Noble in the game. At its peak, Amazon had 90 percent of the trade ebook market in the U.S. By January 2010, the figure was down to about 60 percent for Amazon, and Aiken says it is now closer to 55 percent. "The biggest beneficiary has been Barnes & Noble, who went from just about no market share to 25 percent," he explains. Apple and Kobo, who introduced a basic electronic reader to rival the Kindle in 2010, each hold about 10 percent of the market share.

Amazon also attempted to protect its dominance of the growing ebook market by applying pressure to Macmillan when it shifted to the agency model for selling its books in 2010. Amazon retaliated by shutting down sales of nearly all of Macmillan's books, removing the *buy* buttons from the print and electronic editions of thousands of titles. Macmillan authors, many of whom had linked their websites to Amazon pages, found they were suddenly disabled and useless. Although Macmillan saw its online sales plummet, it stood firm and prevailed. Amazon finally ended the blackout after a week.

The House Wins

Electronic book sales have been a bonanza for publishers, but not so much for authors. Publishers actually have lower expenses with ebooks because they have no printing costs and do not need to

~ Google & You ~

Google's six-year plan to bring all the world's books to the Internet suffered another big setback at the hands of Judge Denny Chin in March 2011. Chin's ruling, filed in U.S. district court in Manhattan, rejected a 2008 settlement that Google forged with several author and publisher groups. The 48-page decision concluded that the deal would give the Internet giant the ability to "exploit" books without the permission of copyright owners.

Chin also suggested a way to revise the deal. Rather than let copyright owners of books opt out of the Google settlement, copyright owners should be asked to opt-in—something Google's lawyers had previously said would not be viable.

Publishers still hope that a settlement can be reached. "We plan to work together with Google, the Authors Guild, and others to overcome the objections raised by the Court and promote the fundamental principle behind our lawsuit, that copyrighted content cannot be used without the permission of the owner, or outside the law," says John Sargent, Chief Executive of Macmillan.

maintain the distribution networks they do for print books. The publishers are "getting proportionately more with those sales than the established authors are," says Auslander. "I can't see a justification for why the publisher's split for ebooks is higher."

"Right now it appears that ebook retailing is going to put downward pressure on authors' earnings for two reasons: because ebooks are already dragging down prices for hardcovers, and because publishers are trying to pay a lower royalty rate on ebooks than they have traditionally paid on physical books," says Scott Turow, author and current President of the Authors Guild. (See the sidebar on page 238–239, "Ebook Royalties: Doing the Math.")

One of the solutions to this problem for authors and agents is to set royalty rates at up to 50 percent of net. "Then the author and publisher would have an equal interest in pushing ebooks," says

~ Ebook Ads ~

You could save $25 off retail for the base-model Kindle, provided you are willing to endure some ads strategically placed on the bottom of the device's home page and on its screen savers. They claim that no ads will appear in the ebooks themselves.

The ad-supported Kindle, a.k.a. Kindle with Special Offers, is now being sold at Target and Best Buy locations for $114. At this point, Buick, Olay, and Visa will be advertising—but it is likely the list will get longer as time goes on. Furthermore, this could set a new precedent that could very well carry over to ad-discounted tablets, netbooks, PMPs, and maybe even advertising-subsidized books as well.

Aiken. "Another way to fix the problem would be to make the author's royalty for ebooks no less than the dollars and cents royalty for physical books. Then the author would never be disadvantaged by the shift to electronic format."

Getting the Best Contract Deals

A publisher's goal is to win as many rights from its authors as possible for the least amount of compensation, whether the book is print or electronic. "When selling rights, your goal is to grant limited licenses for limited durations for maximum gain. In other words, buy low, and sell high," says Jassin. "Remember, a license can cover the entire scope of copyright, or be limited to a particular media, market, language, territory, or period. Clearly, there's much room for negotiation."

Shannon suggests authors pay particular attention to *derivative rights*, the right to adapt your work in some new way. "Don't sign away the right to profit from something new," she says. "You shouldn't bundle dramatic rights, for instance, with electronic rights. I know authors who've had movies developed, things developed for apps or games—and who knows what we'll be doing in five years."

Think about how your work may be bundled with other works and make sure you get paid. "Contracts should have a provision that allows for pro-rata royalties when the work is bundled or put into a collection," says Elia.

Make sure that *net receipts* (sometimes called net proceeds) is defined in your contract. "Writers typically get paid a percentage of net on ebook sales, and the net is the amount after the expenses are paid," says Shannon. "You need to be clear on which expenses are going to be included. Really, the only expense that should be taken out before you get your cut is the bookseller's commission, which is usually 30 percent."

With ebook royalties still in flux, you want to be sure you receive the benefit of increases that may be driven by the market. Literary agent Ronnie Herman says to be sure you have specific language in your ebook agreements: "It is agreed that if the Publisher raises its ebook royalties, the Author's royalties will automatically be increased as well. And/or if the industry standard royalty changes, we have the right to renegotiate these terms. By industry standard, it is understood that this refers to what four major publishers are offering."

Out of Print, Out of Options?

When a book goes out of print, industry practice dictates that rights generally revert to the author. In the current digital environment, the fact that a work is currently out of print is becoming almost irrelevant.

Since there is no physical inventory with ebooks, the sales numbers becomes important in determining a book's status as out-of-print. "It can be keyed to the number of units sold a year or some dollar figure in total sales or revenue per year," says Aiken. "There absolutely needs to be a meaningful out-of-print clause that allows authors to get rights back from the publisher, but it doesn't have to be automatically revertible if the author wants to stay with the publisher or you don't have an immediately better option."

Herman agrees that you and your publisher agree to set a base to determine what would put the ebook out of print so the rights can

~ Royalties: Do the Math ~

Ebooks are becoming the new darlings of the publishing industry. Publishers generally do significantly better on ebook sales than they do on hardcover sales. Authors, however, do worse, at least for now.

So how much better is it for the publisher and how much worse for the author? The Author's Guild has provided some examples of author's royalties compared to publisher's gross profit (income per copy minus expenses per copy), calculated using industry-standard contract terms.

~ *The Help*, by Kathryn Stockett
   Author's Standard Royalty: $3.75 hardcover; $2.28 e-book
   Author's E-Loss = -39%
   Publisher's Margin: $4.75 hardcover; $6.32 e-book
   Publisher's E-Gain = +33%
~ *Hell's Corner*, by David Baldacci
   Author's Standard Royalty: $4.20 hardcover; $2.63 e-book
   Author's E-Loss = -37%
   Publisher's Margin: $5.80 hardcover; $7.37 e-book
   Publisher's E-Gain = +27%
~ *Unbroken*, by Laura Hillenbrand
   Author's Standard Royalty: $4.05 hardcover; $3.38 e-book
   Author's E-Loss = -17%
   Publisher's Margin: $5.45 hardcover; $9.62 e-book
   Publisher's E-Gain = +77%

revert to you in such a case. The base could be a minimum amount earned or a minimum number of ebooks sold in two consecutive accounting periods. She cautions that print-on-demand books should not be a part of ebook deals.

It is important that authors stay on top of all the new publishing trends and be aware of standard practice in these changing times, seeking advice from writers' organizations and experienced agents as needed. Your bottom line depends on it.

~ Royalties: Do the Math ~

Here's the math behind the figures:

The Help has an ebooklist price of $13 and is sold under the agency model. Publisher grosses 70% of retail price, or $9.10. Author's royalty is 25% of publisher receipts, or $2.28. Publisher nets $6.32. ($9.10 minus $2.28 royalties and 50¢ encryption fee.)

Hell's Corner is also sold under the agency model at a retail list price of $15 list price. Publisher grosses 70% of retail price, $10.50. Author's royalty is 25% of publisher receipts, or $2.63. Publisher nets $7.37. ($10.50 minus $2.63 royalties and 50¢ encryption fee.)

Unbroken is sold by Random House under the reseller model at a retail list price of $27. Publisher grosses $13.50 on the sale. Author's royalty, at 25%, is $3.38. Random House nets $9.62. ($13.50 minus $3.38 royalties and 50¢ encryption fee.)

So, all things being equal, publishers are financially motivated to sell ebooks. Every time an ebook is sold instead of a hardcover, it is less likely an author's advance will earn out, meaning the odds a publisher will have to pay royalties diminishes. But take heart. As the ebook market continues to grow, so will the demands of authors and agents to share sales proceeds more equitably.

Source: "The Ebook Royalty Mess: An Interim Fix," February 11, 2011. www.authorsguild.org/advocacy/articles/the-e-book-royalty-mess-an-interim.html

"Everything is in flux and changing so quickly that there are times that the publishers themselves don't even know what they are doing," Herman says. "As agents, we have our authors' and illustrators' rights and terms as our foremost concern. Our goal is to get our clients the best possible terms and the best rights we possibly can."

This article is a general overview of the issues involving ebooks and electronic rights in today's market. You should consult an expert in this area to ensure the proper licensing of your rights.

Resources

~ **American Society of Journalists and Authors (ASJA):**
1501 Broadway, Suite 302, New York, NY 10036. www.asj.org
~ **The Authors Guild:** 31 East 32nd Street, 7th Floor, New York, NY
10016. www.authorsguild.org

Intellectual Property Law
~ **Carter, Leyard & Milburn:** 2 Wall Street, New York, NY 10005.
www.clm.com
~ **The Law Offices of Anthony N. Elia:** 325 Broadway, Suite 201,
New York, New York 10007. www.anelaw.com
~ **The Law Offices of Lloyd J. Lassin:** The Actors' Equity Building,
1560 Broadway, Suite 400, New York, NY 10036. www.copylaw.com

Agent
~ **The Herman Agency:** 350 Central Park West, New York, NY 10025.
www.hermanagencyinc.com

Sizing up the Competition

A Key Component of Your Book Proposal

By Judy Bradbury

When we get excited about an idea for a fiction book project, we are raring to forge ahead. Our spirits are high and ideas brim with promise. We are eager to embark on an adventure in a world made real by our imagination. When we get excited about an idea for a nonfiction book, we are equally as eager to set off on a quest. Our spirits soar and anticipation of delicious exploration fuels our intention. We are itching to write! But first, before we start clicking away at the keyboard, we need to research—and not only the subject of our attention. We must investigate and assess the market.

Hunting Down and Sizing Up the Competition

"Researching the viability of a project for publication is an ever-increasingly important task, and, naturally, it's one that is constantly evolving," says Catherine Frank, former Executive Editor at Viking Children's Books and founder of Catherine Frank Editorial Services, an editorial consultancy specializing in children's books and publishing.

"After researching the topic, you know your book—or at least your idea for the book—pretty well," says Becky Levine, author of *The Writing & Critique Group Survival Guide* (Writer's Digest Books). "But you still need to get out there and evaluate the books already published on the topic. Hit the bookstores and the new-books shelves at your library."

Joanne Mattern, author of more than 300 books for children, mainly nonfiction, does just that. "I have a two-step process when researching a topic," she reveals. "My first step is to see what books are available for the audience. I check our local library system (which in lower New York State encompasses 44 libraries) and also go on Amazon. Then I read any children's books that are out there on the topic to see what authors have already done and what they haven't. I also check how recent the books are. There may be a lot of books on a topic, but if the last one was published 8 or 10 years ago, that could mean it's time for a new voice to speak up and create something more up-to-date. This is especially true when it comes to science," says Mattern, who specializes in science, biography, social science, and sports. "If there are new discoveries, that could make a great updated book. Finally, I look at age levels. For one topic I'm researching now, I've found several YA books, but nothing for younger readers, so that's an area where I can fill a gap."

"Know your competition. It's as simple as that," advises Frank. "What does your book offer that no other book ever has? Be ready to explain—or, more likely, defend—why your book is special, why it is different and better than every other book on the subject ever published."

Current, Timely, Well-Timed, and Targeted

Sharon Coatney, Senior Acquisitions Editor for Libraries Unlimited, a division of ABC-CLIO, stresses, "Uncovering current material on the subject you're interested in writing about must be part of one's research when preparing a proposal. The books I edit have to do with library science or a related field. I keep up on what's new. If I see a proposal in which an author has compared his or her project to 10-year-old books, I know the author has not researched thoroughly in preparation for pitching a proposal." Michael Dahl, Fiction

~ Current & Informed ~

"It's still possible for an unplugged, offline author to write a beautiful story and have it published. And I hope it always will be. But it obviously behooves an author to be as up-to-date as possible on what is being published, what's being well-reviewed, and what books people are buzzing about. These days, that means reading blogs by both other authors and industry professionals, subscribing to e-newsletters, and jumping on the Twitter bandwagon," says Catherine Frank, former editor at Viking Children's Books and founder of Catherine Frank Editorial Services. She can now be found at Twitter@CatherineSFrank.

"It's a time-consuming process, but having an understanding of the publishing business and of the sorts of books people are excited about can be invaluable, particularly to a debut author. In no way do I mean to suggest that a Twitter feed should influence the kind of story an author sets out to write. But could Twitter (and the larger online community) help inform the process of submitting a manuscript? Or how an author pitches and positions her work? Absolutely."

Editorial Director at Capstone Press, echoes Coatney. "The author should include current comparable works out there in the marketplace. I stress the word *current*. If I receive a proposal that compares the project to books published 30 years ago, this does not bode well for the author."

When considering the viability of a project, Coatney also suggests authors search "a little outside the field." For example, she says, "Beyond the library world, there is ASCD [Association for Supervision and Curriculum Development], reading education, and the general education world. These areas are similar, so books published in these realms may compete with those published for the library sciences."

As a result of her stint at Viking, Frank has extensive experience in acquiring and editing award-winning picture books, young adult novels, and nonfiction books. She cautions writers that timing a

~ Research the Competition ~

Here are places to begin researching competitive titles.

- ~ **Online bookstores:** Amazon.com and Barnes & Noble, www.barnesandnoble.com
- ~ **Google Books:** http://books.google.com
- ~ **World catalogue:** www.worldcat.org
- ~ **The Horn Book:** www.hbook.com
- ~ **Publishers Weekly:** www.publishersweekly.com
- ~ **School Library Journal:** www.schoollibraryjournal.com
- ~ **State library systems**
- ~ **University libraries**
- ~ **Large school district holdings**

project can be tricky. "The idea of something being *timely* takes on a whole different meaning when it comes to trade book publication. If an author is inspired by a recent event in the news and writes a story about it, she has to bear in mind that the event won't be remotely recent when the book is published. If an author has a project in mind that ties into an upcoming anniversary or event, it's important that there's more than enough lead time for everyone involved, including publishers and bookstores. For example, the hundredth anniversary of the sinking of the *Titanic* is April 2012. Author Barry Denenberg wrote a book called *Titanic Sinks!* published by Viking Children's Books in fall 2011—months before the actual anniversary of the event. This allows bookstores time to order and promote the book. As an editor, I first learned about Barry's proposal in 2009, more than three years before the anniversary. Barry is an experienced author who knew how much lead time would be needed."

David H. Dilkes, Editorial Director of the educational nonfiction company Enslow Publishers, notes, "If the author is pitching a nonfiction series for the school or public library market, our editors closely evaluate the viability of the project. We look at the publication dates of similar nonfiction series. For example, if someone is pitching a series on presidents of the United States we would like to see that the most recent sets from our competitors are a few years old, because that would mean librarians may be looking to replace them with a newer set. This is especially true of books about hot issues, diseases, or illicit drugs. Because the data is frequently updated, customers tend to look for the most recent books."

"Authors need to show that they understand the current market, not what was published ten, or even five years ago," Dahl says. "Their research can pull in other aspects of popular culture beyond books, such as popular movies, TV, video games, and music—things that can also figure into the fiction young readers are hungry for."

Dilkes concurs. "It helps if the author can time the topic submission with information about an upcoming movie, highly anticipated fiction title, or trend that is becoming popular. It seems that book buyers will purchase nonfiction topics that are relevant to other things that are currently popular."

A Twist on the Familiar Adds Value

Mattern offers insight based on her vast experience. "Along with seeing what's already available, I also consider how easy or hard it will be to find current information on a topic. For that I look at adult books on the topic and also go on the Internet and look for magazine articles online. I might have a great idea, but if there isn't enough information about the topic, I'm just going to frustrate myself and any potential editors. It's better to know that upfront before I delve too deeply into the project."

Mattern recalls one topic of interest that took some time to develop into a viable book proposal. "When I was first starting out I wanted to write about endangered animals, but there were already many, many books about this topic and no one was really interested in yet another collection of animals in danger. Then I read an article about how scientists were breeding a species of endangered condors in captivity and releasing them in the wild, which had resulted in a stable population of condors in the West. I did some research, came up with other animals that were coming back from the brink of extinction with human help, and then I had a whole new angle on a popular topic. I sold that book, *Going, Going . . . Gone? Saving Endangered Animals* very quickly to Perfection Learning, and it is still in print."

"Everything is changing quickly," reflects Coatney. "There is so much more available online for free than would have been found in a book ten years ago, that added value aids a book's competitive edge. This means that in book proposals, we look for evidence that the project offers something above and beyond the book—that it can be used in more than one way, whether that would be professional development or perhaps an online feature. If an author can show more than one way the content can be used—demonstrating versatility, flexibility, and thinking outside the box—that adds value, and the book will be better posed to compete in today's market."

Dilkes agrees. "The Internet has changed the game. We can no longer publish sets about nonfiction topics that read like expanded encyclopedia entries because students can find much of what they need on the Internet. Therefore, we look for authors who submit series or book ideas that revolve around a traditional curriculum area, but also have a twist to make them unique. One example is a set of six books we published a few years ago written by Elaine Landau called What Would You Do? These are American history books on topics that fill a need for the curricula in grades three to five. The twist is that the readers come to a point in the story where they are asked, 'What would you have done if you were George Washington?' in regard to crossing the Delaware for his famous raid. The reader finds out what Washington actually did. These books were unique at the time they were published and that helped them stand out from other books for the age group on similar topics."

Yet, Levine says, "Don't be intimidated if it looks like a lot of people have already covered your topic. Existing books means an existing market. Do you think all those parenting books get published because people don't want to read about raising children? If there's a market out there, it's a market in which you can find a place for your book. As you get to know the competition, you'll see your own book in a new way, in comparison and in contrast to what's already selling. This will set you up for writing the competition section of a solid book proposal, including a brief summary of several published books."

Preparing the Report

"The most important feature in any competition report is evidence that the author has clearly researched the market on their subject," says Dahl. "This single element of market research tells me three things about the author: they're savvy, they're flexible, and they're professional."

Jessica Faust, owner of the literary agency BookEnds, which represents fiction and nonfiction primarily for the adult market, advises choosing books "most people would immediately think of when they think of your subject."

"At the end of each summary, write a solid, specific statement about what *your* book does differently and better than *that* one," Levine suggests. "Show agents and editors how your book adds a missing piece to the market. An important piece." Coatney encourages authors to ask themselves why someone would buy their book instead of others. "Tell what your book will be and how it will be different."

Faust cautions authors to write the competition portion of the book proposal "without bashing books already published on the subject." Levine adds, "Be professional, respectful, and straightforward in your summaries. The strength of this section comes not from putting down other writers, but from understanding the role of their books in the market and then clearly demonstrating why your book is needed."

"What I don't get often, but they're so valuable, are proposals for *standouts*—smaller, cheaper, added-value options to already published material," Coatney reveals.

Levine encourages authors to be thorough. "Don't shy away from the work this part of the proposal requires. The competition report

~ Contact Information ~

- **BookEnds:** www.bookends-inc.com
- **Capstone Press :** 151 Good Counsel Drive, P.O. Box 669, Mankato, MN 56001. www.capstonepub.com. Fiction authors are encouraged to send a query and writing samples to: author.sub@stonearchbooks.com. Nonfiction authors should send a query and writing samples by mail. Guidelines can be found at: http://www.capstonepub.com/content/CONTACTUS_SUBMISSIONS.
- **Enslow Publishers:** Box 398, 40 Industrial Road, Berkeley Heights, NJ 07922. www.enslow.com. Query letters preferred. Accepts unsolicited submissions by mail. Include SASE. For more information, visit /htmlnasp.asp?file=help.html.
- **Catherine Frank Editorial Services:** www.editedbycatherine.com
- **Libraries Unlimited/ABC-CLIO:** www.abc-clio.com

includes some of the most important material you're going to write. This is where you convince agents and editors that you have a book worth publishing. The more you understand what makes your book distinct, the more powerfully you will be able to sell it to your agent, an editor and, ultimately, to readers." This part of your proposal, says Faust, "is where you show how your book shines" against the competition.

Getting your book into the hands of readers is the point of the book proposal, and the competition report is a vital part. "Many, if not most factors that determine viability of a project," says Dahl, "are outside the author's control: sales, marketing, cultural trends, changing tastes, the philosophy and mission of a publishing house, the next new blockbuster that suddenly changes everything, and so on. What can the author control? Their knowledge of the competition, the publishing world, their writing and editing skills, and their voice. Authors will always be needed by publishers; they need to remain skillful and flexible enough to help answer the publisher's changing needs."

Ancient Stones, Early Man, Global Cultures

Researching Anthropology

By Peggy Thomas

E verything that man has thought of, created, or faced in the past, present, and future comes under the study of *anthropology*. It is an enormous and fascinating field ripe with possible writing ideas. Anthropology is broken down into three main areas: cultural anthropology, physical or biological anthropology, and archaeology. Whichever field and anthropological subject you choose to delve into, the material is out there in abundance, from collections to books to journals to websites to experts to interview.

One of the best places to start your research is with the American Anthropological Association (AAA, www.aaanet.org). It is the premier professional organization for all anthropologists in the U.S., and it provides a thorough definition and introduction to anthropology and all it encompasses. The AAA website lists all of the publications it offers, including its academic journal, *American Anthropologist.* Most of the site is accessible to the public, but some areas are restricted to members. Among them is AnthroSource, a searchable database of more than a quarter of a million articles from all AAA publications. From the AAA website you will find links to the sub-organizations under its wide umbrella.

Archaeology

Archaeology is perhaps the most identifiable field in anthropology. Think Indiana Jones without the shoot-outs, Nazis, or snake pits. Archaeologists study past civilizations by digging artifacts out of the ground, and many of the best archaeologists are prolific authors too.

~ Books

For a comprehensive overview of everything archaeology, check out *The Oxford Companion to Archaeology,* edited by Brian M. Fagan. The articles range from "Aerial Surveying" to "Zoo-archaeology." Colin Renfrew's *Archaeology: Theories, Methods and Practices* is a good introduction to the basics. Although it was intended as a college text, if you want to know how to set up a grid, or differentiate bone from rock, this is your book. *Time Detectives,* also by Fagan, is more for the layman and gives a clear explanation of how archaeologists use technology to reveal the past. For a sense of how important archaeology is to our sense of history, read *The Story of Archaeology,* by Paul G. Bahn. It recounts 100 of the greatest archaeological discoveries ever made.

For clear and easy-to-read references that do not sacrifice accuracy or authority, check out these children's books: *Archaeology for Kids: Uncovering the Mysteries of Our Past,* by Richard Panchyk, and *If Stones Could Speak,* by award-winning writer Marc Aaronson, who followed a crew excavating the secrets of Stonehenge.

~ Journals and Magazines

Academic journals are the gold standard for research but they can usually be found only at university libraries. *The American Journal of Archaeology,* however, does offer open access to a portion of its articles on its website (www.ajaonline.org/openaccess). *American Antiquity* and *Latin American Antiquity* are published by the Society for American Archaeology (www.saa.org), but do not offer articles online. Its site does include numerous resources for the general public, and means for connecting with experts.

Discoveries that are published in journals eventually find their way into popular magazines like *Archaeology* (www.archaeology.org), published by the Archaeological Institute of America. The articles are synthesized and give overviews of how a site and its findings fit into an area's timeline and importance. *Biblical Archaeology Review* (www.bib-arch.org) is a nondenominational magazine that focuses on excavations in the Holy Land.

~ *Online Sources*

The Internet is perfect for browsing when researching a subject and brainstorming ideas; one site leads you to other interesting sites, much like shuffling through the library card catalogue in the old days. The *Archaeology* website has links to geographic regions and to specialties within the field, like underwater archaeology and lithic technology. Archaeolink (www.archaeolink.com) has a wide selection of categories. Select a region or site and you will get a brief description and then links to university or museum sites for more information.

Archaeology Online (www.archaeologyonline.net) covers Asia, and specifically, ancient India primarily. For information about Africa try African Archaeology (www.african-archaeology.net), and if you are interested in Australia, look at the Australian Archaelogical Association website (www.australianarchaeologicalassociation. com.au).

For information on Greek and Roman excavations, connect to Archaeogate (www.archaeogate.org); the site is in Italian, but hit the Google Translate button and it will give you English text. Websites that cover other archaeological subjects related to Europe include ArchEurope (www.archeurope.com), and the European Association of Archaelogists (www.e-a-a.org), a professional group that requires membership but has a useful page of links for other resources. In Britain, Archaeology UK has a searchable database called ARCHI (www.digital-documents.co.uk) that provides aerial photographs through GPS and smart phones, maps, historical timelines, place-name finders, and more.

~ Fields in Anthropology ~

The following list is based on the sections of the American Anthropological Association. This may suggest areas for you to research and develop specific ideas for articles or books. The sections have their own websites: Check them for more subject possibilities.

- American ethnology
- Anthropological sciences
- Anthropology & environment
- Anthropology of consiousness
- Archaeology
- Biological anthropology
- Black anthropology
- Evolutionary anthropology
- Feminist anthropology
- Food & nutrition anthropology
- Culture & agriculture
- Cultural anthropology
- Geographical anthropology sections: Africa, East Asia, Europe, Latin America and the Carribbean, the Middle East, North American

- Humanistic anthropology
- Indigenous anthropology
- Latina and Latino anthropology
- Linguistic anthropology
- Medical anthropology
- Museum anthropology
- Political and legal anthropology
- Psychological anthropology
- Queer anthropology
- Religion anthropology
- Senior anthropology
- Urban , national, global anthropology
- Visual anthropology
- Work anthropology

Once archaeological field work is complete, the excavation site is filled in and the knowledge that remains consists of artifacts kept in museums or other collections and a written analysis, which in the past was often boxed up and stored in a museum or university basement. But more and more research teams are storing their work online. One of the best examples of this is the Chaco Research Archive (www.chacoarchive.org). Maps, diagrams, photos, and written analysis about the history of archaeological research in Chaco Canyon, New Mexico, are all available for the viewer.

~ *Hands-On Experience*

Your writing is always more likely to be at its best when you have firsthand knowledge of your subject. Visit an archaeological site, volunteer on a dig near your hometown, or take a working vacation in a far off land.

To locate a preserved state or federal archaeological park, log on to Archaeological Parks in the U.S. (www.uark.edu/misc/aras/index.html). Most archaeological parks have aboveground remains. Among the preservations are an Iroquois long house at the Ganondagan State Historic Site in New York State; the many mound complexes throughout the Midwest or the Sanilac petroglyphs in Michigan; and the Gila cliff dwellings in New Mexico.

The Arizona State Museum at the University of Arizona (www.statemuseum.arizona.edu) relies on volunteers to dig in the field and analyze artifacts in the lab. Volunteers have worked on a Hohokam compound in Northern Tucson and a survey of ancient pueblo in northeastern Arizona.

Outside of the U.S., Projects Abroad (www.projects-abroad.org) staffs ongoing digs in Romania and Peru from two weeks to three months or more. Earth Watch (www.earthwatch.org) organizes cultural heritage trips all over the world, including Italy, England, and Mongolia; other of the expeditions study climate change and ecosystems. The Israeli Ministry of Foreign Affairs lists all of the volunteer projects being conducted in its country, including in early 2012, Ein Gedi, an oasis on the western shore of the Dead Sea (www.mfa.gov. il/MFA/History/Early+History+-+Archaeology/Archaeological_ Excavations_Israel_2011.htm)

If you cannot get away, consider volunteering for the Archaeology Channel (www.archaeologychannel.org) updating its website, researching content material or providing promotional outreach.

Physical Anthropology

Physical anthropologists conduct primate research and forensic analysis, and study the evolution of early man and the adaptation of the human body. The fame of the fictional forensic anthropologist on the television series *Bones* has probably surpassed that of Louis Leakey, although he and his family discovered many of the first early hominid remains in Africa. There is a lot of material for the layman about forensic work because of its popularity, but here are some books that will introduce you to all facets of the field.

~ *Books*

Biological Anthropology: The Natural History of Humankind, by Craig Stanford, John S. Allen, and Susan Anton, was meant to be a textbook, but is an excellent introduction to the field. *Biological Anthropology: An Introductory Reader,* edited by Michael Park, contains classic historic and contemporary articles on a variety of subjects. For another fascinating read, try *Death's Acre: Inside the Legendary Forensic Lab, the Body Farm Where the Dead Do Tell Tales,* written by one of the legends in forensics, William Bass, with Jon Jefferson. Carl Zimmer's *Smithsonian Intimate Guide to Human Origins* is a comprehensive overview and a beautiful book to look at. And Jane Goodall's seminal title, *The Chimpanzees of Gombe: Patterns of Behavior,* paints a vivid picture of an anthropologist's life in the wild.

~ *Journals and Magazines*

The American Association of Physical Anthropologists (AAPA, http://physanth.org) is the primary organization in this country, and there are similar professional groups across the globe. AAPA publishes the *American Journal of Physical Anthropology* and *Yearbook of Physical Anthropology.* Forensic professionals are board certified through the American Board of Forensic Anthropologists (www.the-abfa.org), which does not publish a journal, however, its articles appear in the Journal of Forensic Sciences.

~ *Online Sources*

From the American Anthropological Association website (www.aaanet.org/cmtes/commissions/aec/Biological.cfm) you will find links to other professional organizations, publications, and websites. Biological Anthropology Web (www.bioanth.org) also features dozens of links, as well as book reviews, and full-text documents of out-of-print books.

Other sources for older titles are the Internet Archive (www.archive.org), which is a collection of downloadable full-text documents, and the World Digital Library (www.wdl.org). The WDL was created by UNESCO with more than 30 participating national, university, and research libraries and archives, such as the Library of Congress, and the Bibliotheca Alexandrina of Alexandria.

~ *Hands-On Experience*

Unlike pottery shards and arrowheads, human remains are usually handled by professionals. Finding a place to get firsthand forensic anthropology experience may be difficult, but many museums have excellent skeletal collections and exhibits that you can visit. Until January 2013, the Smithsonian is hosting an exhibit called *Written in Bone* that reveals history through seventeenth-century *bone biographies*. Visitors can get a sense of anthropological work as they try their hand at piecing bone fragments together and identifying bone injury in the lab portion of the exhibit. An preview is available online at http://anthropology.si.edu/writteninbone/inside_look.html).

The Museum of Man in San Diego (www.museumofman.org) houses several invaluable research collections of bones showing human evolution and environmental adaptation, and the Cleveland Museum of Natural History (www.cmnh.org) owns the Hamann-Todd Osteological Collection, the largest of its kind in the world. It consists of 3,100 modern human and more than 900 nonhuman primate skeletons.

Cultural Anthropology

Cultural anthropologists look at the way we arrange our world and how we interact with it. From art to political systems, childbirth practices to corporate office interactions, anthropologists observe from within. Picture Margaret Mead living with the Samoans, or yourself watching an episode of *Survivor*. Mead wrote about her experiences in *Coming of Age in Samoa*.

~ Books

Published anthropological studies are called *ethnographies* and there are several classic examples, in addition to Mead's. To get a feel for what it is like to be a foreigner going into a community without knowing the language or customs, read *The Yanomamo*, by Napoleon Chagnon, for case studies about a Brazilian tribe, or *The Forest People,* by Colin Turnbull, about his time spent among the Mbuti Pygmies. More recent titles are *Veiled Sentiments: Honor and Poetry in a Bedouin Society,* by Lila Abu-Lughod, and *Laughter Out of Place: Race, Class, Violence and Sexuality in a Rio Shantytown*, by Donna Goldstein. Other classic anthropology titles include Ruth Benedict's *Patterns of Culture,* and Claude Levi-Strauss's *The Savage Mind.*

Remember that cultural anthropology also embraces social relationships, like marriage and parenting, as well as individuals and institutions, like government or religion. The Society for Applied Anthropology gave its annual Margaret Mead Award to Frances Norward, who studies medical anthropology, such as end-of-life care. Other subjects studied by recipients of this award in recent years have included child fostering and adoption in Peru, corruption and popular discontent in Nigeria, the many forces behind the death of a mentally ill woman in an asylum in Brazil, and the African American community in Muncie, Indiana.

The Society for Applied Anthropology website includes a list of useful links (www.sfaa.net/sfaaorgs.html).

~ Journals and Magazines

Cultural Anthropology, the journal of the Society of Cultural Anthropology, has what it calls Virtual Issues on its website (www.culanth.org) that include full-text articles and interviews with their authors. *Global Ethnographic* is a peer-reviewed online journal (www.globalethnographic.com) that features articles written by social anthropologists across a wide range of topics.

Popular Anthropology (www.popanthro.com/index.php/en/home) launched in 2010 and is designed to give the novice access to anthropological research in a variety of languages. The quarterly is available by paid subscription, or archival issues can be downloaded three months after they are published. *Anthro Now* (http://anthronow. com) has a similar mission, making anthropology available for the average person. Its most interesting feature is a section called Fieldnotes, which are a series of articles posted by an anthropologist currently working in a foreign culture.

～ Online Resources

One of our national treasures is the Library of Congress, which contains a vast amount of anthropological information. In particular, the Resources in Ethnographic Studies section (www.loc.gov/folklife/other.html) contains material about ethnomusicology, folklore, and folklife.

Similarly, the National Anthropological Archives at the National Museum of Natural History (www.nmnh.si.edu/naa/index.htm) is a rich storehouse of field notes, journals, maps, photos, recordings, and film created by anthropologists at the Smithsonian and around the world. Anthro Base is a multilingual database of anthropological texts (www.anthrobase.com), and Native Web (www.nativeweb.org) is a site about and for indigenous cultures around the world, with anthropological information and contacts.

～ Hands-On Experience

Anthropologists look not only at other societies, but to their own cultures too. In fact, pop culture may be more documented than most ancient civilizations. It is discussed by academics in journals like *American Popular Culture* (www.americanpopularculture.com), but it is more fun to relive our own pop culture by visiting one of several museums such as the Arizona Pop Culture Museum (www.azpopculturemuseum.com) in Phoenix, and the Geppis Entertainment Museum (www.geppismuseum.com) in Baltimore, Maryland.

Interview Contacts

When you are ready to contact an expert or two to interview, besides relying on the list of names gathered from your research, you can also search for an anthropologist with a particular specialty using the Worldwide Email Directory of Anthropologists (http://wings.buffalo.edu/WEDA). WEDA was developed by the anthropology department of the University of Buffalo.

Another handy site is AnthroBlogs (www.anthroblogs.org/ anthroblogblog) hosted by Scripps College, which offers free hosting to anthropologists who blog. It occasionally has guest bloggers and lists links to others.

For current news in anthropology, bookmark sites like the *New York Times* anthropology page (http://topics.nytimes.com/topics/ news/science/topics/archaeology_and_anthropology/index.html), *ScienceDaily* (www.sciencedaily.com), or the National Science Foundation's news website (www.nsf.gov/news).

So, go wandering among ancient or modern cultures, dig through books and dig in fields. Turn over the many possible fascinating subjects among the disciplines of anthropology to intrigue readers young and old.

Charles Darwin Would Have Loved Facebook

By Darcy Pattison

C harles Darwin would have loved Facebook.
We may think of Darwin as a famous scientist, but he was also a writer who produced more than a dozen books and many more articles. Publicity and networking were just as important for Darwin as for any writer today. With the publication online of his complete works (http://darwin-online.org.uk/), including 1,131 pieces of correspondence, we can start to see how much networking is needed for authors of any time period. Biographer Deborah Heiligman writes of Darwin, "During his lifetime he had two thousand correspondents. He wrote at least seven thousand letters and received as many." *(Charles and Emma: The Darwins' Leap of Faith*, Henry Holt, page 195)

Does that mean he would have had 2,000 friends on Facebook? Likely more.

Networking takes time. Today, we use blogs, tweets, Facebook posts, Flickr photos, or YouTube videos. Overall, the purposes of the networking are the same as Darwin's, who chose to write arguments, detail his frustrations, encourage others, answer objections, share interesting information, and generally live a social life. When distance separates us, we find ways to connect. As authors, we must work especially hard to make those connections with our audience—and that work is also fundamental research that will contribute to our success as writers.

Five Questions Before You Start

~ *What kind of content do you like to create?*

Everyone creates some content online these days. You may post original articles, comments on blogs, provide short updates via Twitter or Facebook, post photos or videos, or make your art available online. You may only write emails. But you do some kind of online communications.

But research yourself further and find out what you like to do online: Keep track of your online activities for a week and evaluate which you must force yourself to do and which you are eager to do.

Cynthia Leitich Smith, YA author of *Tantalize, Eternal,* and *Blessed* (Candlewick), says Twitter is her playground. Her blog and Facebook are community outreach, but Twitter is what she most enjoys, the challenge of saying something useful in 140 words.

~ *With what audience do you want to connect?*

As authors and illustrators, we have many possible audiences: readers interested in the topics or stories that interest us, other writers and illustrators, readers, educators, single people, seniors, parents, teens, kids, men, women. With whom do you want to connect? With what audience can you envision yourself interacting on an ongoing basis? Where can you join a conversation? For whom do you want to write, and what more do you want and need to learn about them?

You may not be able to answer these questions directly. Go back to the journal of your online weekly activities. Who were you talking to? Did you talk at them, or did you have a conversation? Especially notice places where you were comfortable and eager to have a conversation, because social media is about connecting with people in a two-way conversation. What did you learn? What directions will you go in the next conversation you have? Will you look for a different or new audience?

Alternately, start a blog on a free site such as WordPress and write five to ten posts. Do not think about your target audience yet; just write what you *want* to write. Then, go back and ask yourself: Who would want to read this? Your parents, a teen, a thirtysomething? If you can identify the prototypical reader of your posts, go back and create another five to ten posts with that reader in mind.

Be aware that your preference may change over time. Martha Brockenbough, author of *Things That Make Us [Sic]: The Society for the Promotion of Good Grammar Takes on Madison Avenue, Hollywood, the White House, and the World* (St. Martin's Press) and a forthcoming picture book, says "My website is mostly static information about my book. I am not blogging much these days. I am on the SCBWI (Society of Children's Book Writers and Illustrators) national blog team and love covering events live. That will be my focus for now. There are a lot of excellent bloggers out there and after doing it myself for more than 10 years, I don't feel compelled to add anything more right now."

Where do they hang out online?

If you can identify an audience you want to pursue, the next step is to find that audience online. They may be conversing in blogs or forums, on Facebook or LinkedIn, in email listservs or on Twitter, on Goodreads or LibraryThing, or maybe even with video on YouTube. With luck, your audience will be in several places. Take some time— a month or two or more—to research and find the most active and interesting (to your way of thinking) communities. Try interacting within these communities for a while to see if they keep your interest.

What blend of social media will let you optimize your reach, use your strengths, and best cross-pollinate your efforts?

Now, try to put it together. You know what type of content you like to create, your audience, and where they hang out. Maybe you want to do a photo-blog, or maybe you just want to post reviews on Goodreads or Amazon.

Prioritize and find a home base. Lisa Yee, author of *Absolutely, Maybe* and *Warp Speed* (both from Arthur A. Levine/Scholastic), says, "Blogging is my home base. It's meatier and gives me a chance to really say or show what is on my mind. However, I flirt with Facebook far too often and am totally addicted to it. If I need instant answers to something I'm working on, I'll often ask my Facebook friends."

You may go wrong here in one of two ways. First, the temptation may be to think that what you like to do is unimportant. If you like to post comments on blogs, for example, you may think it has no impact. But as a blogger (www.darcypattison.com), I can tell you we always wish for more comments. We would love for our post to start up a real conversation. Writing a comment adds real value as you agree or disagree with the post.

Second, you may be tempted to learn a new skill. I've tried to learn to post videos on YouTube and I have some success at it. But video is a steep learning curve and not the most comfortable place for me. For illustrators, you may be urged to start an Etsy shop (a handmade marketplace, www.etsy.com) to sell your artwork, but you hate marketing. If so, it is not a good fit.

Your social media efforts will live or die on this question: Can you find a place online where you can consistently and comfortably join the conversation?

Another issue is how your efforts cross-pollinate. *Billboard* has reported that social media affects online viewers. One study showed that "fans linking to online videos via Twitter watch an average of 2:30 minutes, compared to 1:30 minutes on average watched by those finding the same videos via a search engine. Yet 76 percent of streams on artist or label sites come as a result of online search, such as Google." ("A Look at the Numbers: Trends in Online Video Consumption," Anthony Bruno, April 12, 2010. www.billboard.biz/bbbiz/content_display/e3i10a8ce4131a6378aafbd212950e5edd6).

In other words, more online users come to videos (and presumably to blogs and other content) through individual websites that interest them and were found via search engines. So, if you are going to use Twitter or Facebook or YouTube to connect to an audience, and do research into them and into subjects that interest you and them, do not forget search engines. Remember to mention your efforts on one social media platform on the other platforms where you participate.

Can you find a place online where you can consistently and comfortably join the conversation?

~ What are your goals for this particular bit of connection?

Once you decide on a social media home base, go one step further and articulate your goals for your social media. It may be as simple as you want 1,000 friends on Facebook. Or your goal may be more complicated: Join the conversation about the importance of nonfiction for elementary kids. Focus again to another level, and find the topics you want to converse about this year. Then you will then be in a position to provoke conversations, add to them in interesting ways, and learn from them.

You probably will have multiple goals over the course of a year. Expect your goals to change, perhaps rapidly at first, as you get used to what is possible online. The key is to make your goals conscious so you can direct them.

Try to find ways to measure your success in some way. Maybe your website should use Google Analytics, which gives you counts of traffic and how people found you online. The number of Facebook friends is another indicator of online success. Tie your measure to your goals and adjust both as often as needed to focus your time and efforts online.

~ Social Media Basics ~

Your Writing

~ **Domain.** Get your own domain, yourname.com, at a site such as GoDaddy.com. Consider buying the domain name for any or all of your published books too. One author was chagrined to find that her book title led to a porn site, so be careful. Even if you do not develop the site, protect your book's title by buying the domain.

~ **Web page.** Some people still create an HTML (Hypertext Markup Language) website, but the trend today is toward a blog because it is easier to keep updated. Some combine the two. You probably need some sort of online brochure as a minimum presence if you are a writer.

~ **Email Newsletter.** When people visit you online, you should be asking for their name and email—these are people who say they want to hear from you. Such a list is invaluable when you want to promote a new book, ask for support for your causes, stay encouraged, do research—or create an email newsletter to send out to readers and/or other writers. Three popular sites that automate all activities needed to set up an email newsletter include Mailchimp.com, Aweber.com, and ConstantContact.com.

Find Connection Points

~ **Blogs.** Look at Alltop.com. Choose a category to find blogs in your topic of choice. Follow a couple of blogs, friend the authors on Facebook, etc. to find your community.

~ **Facebook.** Share updates on your life, upload photos, and chat with friends. Deciding which Face to put forward? You have four options for using Facebook. Be sure to understand the advantages and disadvantages of each:

- Individual Profile: Just sign up.
- Fan Page: Business of all kinds use fan pages to provide relevant

~ Social Media Basics ~

information about them and promote their businesses. Click on Advertising to begin creating a fan page. You can add videos, apps, an RSS feed, and more. You will need to invite people to become a fan of your page, which you can do via your Facebook profile and Twitter.

- Group Page: Users of a Group page can communicate about subjects of interest and share content. Consider starting a group about an issue of importance to you and your writing, and to learn more through others' input.

- Facebook Events: Report and magazine events of importance to you and your writing.

~ **LinkedIn.** Connect with other professionals. It is reported that educators are more likely to be on LinkedIn than on Facebook.

~ **YouTube.** Upload videos for public viewing. Here is a tutorial on editing and customizing your channel: www.google.com/support/youtube/bin/answer.py?hl=en&answer=174555

~ **Twitter.** Try this platform if you like to be the most up-to-date possible. For the hottest hashtags of the week, see www.twitter.com/HottestHashtags (*Note:* A hashtag is the # symbol, followed by a short word or phrase. Twitter uses hashtags as a way to categorize tweets.)

~ **Book-related sites:** Numerous book-related sites allow readers to find good books, review books, and talk about their favorites. Try Goodreads.com, RedRoom.com, Shelfari.com, and LibraryThing.com.

~ **Illustrator sites:** The needs of illustrators are slightly different than those of authors. Many find it easy to sell their artwork on Etsy.com. DeviantArt.com is a gathering place for artists.

Be prepared to fail at times too. Sometimes, you need to experiment with a different mix of social platforms until you find the right one for you. If you hoped to gain 100 Facebook friends in a month but you only got 10, something is not working. Maybe Facebook is not right for you and you need to switch to Twitter.

Pitfalls of Social Media

While you are getting involved, be careful. If you only think of using social media as a means of self-promotion, rather than as a place to connect, interact, and communicate, this warping of the purposes of the communication tools we use is self-destructive. Social media can make for a self-absorbed life—all about *me*, the antithesis of *social*.

Remember this additional caution: What happens in Vegas stays . . . on YouTube, Facebook, and so on.

Keep Emily Dickinson as your model: Would you characterize your tweets as "warm, loving, marvelous"? Ultimately, social media is about people and joining a community with a common interest.

Researching the Story of a Life

By Barbara Kramer

"The best biographies are those that peek into the heart and soul of their subject," says Candace Fleming, who has written about people such as Benjamin Franklin, Eleanor Roosevelt, and Amelia Earhart. "They delve deep beneath the surface of *fact* to find the real human story."

Successful biographies bring their subject alive on the page through details, interesting anecdotes, and lively quotes. The profiler or biographer may begin with general sources to get an overview of the subject. That could include an Internet search focusing on reliable sites such as those maintained by government agencies, universities, museums, and historical societies. It could also include encyclopedias and substantial, accurate books written about the person.

General sources provide basic facts such as the subject's achievements and important dates. All of that information has a place in a biography, but to bring a subject to life, the writer to needs to go deeper, with the research in primary sources.

Primary sources include letters, diaries, journals, scrapbooks, manuscripts, speeches, and interviews. They also include newspaper and magazine articles contemporary to the time in which the subject lived. Authors may examine other original documents such as maps, patents, and vital records to put together the details of a person's life.

One way to go deep with the research and find good primary sources is to use the bibliographies of other books. Sue Macy, the author of biographies about Nellie Bly and Annie Oakley, and of *Wheels of Change: How Women Rode the Bicycle to Freedom (With a Few Flat Tires Along the Way)* (National Geographic), says she reads other books about her subject for background information as well as for learning what sources the author used. "Often, I'll use his or her bibliography to continue my own research, looking at the articles and books the author used to add to my background on the subject," she explains.

Sometimes no books have been published about your subject. That was what happened to Macy when she was writing her book, *A Whole New Ball Game: The Story of the All-American Girls Professional Baseball League* (Puffin/Penguin). There was only one other book published about the league at the time Macy was writing. So she began her research by locating magazine articles published from 1943 to 1954, the time of the league's existence.

Macy's magazine research uncovered an important clue when she found a Letter to the Editor in a women's sports magazine. It had been written by a former player in the All-American Girls Professional Baseball League. Macy called the letter writer, who referred her to another player who had a mailing list of about 120 former members of the league. "I sent all of them a written question-naire about their playing days," Macy says. She got more than 100 replies. "After reading them, I decided which players to contact for interviews."

Discovering the Letter to the Editor was a big break in Macy's research. But it happened only because she did her legwork in researching magazines current to the time when her subjects were making the news.

~ Select Biography Resources ~

~ **Biogs:** http://biogs.com. Started and written by a researcher and documentary producer, this site has international content in subject areas such as actors, artists, authors, broadcasters, business, composers, fashion, sports, music, law and crime, religious, politics, etc.

~ **BBC Audio Interviews:** www.bbc.co.uk/bbcfour/audiointerviews. 150 audio interviews from figures in the arts in the twentieth century.

~ **Lives:** www.webofstories.com/lives. Lives is the flagship site of Web of Stories, and includes videos with the life stories of influential people of many kinds. A sample includes physicist Jeremy Bernstein, illustrator Quentin Blake, master watchmaker Georges Daniels, author Julia Hartwig, computer scientist Donald Knuth, author Doris Lessing, comic book creator Stan Lee, and artist Paula Rego. The Web of Stories section is broken down into categories like architecture, education, family, literature, politics, science, work life, and many more.

~ **New York Public Library:** http://legacy.www.nypl.org/research/chss/grd/resguides/biography/introduction.html. This site offers extensive leads for biographers beginning their work, including sources from around the world, and specialized biographical sources, such as the *Annotated Index of Medieval Women* and the *Dictionary of Scientific Biography*.

~ **The New York Times Article Archive:** http://www.nytimes.com/ref/membercenter/nytarchive.html. Articles from 1851 to today. Individual articles and subscriptions available.

~ **WBIS (World Biographical Information System):** www.degruyter.de/cont/fb/nw/nwWbisEn.cfm. An online subscription database that claims to be the most comprehensive collection of biographical information in the world. Its content includes materials from the sixteenth century to the present day.

Finding Newspaper and Magazine Articles

Some articles are available online and can be located with a basic Internet search. More often writers find they need to search newspaper or magazine databases such as EBSCOHost, Lexus-Nexus, Infotrac, and ERIC to find the information they need. It is possible to subscribe to newspaper or magazine databases available online. Or to save money, you can check with your local library to find out what online research databases they have available.

When you type your subject's name into the database's search bar, you will get links to magazine and newspaper articles about that person over a span of several years. In many cases, you can get the complete text of the article. Other times only a citation and a brief summary is provided and you will need to go to the source for the full-text of the article.

Obtaining back issues of magazines is getting more difficult as space limitations and budgets force public libraries to make hard decisions about how much material they can keep. Some may have magazines on file for only a couple of years and newspapers for only a few weeks. If you live close to a university or college library, they may have bound copies of magazines covering a wide span of years going back to the early 1900s. They may also have newspapers on microfilm. Or, for a small fee, you can often obtain photocopies of articles from your local library through interlibrary loan.

A drawback to using computerized databases is that many of them only index fairly recent materials, about the last 30 years. For older materials, you may need to use printed annual indexes such as the *Reader's Guide to Periodical Literature* or its precursor, the *Cumulative Book Index (CBI)*. There is also a *Biography Index,* which indexes articles about people. Many libraries no longer have these guides, so you may need to travel to a university or college library to locate them. Using one of these guides means checking indexes for each year when there might be something about your topic and jotting down the magazine name and issue. Then you need to find the articles.

Searching Archives

Another way to research deeply is to use archives. These special collections might be housed in a university library or at a museum or historical society. An Internet search about your topic should lead to information about where the subject's papers are kept. Experienced researchers travel to those archives and almost always find it is worth the trip. The archivists are often "incredible" Fleming says.

> "**A**rchivists know so much about their subject, and they're always eager to share their expertise and knowledge. Often, they'll tell you something you might never have discovered on your own."

"They know so much about the subject, and they're always eager to share their expertise and knowledge. And often, they'll tell you something you might never have discovered on your own."

That is what Macy learned when she traveled to Annie Oakley's hometown of Greenville, Ohio, and visited the Garst Museum. Macy knew the museum had some of Oakley's papers, but what she uncovered was better than she could have imagined. "I found [Oakley's] unfinished autobiography in a random folder that the archivist pulled out for me," Macy recalled. "At that point, I didn't even know she had written an autobiography, so I never would have asked to see it. Being there meant all the difference in that case."

Penny Colman took an 880-mile research trip to sites in New York State for her book about Elizabeth Cady Stanton and Susan B. Anthony. It included stops at Anthony's childhood home in Battenville and Stanton's birthplace in Johnstown. "Immersing myself in their places is one of the ways I brought Elizabeth and Susan to life for me," Colman says, "and of course, I hope for everyone who reads *Elizabeth Cady Stanton and Susan B. Anthony: A Friendship That Changed the World* (Henry Holt)."

Visiting archives can uncover some unexpected treasures for researchers, but traveling is not always possible. Writing is after all a business, and you do not want to invest more on researching a topic than you can expect to earn from the project. That does not mean archived material is not available to you. Some museums and libraries are putting at least part of their collections online.

You can also write to archivists and request photocopies of materials. The staff will charge you for the photocopies and may also charge an hourly research fee. However, if you are specific in your request, it does not take a staff person long to find materials and photocopy them.

Problem-Solving

Contacting archives is a good way to handle one of the biographer's most frustrating problems: what to do when the facts do not match. That is a problem Fleming encountered when she was writing her biography, *Amelia Lost: The Life and Disappearance of Amelia Earhart* (Schwartz & Wade). "Time and again, I unearthed a telling detail, or a charming anecdote only to learn that it wasn't true, that Amelia had made it up to maintain her public image," Fleming notes.

An example was Earhart's around-the-world trip with Fred Noonan. "According to Amelia, Fred was confined to the navigator's station in the rear cabin and could communicate with her only in notes passed forward over the fuel tanks by means of a bamboo fishing pole," Fleming explains. Through further research Fleming learned that anecdote was not true. "Fred spent much of his time in the cockpit with Amelia, clambering over the fuel tanks in the rear cabin only when he needed room to spread out a chart."

The best way to resolve discrepancies with the facts is to contact experts on the subject. For example, if there is conflicting information about a former U.S. President, you could contact the presidential library. If the person you are writing about is still living, you could try to interview that person or people who know the subject.

Sometimes, it is not possible to get to the truth in spite of the researcher's best efforts. That was the problem Colman encountered when researching her biography *Fannie Lou Hamer and the Fight for the Vote* (Millbrook Press). She discovered there were two dates for Hamer's death, March 14 and March 15, 1965. Determined to get to the truth, she called a clerk who worked in the records division of the county in Mississippi where Hamer died. The clerk checked the original death certificate and came up with a third date, March 13. As the clerk explained, mistakes are made even on official records. Then the author must make a decision based on all the research. Colman used the date on Hamer's headstone, March 14, 1965.

Get Creative

Sometimes biographers run into blocks with their research when it seems almost impossible to find the information they need. When that happens, it is time to get more creative by trying new angles.

Author Wendie Old has found unexpected leads by talking to people about her projects and asking many questions. "For every book, I run into people who know tidbits of information that make my person more human," she says. When she was researching *To Fly: The Story of the Wright Brothers* (Clarion Books), she shared information about her project with online writers groups. "Much to my surprise, people there *knew* some people who were involved in some way with the Wright brothers," she says.

Charles J. Shields interviewed Kurt Vonnegut and people he knew for his biography *And So It Goes: Kurt Vonnegut, A Life* (Henry Holt). But finding Vonnegut's personal correspondence was tricky. "He told me he had lost all of his correspondence in a fire in his study," recalls Shields, who then tried a different angle. "Over the next three years, every time I spoke to one of his friends—and he had many—I asked whether they had copies of his letters." Shields's strategy worked and the letters began to arrive. "Sometimes, I received as many as 200 at a time."

Be Persistent

Shields encountered a different challenge while researching his biography *Mockingbird: A Portrait of Harper Lee* (Henry Holt). The Pulitzer Prize winner Harper Lee, author of *To Kill a Mockingbird,* has been notoriously private and has not given any interviews since 1964. So Shields started his research knowing he would not have her help with the book.

He followed Lee's paper trail as far as it led, finding archived materials that included newspaper and magazine articles. Knowing that Lee had helped Truman Capote with his research for the book *In Cold Blood,* Shields went through Capote's papers at the New York Public Library as well as the papers of Lee's agent, Annie Laurie Williams.

He also set out to contact people who had known Lee. She had attended Huntingdon College for one year and then went on to the University of Alabama. Shields got their alumni directories and emailed about 200 people who had attended those schools in the mid-1940s when Lee was a student. He used the Classmates.com website to find people who had attended elementary and high school with Lee in her hometown of Monroeville, Alabama, and contacted them as well. Many of those people were not willing to talk to Shields, and in fact, Harper had asked friends and family members not to cooperate.

It was an interesting problem, but Shields did not get discouraged. "Actually, the obstacles I kept running into made me more determined to deliver a fair, accurate, and comprehensive account of her life," he says. The result of his hard work: "Fifty to 75 interviews by phone and in person."

Researching a biography is an interesting challenge that requires problem-solving abilities, some creativity, and often a little detective work. It also requires a determination to not stop until the biographer has found the *story* of a person's life. It is the story that brings a person alive on the page and that is the biographer's goal.

Bacon & Eggs in Mesopotamia

Historical Resources

By Christina Hamlett

I must have been a source of great mirth to my English teachers in elementary school when I would pen elaborate stories about ancient settings in which my characters played instruments that had not been invented, ate modern breakfasts, and rode around on horses named Rex and Buttermilk. In that pre-Internet age, the *Encyclopedia Britannica* gave readers only a cursory view of the past that was largely defined by the major history-makers, not all those workaday folk who obscurely toiled in the background. The absence of accessible resources seemed to give my young imagination *carte blanche* to make up whatever best fit the demands of the plot.

Today's writers—of any age—can no longer tap the *how could I possibly know* excuse. If your fictional characters are going to rub shoulders with historic luminaries, engage in eighteenth-century courtship rituals, storm a medieval castle, or stalk a wooly mammoth, discerning readers will expect you to do the background work and infuse your text with enough accuracy to make the whole tableau sound plausible. Fortunately, there is no shortage of websites and reference books to help you accomplish that.

Food, Glorious Food

~ *Food in History*, by Reah Tannahill. Eating habits, food fads, and culinary influences on mankind's evolution from prehistoric times up to the present.

~ *Much Depends on Dinner: The Extraordinary History and Mythology, Allure and Obsessions, Perils and Taboos of an Ordinary Meal*, by Margaret Visser. Who knew all the baggage we were bringing to the table?

~ The Food Timeline (www.foodtimeline.org/food1.html) is an online journey of epicurean proportions that covers such courses as dining with Romeo and Juliet, the invention of restaurants, breakfast at Monticello, Ellis Island canteens, and dining room rules at Alcatraz in the 1950s.

~ At FoodReference.com (www.foodreference.com), you will learn such historical trivia as the fact that celery was used medicinally by the ancient Chinese, mince pies made their debut at medieval tables, the Visigoths demanded 3,000 pounds of pepper as ransom for Rome, and bread slicers, invented in 1928, were banned during World War II because the metal required to operate them was needed to build tanks.

Dressing the Part

~ Fashion Era (www.fashion-era.com) covers fashion topics head to toe, from the Regency period to the twenty-first century, along with articles about the duties of 1900s seamstresses, cloth rationing in the 1940s, and the influences of *Dynasty* and *Dallas* on power dressing, just to name a few.

~ The Timeline of Fashion (http://aspees.students.cofc.edu/time-line.html) takes a nuts-and-bolts approach to the fabrics and structure of men's and women's apparel through the centuries, and speaks to concepts of modesty, social status, and comfort.

~ The Costume Gallery Research Library (www.costumegallery.com/research.htm) requires a subscription to browse but is well worth the price. Everything from hats to shoes is covered in this fashionable compilation that also includes textile and color references, etiquette primers, notable designers, paper dolls, vintage photos and fashion catalogues, needlework, and film costumes. The cost ranges from $18 for three months to $55 for a year.

Associates of mine who design costumes for theatrical productions have told me that the following two texts are indispensable for writers who want to get all the details right for their historical novels:

~ *What People Wore When: A Complete Illustrated History of Costume from Ancient Times to the Nineteenth Century for Every Level of Society,* by Melissa Leventon.
~ *Fashion in Costume, 1200-2000,* by Joan Nunn.

Everyday Life

During the 1990s, a remarkable series about what it was like to live during different periods of American and English history was published by Writer's Digest. In addition to their detailed coverage of transportation, housing, occupations, currency, courtship, amusements, health/medicine/hygiene and housekeeping, some of the books also include colorful slang and colloquialisms. Did you know, for instance, that in the 1800s *absquatulate* meant to disappear; *the biggest toad in the puddle* was the most important person in the room; a cheerful person was *chirk;* or that a *gallnipper* was a mosquito?
The titles are:

~ *Everyday Life in the Middle Ages: The British Isles 500–1500,* by Sherrilyn Kenyon
~ *The Writer's Guide to Everyday Life in Renaissance England from 1485–1649,* by Kathy Lynn Emerson
~ *The Writer's Guide to Everyday Life in Colonial America from 1607–1783,* by Dale Taylor
~ *The Writer's Guide to Everyday Life in the 1800s,* by Marc McCutcheon

~ *The Writer's Guide to Everyday Life in Regency and Victorian England from 1811–1901,* by Kristine Hughes
~ *Everyday Life Among the American Indians 1800–1900,* by Candy Moulton
~ *The Writer's Guide to Everyday Life in the Wild West from 1840–1900,* by Candy Moulton
~ *Everyday Life During the Civil War,* by Michael J. Varhola
~ *The Writer's Guide to Everyday Life from Prohibition Through World War II,* by Marc McCutcheon

That same decade, Time-Life Books published its own series, called What Life Was Like. Sample titles include:

~ *What Life Was Like: At the Dawn of Democracy: Classical Athens 525–322 BC*
~ *What Life Was Like: When Rome Ruled the World: The Roman Empire 100 BC–AD 200*
~ *What Life Was Like at the Rebirth of Genius: Renaissance Italy, AD 1400–1550*
~ *What Life Was Like in Europe's Golden Age: Northern Europe, AD 1500–1675*
~ *What Life Was Like in the Jewel in the Crown: British India, AD 1600–1905*
~ *What Life Was Like at Empire's End: Austro-Hungarian Empire, AD 1848–1918*

Everyday life is also covered in the following titles and websites:

~ *The Household Cyclopedia of General Information* (www.public-bookshelf.com/public_html/The_Household_Cyclopedia_of_General_Information). How did people in the nineteenth century manage routine chores like cooking and cleaning without all the modern conveniences? This website has the inside scoop, along with must-have tips about how to breed canaries, how to avoid drowning, and how to clear up a bad complexion.

~ Authentic Historical Designs (http://historicaldesigns.com) offers plentiful vintage floor plans. Although this website is primarily targeted to people who want to recreate the facade of an old house with all the nifty interior conveniences of a modern one (indoor bathrooms, for instance), the line drawings and layouts provide a clever sense of different architectural styles such as Tudor, Georgian, Federalist, and Victorian.

~ *110 Turn-of-the-Century House Designs,* by Robert W. Shoppell. If you are seeking the real deal in late nineteenth-century architecture, this book contains floor plans as well as overviews of materials used, color schemes, and estimates of building costs based on 1897 prices.

~ For her four-part BBC series, *If Walls Could Talk,* Dr. Lucy Worsley, Chief Curator of the Historic Royal Palaces, offers insights on the evolution of bedrooms, bathrooms, living rooms and kitchens throughout history. Capsule summaries of this program can be found at www.bbc.co.uk/history/british/middle_ages/history_of_home.shtml. A hardcover version is slated for publication this year.

Everything Old Is News(worthy) Again

Is staying on top of current events critical to the characters in your yesteryear plots? Until the advent of high-tech media, people primarily learned about social, political, and economic happenings through regional gazettes.

~ The Library of Congress's Chronicling America website (http://chroniclingamerica.loc.gov) now has digitized versions of American newspapers from 1860 to 1922, as well as a comprehensive directory that covers U.S. newspapers published between 1690 and the present.

~ If your story's focus is eighteenth-century America, you will find first-person accounts, newspapers, magazines, letters, maps and timelines at Archiving Early America (http://www.earlyamerica.com).

~ Eyewitness to History (www.eyewitnesstohistory.com) paints even broader historical brushstrokes by providing users with a front row seat to events ranging from the ancient world to the twentieth-century. Examples include traveling the Erie Canal, looking over Victoria's shoulder on her first day as queen, getting caught up in the hysteria of the Salem witch trials, and spending Christmas in the trenches with World War I doughboys.

Meanwhile, in Another Part of the World

I am putting this next historical resource in a category by itself simply because it is one of the most useful books I have ever found insofar as putting world affairs in a comparative context. *The Timetables of History: A Horizontal Linkage of People and Events* was compiled by Bernard Grun and based on a 1940s German tome called *Kulturfahrplan*. Formatted in a matrix style, it covers politics, literature/theater, religion/philosophy/learning, visual arts, music, science/technology/growth and daily life from 5,000 BC to 1978.

In 1939, for example:

- King George VI and Queen Elizabeth visited the U.S.
- C. S. Forester wrote *Captain Horatio Hornblower.*
- Pope Pius XI died.
- *Gone with The Wind, The Wizard of Oz,* and *Stagecoach* debuted.
- Germany invaded Poland, causing Britain and France to declare war on Germany.
- Aaron Copeland wrote his *Billy the Kid* ballet.
- Polyethylene was invented.
- Baseball was first televised in the U.S.

The book also contains a reverse-engineering index for looking up specific names, titles, events, and inventions to learn the related year. If, for example, your character is going to compose a letter on a typewriter, you need to confirm whether typewriters were in circulation at the time. (Here is some interesting trivia: The first company to start producing the typewriter device was better known in the 1870s for its manufacture of guns: E. Remington & Sons.)

Virtual Field Trips

~ BBC's Interactive Virtual Tours (www.bbc.co.uk/history/inter-active/virtual_tours) invites visitors to step aboard Henry VIII's flagship, the *Mary Rose;* take a tour of Windsor Castle; and see how Vikings farmed their land. This site also has an abundance of links to archival clips and vocal recordings from BBC programming pertaining to both World Wars.

~ History.com (www.history.com/topics) has an expansive list of topics, many of which come with videos that include reenactments, archival footage, photographs, letters, music, and interviews with notable experts. The lineup covers eras and decades, luminaries, wars, science and technology, famous places, and events such as the Black Death, the Triangle Shirtwaist Factory Fire, the St. Valentine's Day Massacre, and the Great Depression.

~ The Worldwide Web Virtual History Library (http://vlib.iue.it/history/index.html) covers continents, eras, and epochs, and history by topics such as anthropology, cartography, religious missions, indigenous peoples, and women's history.

~ Discovery Channel's Virtual History website (www.yourdiscovery.com/virtualhistory/_home/index.shtml) encourages browsing on diverse subjects such as classic cars, dinosaurs, crime, history, and the natural world.

~ At 3D Ancient Wonders (www.3dancientwonders.com), you can stroll around the Parthenon, Stonehenge, and an Aztec temple, just to name a few. The most helpful aspect of this 3D technology is that it provides a frame of reference on the size of these structures.

~ Crazy for castles? TimeRef.com (www.timeref.com/v699.htm) has 3D tours as well as timelines and multiple research articles on medieval life, royals, and the power of the church.

~ Enjoy the exhibits of the Smithsonian Museum of Natural History (www.mnh.si.edu/panoramas) without leaving home. Click on the Research & Collections tab or Explore a Topic to narrow your research.

Note: Many of the websites that use 3D graphics require a VRML plug-in. This is available as a free download on each site and is easy to install.

The World in a Nutshell

~ The Ancient World (www.ancient-world.org) provides links and mailing addresses of research museums, university scholarly associations, and websites focusing on antiquities and Mediterranean civilizations.

~ Essential Humanities (www.essentialhumanities.net) offers byte-sized summaries of worldwide history and art from the beginning of mankind.

~ Macro-History & World Report (www.fsmitha.com) has everything you would want to know about the world from 4.3 million years ago up to today.

~ The British Museum (www.britishmuseum.org/default.aspx): More than two million artifacts call this iconic London museum home. Go armchair exploring in the online tours of its exhibits.

~ Librarians are your friends and never has this been more solidly proven than by the Ask a Librarian feature at the Library of Congress (www.loc.gov/index.html). The virtual reference shelf covers just about every topic you would ever want to research; the breadth of digital collections is astonishing.

Verifying the authenticity of any historic research is essential. As useful as Wikipedia, Ask.com, and Ask Jeeves are in providing instant answers to whet your curiosity, they should never be considered as more than just a starting point. Too often, the contributors pepper the content with their own 20/20 hindsight interpretation of the truth or engage in recitations of so-called facts that have never been fact-checked. Nor should you rule out the possibility of typos missed during proofreading on these sites. Whatever research tidbits you decide to incorporate in your story should always be confirmed by two additional independent sources.

IDEAS

IDEAS

IDEAS

Ideas

I
D
E
A
S

IDEAS

IDEAS

IDEAS

IDEAS

Ideas

IDEAS

IDEAS

Loosening the Ligaments

A Writer's Journal

By Judith Logan Lehne

Before a runner begins a race, he stretches his muscles. Before a dancer performs, she does warm-up exercises. Before a game, baseball players have batting practice and basketball players run lay-up drills. Loosening up before a main event is standard preparation for performers and athletes, but how can writers exercise creative skills to prepare for their work? Many writers find that journaling is the perfect warm-up to tune into the world, find focus, unblock a reluctant muse, and unlock hidden word treasures.

Virginia Woolf wrote in her diary, "The habit of writing for my eye only is good practice. It loosens the ligaments." Woolf makes a good point. When you are writing professionally, you must constantly edit, rethink phrasing, check spelling and punctuation—and recheck. All this attention to detail puts the *professional* into the writing. However, creative journaling, the loosening-the-ligaments type of writing, is unpressured and uncensored, allowing words to tumble out of hiding and flow freely, a kind of scribe-aerobics.

Long before I ever thought of writing professionally, I scribbled thoughts on paper. I still have the plastic diary with the lock-and-key closure I received for my twelfth birthday. I have a narrow spiral

287

notebook filled with the secrets of my high school days scribbled upon lined pages, dutifully penned daily for four years. I have stacks of hardbound and paperback journals in which I have recorded decades of life and family milestones, travel memories and dreams. All of these notebooks have come out of free-writing—a casual spilling of words onto pages. I never thought of those writings as preparation for creating novels and nonfiction, and that was surely not the intent. But looking back, I am convinced that this process, over the years, has positively affected my professional work. And while I have not used any actual entries from my journals in my novels, I did review my plastic diary when I wrote *Coyote Girl* (Marcel Dekker) to get a sense of how Billie might put pen to paper during her wilderness journey.

Loose or Structured

Whether you call them journals or diaries or notebooks, journaling can document important happenings in your daily life, process emotions, and keep track of information. Any type of journal can be fertile soil in which seeds of creativity can sprout. Certainly writers' personal diaries and journals can be a great source of inspiration and may even guide a writing project. But writing journals are different from personal journals. These notebooks or even just scraps of paper (informal and spontaneous works, too) are specifically intended to hone a writer's skills and fuel the writing process.

Journaling can be as loose or as structured as suits you, but as a writer's tool, it is best to have some goal at the foundation of the writing. The goal might be to free a resistant muse or tune into the sensory details of a wintry night. Or the goal can be directed at a work in progress: getting to the heart of a character or working through plot problems.

"Keeping a journal is an essential part of my writing life," says author and editor Ellen Dreyer, but her method varies. She may write in her journal regularly for long periods of time, then set it aside. Even if she does not pick it up again for many months, she knows it is "always there as a safe haven and a seedbed for ideas." Dreyer's writer's journal is her place to jot words or images that come to her in dreams; some even grow into scenes or ideas for novels.

She also uses her journal to write reminders, helping her maintain balance and focus. "The words 'take your time!' occupy the center of one page in my current journal," Dreyer says."I wrote it when I felt particularly impatient to finish a draft of a novel and found myself rushing through the final chapters."

If she is feeling creatively blocked, Dreyer will use her journal for free-writing. "In one instance a free-write started in my journal with the dream image of a girl lost in a cave." She wound up filling several pads of paper with those free-falling words, which became the first draft of her novel, *The Glow Stone* (Peachtree Publishers).

Author and writing instructor Patricia Curtis Pfitsch also keeps journals. "I have a book that I write in every night." She dates each entry and records specific events of the day. "This is a personal journal," she says, "but I may include notes about struggles with a novel or document conversations with my agent or editors." Her writer's journals are usually directed at fleshing out issues around a work in progress. These are written more sporadically, on scraps of paper, pages from notebooks or legal pads, notes tapped into her computer or smartphone, or the notepad she keeps in her purse. While she admits this is not very organized, she does not feel it necessary to keep track of her thought-writing. "The purpose isn't to ever go back and look at those notes again. The mere act of the writing secures the thoughts. Then they seem to come to me when I need them."

That is exactly how Pfitsch works through plot structure and characters for novels, including *Riding the Flume* (Simon & Schuster). "I scribbled down over-arching questions and then answered them: What does Francie want more than anything else? What's standing in her way? How does she grow?" Many of the answers to those questions never became part of that book, but the process was the key in charting a clear course for the plot.

Pfitsch uses similar techniques for fleshing out characters, free-writing descriptions as they come to mind, or she creates a *character wheel*. "The character's name goes in the center. As I imagine her characteristics, they become the spokes: What's her age? Who's in her family? Hair color? Nicknames?" She laughs. "Lots of questions, lots of spokes." Lots of spokes—excellent exercise routine!

Get Moving

While journaling can be directed at a current writing project or become a seed for a work in the future, other techniques can get and keep a writer in good creative shape. The first step: Just do it! If you are going to work out, you have to tie on your Nikes, go to the track or gym and get moving. Likewise, if you want to exercise your creativity, you have to get paper, grab a pen and get your hand moving. The thing about journaling is that it is convenient. Anywhere in the world can be your gym: a quiet place in your home, a bench at a busy park, in your car waiting for your kids, an arboretum or wildlife preserve. Each location can be a jogging track for the mind, taking your writing into very unique and distinctively different places.

An athlete who wants a thorough and well-rounded exercise program does not spend all the time lifting weights, but uses a variety of routines. Writers looking to exercise their creative muscles do well to experiment with various journaling techniques. Each will likely elicit different reactions and responses, stretching mind ligaments you may not yet know you have.

~ *Free-writing*. I compare this writing to a skydiver's free-fall before deploying the parachute. Give yourself a set period of time and write continuously—whatever comes to mind, without editing, correcting, or evaluating. For a different free-write experience, begin with a topic or emotion and let your words tumble willy-nilly as you think of that subject in stream-of-consciousness writing. The beauty of for-your-eyes-only writing is that there are no rules. So, pick a timeframe and location that works for you and free-fall onto the page. No parachute needed for safe landing!

~ *Prompts.* While it may seem contradictory to use contrived prompts for journaling, they can often get your mind limbered up and racing down a path of thinking you had never been on before. Prompts are statements or questions intended to spark your imagination. You can create prompts around morals or values you believe in, or those you have never considered. You can find prompts by thinking back over your life. If you only recall a snippet of a time or place, it could be a journal prompt that will bring the memories into clearer, more colorful focus. A subject in the news, your own personality traits, people you know, people you do not know but see every day on the train, a color, flavor or aroma, all can be valuable prompts to get your hand moving and your mind spinning. ("Spin Zone: Remixing the Headlines, Brainstorming Ideas," beginning on page 287, offers hundreds of prompts.)

~ *Dialoguing.* These are imagined conversations between two or more entities. The dialogues can be between two different sides of yourself or another person, between varying opportunities or challenges, or between inanimate objects. (Hmmm. What does the refrigerator say to the stove when I am not in the kitchen?)

Ira Progoff (1921-1998), a psychotherapist and author of *At a Journal Workshop*, developed a reputation as the grandfather of personal journaling and an impressive list of possible dialogues that would help people learn more about themselves, including:

- dialoguing with a person from a current or past relationship
- dialoguing with yourself in your work role, your role as a parent or sibling, your creative side
- having a "conversation" with a specific emotion you are experiencing
- dialoguing with a resistance-point in your life. ("Okay, Novel. Why won't you let me write the story?" "Because I want you to think about it first." "But I have thought about it – for weeks." "Well, if it's gonna be great, you gotta think longer!")

As writers, the more we know ourselves, the more substance goes into our work. Dialoguing can be a solid substance-building exercise.

~ *Jump-start quotes.* Sometimes when we are at a loss for words, the words of others can get our blood pumping. What are some of your favorite quotes? What do some of the great thinkers have to say about a topic or theme? How about first-lines in books? Place the quote at the top of the page, then do that free-fall thing, letting your mind carry on beyond the quoted words. Try one of these:

- "Do or do not. There is no *try*." (Yoda, *The Empire Strikes Back*)
- "Now the earth was formless and empty, darkness was over the surface of the deep." (The Bible, Genesis 1:2)
- "It's kind of fun to do the impossible." (Walt Disney)
- "I died once." (*The Glow Stone*, Ellen Dreyer)
- "Eleven-year-old Muhammad Bilal flinched." (*The Glory Field*, Walter Dean Myers)
- "The edge of the world." (*Keeper of the Light*, Patricia Curtis Pfitsch)

Just as starting a physical exercise routine can be a struggle, exercising your writing may take some perseverance and a concerted effort initially. But the more you journal, the more comfortable you will become with the process, and the more benefits you will see spilling into your professional life. The ligament-loosening that comes from spontaneous personal writing has a way of opening our minds, perking up our antennae, tuning us in to notice and absorb more, and, somewhat subconsciously, build our confidence. The miracle of keeping on a little past your comfort zone when you are writing only for yourself is that something powerful and strong can emerge.

So the next time you need to wake up a sleepy muse or loosen creative ligaments, journal aerobics might be the prefect exercise to enlighten and surprise you.

Self-Inspiration

Keep Yourself Writing Until Your Big Break

By Sue Bradford Edwards

Maybe your goal is a novel sale or maybe it is a byline in *Scientific American.* Either way, the journey from beginner to your big break can be discouraging. After all, who knows how long it will take? How many times will you almost make it only to get a rejection? In spite of this uncertainty, you can succeed if you keep yourself inspired.

Just how to stay inspired varies from writer to writer. Some writers seek out the company of fellow writers. Others make time for various creative pursuits. Still others set specific goals. Inspiration is not the same for everyone, but perhaps what works for one of these writers will keep you writing until you reach your big goal.

Do not overlook the importance of your goals. Goals are, after all, powerful motivators.

Checklists and To-do's

Goals provide inspiration by giving you small, measurable successes. How many times have you added an almost completed chore to your to-do list so you can check it off?

Vague goals or goals that cannot be measured sap creative energy.

293

Avoid goals like "work harder on my writing." Do you want to increase production or study something new? Make your goals very specific so you will know when you have succeeded.

Next, make sure you have the power to achieve the goals you set. You cannot control how many new markets you break into each year or whether or not you win a specific prize. You do have power over the work you do.

"My system is 'Keep 13 in Play': Make sure 13 queries are always outstanding. Receive a rejection or acceptance, and submit another query."

Some authors measure their work in terms of submissions. "I started writing freelance articles for income, with the novel being *dessert* once my work was done," says C. Hope Clark, an author of suspense and the editor of Funds for Writers (www.fundsforwriters. com). "My system was 'Keep 13 in Play.' I'd make sure 13 queries stayed outstanding. When I received a rejection or acceptance, the number dropped. So I'd submit queries until I had the 13 queries back in play."

Other writers set word-count goals. "I take my laptop to a coffee-house without open Internet access, order a vanilla latte, and force myself to write 1,500 to 2,000 words, no matter how lousy they sound as a first draft," says Mitali Perkins, whose most recent book is *Bamboo People* (Charlesbridge). "The next day I edit and revise those words, cutting most of them, and add 1,000 to 1,500 new ones—mostly nonkeepers—and so on." Pages of text add up, encouraging Perkins to keep writing, refining her work as she goes.

Some writers create annual goals. "At the beginning of each year, I get clear on what this year is about for my writing. Some of my foci have been: revision, completion, promoting existing work," says

~ Brave New Goals ~

Money cannot be the lone determining factor when you choose a writing project, but what if what you love to write fails to bring that contract? Edie Ramer had a track record but no book deal. She did not give up. She altered her goal.

"I made my big break. After four agents, contest wins and finals, and near misses, I self-published my first book in August 2010. Since then I've published two more books and one short story," says Ramer.

Self-publishing is not the answer for everyone but for a writer, like Ramer, who already has a fan base looking for more of her work, it can pay off. Says Ramer, "For the last two months, I've made over $2000." Sometimes you can earn a living writing what you love but for some writers, like Ramer, it means making your own big break.

Cynthia Morris. "From that big picture focus I get specific on quarterly, monthly, and weekly levels. I recently completed my novel, *Chasing Sylvia Beach*, and used a deadline to help focus to the finish." Short-term goals give Morris the jazzy feeling of achieving something easily measured while working toward larger goals.

Remember that goals that work today may not work tomorrow. "I divide my year into academic quarters, focusing on author visits and appearances during the fall and spring and on longer writing projects during the winter and summer," says Perkins. A goal of 2,000 words a day when she has several school visits would weigh Perkins down instead of buoying her up. The birth of a child, an impending move, or even hosting Thanksgiving dinner may mean having to re-examine and reset your goals. But even realistic goals cannot keep you inspired if the problem is what you are writing.

The Writing Itself

Even if you love writing more than any other job, writing the wrong things can leave you uninspired. Most often, this happens when you accept an assignment not for love of the topic, but because you have been lured in by dollar signs.

"Money certainly does influence me to the extent that I make my living from writing," says Beth Revis, who writes YA science fiction and fantasy, including the Across the Universe trilogy (Razorbill/Penguin). "It influences me to make sure the work I make is perfect. But I write only the books that I want to write." We all need to earn a living but this should not be the only determining factor when it comes to your writing.

Yet the lure of a check can lead us off the path and away from the long-term goals that we set for ourselves. Writers combat this temptation in a variety of ways. "I take annual silent prayer retreats to focus on my call and contribution in this vocation. This allows me to discern which projects might contribute to that vision and which might be distractions," says Perkins, who seeks out advice from a respected source. "Also, my agent helps to sort through and prioritize potential projects."

No matter what your goals are, the focus has to be on more than the money. "You have to love the work more than the income. Otherwise, find another profession where enthusiasm doesn't matter so much. In the arts, you have passion or you die," says Clark, whose writing focus has changed over time. "It's a constant juggling act—a give and take, money versus creativity. But you can try to keep your money-making work entertaining. Frankly, I enjoy writing almost anything. It beats going back to the nonwriting employment."

Even if writing is your favorite activity, nonwriting activities keep writing energy high.

Recharging Your Batteries

No matter how much you love writing, sometimes you need to recharge. "Whenever I get stuck, I do something else," says Revis. "Usually driving. Something about driving around makes me think. Mowing the lawn, gardening, and housework also do the trick. My house is cleanest when I'm working on a complicated scene."

For some people, recharging means other artistic pursuits. "What feeds my creativity is giving myself time to play. Watercolor, illustration, calligraphy, and other media help me loosen up and be messy. Writing demands a certain kind of attention and these other forms allow me to be more playful and to have a greater sense of fun," says Morris.

Jacqui Lofthouse's newest form of expression takes her outside. "I'm just getting into photography at the moment. I enjoy taking photographs of birds and the natural world. I like being out in nature; it's a great contrast to being at the computer screen, and, when I have a camera with me, I become more observant which is good for the writing too."

Clark also recharges outdoors. "I'm a gardener and I raise chickens," she says. "I adore the outdoors and live on three acres beside a lake so I'm drawn outside often."

Some writers push themselves physically. "Being in my body, whether playing tennis, biking, or at yoga, really helps keep me sane and balanced," says Morris. "These challenging activities help me be a better writer. I'm able to cope with demanding situations with more grace and patience because of these physical practices."

Other writers turn to the thought-provoking. "I enjoy studying art history and visiting art galleries. Visual images inspire my writing work and I love the connections that I end up making when I look at art; art seems to spark me in a way that nothing else does. Whenever I look at paintings, I'm thinking of the stories they might inspire. References to paintings are scattered throughout my work. If I'm stuck, I'll always go to a gallery," says Lofthouse.

If writing is your creative soul pursuit, attend a writing-related event. "I attend conferences. Now I'm speaking at them, but they are rejuvenating and thrilling. Every writer needs to attend one per year to get that shot in the arm that makes one feel part of a bigger world of like individuals, and learn from the experts. It helps you improve faster, or learn that you've actually been on the right path," says Clark.

Finding Fellowship

Inspiration can come from a writing event simply because it puts you among like-minded individuals who understand the writing life. "Networking with other writers was invaluable to me," says Revis. "People who aren't in writing don't understand that you have to celebrate the little things. I would tell my friends and family that I got ink on a rejection letter, and they would say 'Who cares? It's still a rejection.' My writer friends would realize how important it was. They would buoy me up when I felt down, encourage me when I needed it."

Another way to tap into the inspiration of other writers is to join a professional organization. "Eight years ago, I joined Romance Writers of America (RWA). That made a huge difference in my writing life. It was if I was wandering alone in a desert, and suddenly I wasn't alone anymore," says Ramer. "I met my brilliant critique partners through RWA."

Critique groups offer both feedback and regular contact with your fellows. When Clark started writing full-time, she joined a women's writing group that met monthly in her area. "I took an interest in one fellow writer in the local group, and we had a biweekly morning writing breakfast for three hours. Oh how I looked forward to all that interaction," says Clark.

You can also find a writing team at your local college or university. "When I was in my mid-twenties, I studied for an MA in Creative Writing at the University of East Anglia (UEA)," says Lofthouse. "It was fairly competitive but in fact that pushed me to produce my best ever work and the work I did that year led to my first novel, *The Temple of Hymen* (Penguin). I also made some close friends in that group and having writing colleagues helped to deepen my seriousness about literature."

If you need the inspiration of your fellow writers but cannot find a face-to-face group or a local university with applicable classes, look online. Twitter, Facebook, and various blogs enable writers to interact. Many blogs and online communities are sponsored by groups of writers who offer classes and lead online workshops. These will not work quite the same as local groups and courses but they will give you the interaction that many writers need to write until they get that big break.

When it comes to inspiration, do not underestimate what you can gain from fellow writers. "Writing is solitary. You need cohorts for feedback, to judge if you are on track, to raise your spirits when you hit brick walls with rejection. And having other eyes on your work is the best way to improve. So when I'm not sure about my work, I turn on the computer and shoot a message to someone who cares, knowing the feedback is genuine and for my own good," says Clark. Not only does this feedback enable Clark to improve, it also inspires her to keep writing.

Do not wait for inspiration to strike. Use your goals, creative pursuits, and your interactions with other writers to keep you going. But remember, you will have to find the combination that works for you where you are now.

"I coach others to get clear and stay connected to their own motivation for creating. It's important for us to trust our own instincts. We spend too much time absorbing advice that isn't right for us," says Morris. "I invite people to know and follow their playful urges."

Writer, know yourself. From there you will find what you need to keep writing from one day to the next.

The Key to Writing a Book that Makes an Impact

Ideas & Theme

By Patricia Curtis Pfitsch

The Newbery. The Pulitzer. The National Book Award. Have you imagined the call, the acceptance speech, the satisfaction of knowing that at least one of your books will not go out of print? Or perhaps your goal is not that lofty. Maybe you just want to write a book that makes an impact. "Will this be the one?" you whisper as that creative spark hits. You begin the journey already knowing it is likely to be painful and that there are no guarantees of success. But you are sure it will be worth the struggle. Just don't forget your key.

The Key to the Kingdom

The conflict will keep us turning the pages. We might love, or hate, the characters. But it is the theme that makes a book reverberate down the generations. That is the key to fiction that touches readers.

"Theme is what makes all kinds of books resonate with readers today," says Kathleen Ernst, who writes historical fiction and mysteries for children and adults. "They might not know or care much about

301

history, or about an imaginary planet in a science fiction book, but the themes, which are based around human emotions, those things are the universals—that's what makes a book so compelling."

Theme is elusive. It is sometimes easier to understand by thinking about what it is not. For example, even though the theme is often what makes a book powerful for readers, it is not the moral. "A moral is something I try to stay away from," says Stephanie Golightly Lowden, author of the historical novels *Time of the Eagle* and *Jingo Fever* (both from Midwest Traditions). "I picture someone shaking their finger and teaching me a lesson. A moral is more of a statement, what the reader should or shouldn't do. A theme develops organically from a natural place."

Donald Maass calls a novel's theme "its animating spirit" in *Writing the Breakout Novel*. It starts, he says, "with having something to say."

The Passion at the Core

One way to find something to say is to ask yourself what you are afraid of, says Sheri Sinykin, author of 19 books for middle-graders and young adults. Her most recent novel, *Giving up the Ghost* (Peachtree Press), began with her attraction to New Orleans and several plantations she visited. "But I was in desperate need of a character with a problem, and an emotional connection with me." When she thought about her own fears, she found the link. "At that time I was really afraid of my mom dying from her cancer." From that spark came 13-year-old Davia. Davia's mother's cancer is in remission and she is helping to care for her great aunt who is dying of cancer on her spooky Louisiana plantation. Davia's fear of death, her own death as well as her mother's, was the connection Sinykin needed. The book has been praised for its honesty in the way the characters deal with the dying process as well as for its exciting plot line.

In her new picture book *Zayde Comes To Live* (Peachtree), she tackles the dying process for younger children with a story featuring

~ Book Advice ~

"When I write," says author Laura Fitzgerald, "and especially when I revise, I refer to these books over and over. If you follow their advice, you can't go wrong."

~ *Emotional Structure: Creating The Story Beneath the Plot,* by Peter Dunne (Linden Publishing).
~ *Techniques of the Selling Writer*, by Dwight Swain (University of Oklahoma Press).
~ *The Third Act; Writing a Great Ending To Your Screenplay, by Drew Yannow* (Continuum).

a young girl whose dying grandfather comes to live with them. A talk by a hospice rabbi at Sinykin's temple sparked the idea for the book. "The rabbi said that Jewish patients in hospice are the worst-case patients spiritually because nothing in their religion prepares them for dying. All the focus is on the living, good deeds on earth; nobody talks about the hereafter." That, combined with a conversation she overheard between some Jewish and Christian children, resulted in her story about a Jewish child who is anxious about where her Jewish grandfather will go when he dies. "She asks her Christian friend, who says, 'if you believe in Jesus he'll go to Heaven,' and she thinks, 'but we don't.' She asks another friend who's Muslim and he says, 'If you believe in Allah, you'll go to Paradise.' And she thinks, 'but we don't.'" The child's search leads to her discovery of what Jews believe about death, and she is reassured. "Maybe kids will grow up having more comfort when their grandparents die," Sinykin says.

When you find the same theme appearing in all your stories, then you know you have found something you feel passionately about. "One of the themes I return to again and again in my novels is the whole question of identity," says Ernst. "Who am I? Who do I want to be? What kind of decisions do I want to make about what kind of person I'm going to be." Her new mystery series for adults explores different aspects of that larger theme. In the first book of the series, *Old World Murder* (Midnight Ink), Chloe Ellefson is recovering from some wrenching emotional experiences and struggles with the question at the most basic level. Does she even want to go on living? "In book two," says Ernst, "her old boyfriend comes back and she really has to wrestle with, 'What do I want in a relationship?' And in book three she'll be on an island. She goes there to be alone, but she discovers she really needs to have people around sometimes."

Out of the Corner of Your Eye

Philip Gerard, author of *Writing a Book That Makes a Difference* (Story Press), refers to theme as "the unconscious of the story" and suggests that sometimes it is easier to get at the theme by looking at it "out of the corner of your eye rather than straight on."

> **"The story is like the river, and the mist that rises from the river is the theme."**

Sinykin agrees. "I've heard it said that the story is like the river, and the mist that rises from the river is the theme. In other words, you don't set out to create the theme. You find stories that seem important, that resonate with you." Then, Sinykin says, "focus on the character and the story. Ask yourself, 'What did my character learn?' and the theme will come from the journey."

Picture book writer Dori Chaconas never thinks about theme when she begins a book. "When I set out to write the very first Cork and Fuzz easy-to-read book (Viking), the characters came first. I chose a muskrat and a possum, each with a distinct personality that often brought them into conflict." Cork is a vegetarian and Fuzz eats beetles and worms. The games they enjoy are different. They appear to have nothing in common.

Each time she starts a new book in the series, Chaconas puts Cork and Fuzz in a situation that early elementary children will understand—making new friends, physical differences, sharing, and so on. "Cork and Fuzz's personalities mix like oil and water," explains Chaconas, "and the conflict comes out of the situation and how each reacts to the other. The characters learn to understand and accept each other's different ways of thinking or behaving. The reader wants them to succeed and when they do, the resolution and ending are satisfying without being didactic." The theme, accepting differences and getting along, comes out of the conflict rather than being superimposed upon it.

Which Comes First?

Other writers focus more directly on the theme. "I'm really big on theme," says Laura Fitzgerald who writes for adults. Her novels include a national bestseller, *Veil of Roses* (Bantam). "The whole plot of the book should focus on what that theme is," she says. "Every character plays a part in addressing the theme, whether they're opposite to the theme or a challenge to the theme or support the theme. Working this way gives you a structure; it keeps you on a tight leash."

She points to her second novel, *One True Theory of Love* (NAL Trade), as an example. "That book is all about second chances. If you have the courage to take a second chance at happiness once life has screwed you over, you might not get your happy ending, but life is richer for the attempt. Every character in the book is playing off the theme of having the courage to take a second chance," she explains. In the novel, every character is a variation on the theme, either changing and growing or resisting change. "That allows the main character to bounce off of all of them."

Fitzgerald says that whether she begins with the theme or with the story varies with each book she writes. "But I can't get too far in one without the other holding up a stop sign to say, 'Wait! What about me?' I need to know in the larger sense what story I'm trying to tell. If I continue on with the plot too long without knowing what the larger story is about I could be wasting my time. That's when burnout sets in."

Once she is done with the first draft, she does an exercise she calls 'The First 50 and the Final 50.' She starts revising from the end of the book—the last 50 pages. "I'll work on that, making sure my theme and my premise are there and build up to the conclusion." Then she goes back to the first 50 pages and makes sure everything that comes up in the last 50 is hinted at in the first. "I'm able to cut out a lot of waste," she explains. "By figuring out what's wrong with the ending, I'm able to go back and quickly fix the beginning and the middle. It becomes really easy to get a book tight."

Ernst also thinks about the theme early in her writing process. "I don't do a lot of extensive outlining before I write. I may just have the kernel of an idea and I'll wade right in and see where it goes. But at some point I decide in very broad terms what this book is going to be about. Then I look for ways where a plot that may seem to have nothing to do on the surface with the theme—how I can manipulate that plot in ways that address the theme. Are there things I can do to help shine a light on a facet of that broad theme?"

Her middle-grade historical mystery, *Whistler in the Dark* (Pleasant Company), is set in Colorado in the years after the Civil War and addresses another theme that appears often in Ernst's books, the challenges strong women faced in the past. In the first chapter, 12-year old Emma is embarrassed by her mother's reform dress, the newfangled *bloomers* that many at the time thought inappropriate for a woman. "Emma has to figure out for herself what is appropriate for a woman," explains Ernst. "The mystery has to do with the printing press, which has nothing to do with reform dress, and the one thing I knew when I started developing that plot was that by the end of the book I wanted to get Emma in trousers." She brainstormed possibilities and ended up with a scene in which Emma needs to climb a tree in order to solve the mystery. "She tries to do that in a long skirt and it doesn't work so she gives in and puts on the reform dress her mother had made for her."

Avoid the Pitfalls

Normally, Lowden does not think about theme when she is writing. "It's character, or it's a scene or place," she says. *Time of the Eagle* grew from her love of the north woods of Wisconsin and a story she had heard about a young Native American girl whose family all died of smallpox; she had to spend an entire winter alone in the woods. The theme—the clash of cultures and the upheaval the Native American culture experienced with the arrival of Europeans—is a subtle undercurrent to the survival story.

But the conception of her just-published historical novel *Jingo Fever* was different. "I probably thought more about theme than in anything I've ever written," says Lowden. The idea started to percolate when her mother told her that during World War I, the teachers at her school in Milwaukee, Wisconsin, burned all the German language books. Then, when she was doing research for a University of Wisconsin history professor, Lowden learned that during the same time period German professors in Ashland, Wisconsin, had been tarred and feathered. "I saw the theme right away: how tolerance goes by the wayside during wartime."

She had problems with the first few drafts. "The trouble is that you can get really didactic and run away with the theme, forgetting about your character, the 12-year-old girl who is supposed to be the focus." In fact, her editor rejected the manuscript the first time he read it because the ending was not hopeful. "The whole thing was a downer because of the intolerance and the war," Lowden says. "He pointed out that my character, Adelle, can't have an effect on any of it."

Lowden solved the problem by refocusing on the story. In a later revision she added a boy who is changed through Adelle's influence. "I said, okay, a 12-year-old girl can't change the world but maybe she can change one kid's ideas. And that is what sold the book. The first ending was depressing, but now there's hope. People can change."

Embrace the Paradox

When you've found the issue you are passionate about, you want to be sure the reader gets the point. It is tempting to include a clearly stated message, a moral. But as Lowden discovered, that actually lessens the book's impact.

"Instead of focusing on what the reader will learn from your story," says Sinykin, "focus on the characters. To me, theme is what the characters learn from what they go through." The best way to influence readers, then, is to stop thinking about influencing readers. That's the contradiction at the heart of all powerful stories.

"I think that at some point we have to put things out there and then let the readers come to it at whatever place they are," says Ernst. "One child might read *Whistler in the Dark* and just think of it as a good adventure mystery and another child of the same age who may be struggling with some of the same issues would come away with a different take on what the book is about."

Most readers, no matter what their age, do not sit back and analyze a story after they finish it. "But we hope that on some level they're seeing models," says Ernst. "Even if they don't concretely process it, we give them a reason to feel a little stronger and perhaps subconsciously apply some of those things to their own lives." That is the theme at work—the key to writing a book that makes an impact.

Spin Zone: Remixing Headlines, Brainstorming Ideas

By Meredith DeSousa

The truth often is stranger than fiction, which is why news headlines are often called a major source of inspiration for writers of all kinds. Now, thanks to the proliferation of Web-based technologies, news from anywhere and everywhere reaches writers all around the globe, turning what were once neighborhood oddities into national and international curiosities.

It does not stop there. One simple headline can lead writers down any number of fantastic paths—both real and imagined—where characters converse, lives intersect, and events have consequences. A letter in a bottle found after 24 years becomes the premise of a fiction writer's fantasy world, the theme of a history lover's narrative nonfiction, or a backdrop for romantic dialogue in a play's final act. For writers, nothing ever "is what it is." What might it be?

In the spirit of twenty-first century newshounding, we offer a literary mashup designed especially for the year 2012. Following are 10 real-life news headlines, each followed by 12 types of writing prompt. The prompts are based on modern technology terms that echo specific elements of story building. So go ahead—mind map, mashup, and meme the news to your heart's content. It is your unique user experience that the world is waiting for.

First, here are the tech terms used for this brainstorming session, correlated to the idea generation tasks we suggest for each one of the 12 headlines.

1. *Keywords* = words and phrases taken from the headline story to research
2. *Search engines* = research sources for you to investigate for ideas
3. *App(lications)* = themes to explore
4. *Mashups* = premises (fiction) or slants (nonfiction)
5. *Virtual worlds* = potential plots
6. *User experiences* = point-of-view (POV) to experiment with
7. *GPS data* = setting possibilities
8. *Tweets* = dialogue to inspire more ideas
9. *Tag clouds* = imagery and inspirational words and phrases
10. *Blogmeme* = character development, or a nonfiction audience
11. *Bits and bytes* = first lines to try
12. *Links* = items of interest related to the headline

Headline 1: "What If the Biggest Solar Storm on Record Happened Today?"

National Geographic Daily News, March 2, 2011 (http://news. nationalgeographic.com/news/2011/03/110302-solar-flares-sun-storms-earth-danger-carrington-event-science)

Scientists predict that the sun's activity cycle is about to peak, which could mean the onset of solar storms. The famous solar storm of 1859 caused geomagnetic disturbances on Earth (enough to disrupt telegraph machines), and a storm of similar size today could seriously affect many aspects of our daily life, potentially disrupting everything from satellite communications and electrical power grids to financial and medical services.

↝ *Keywords:* solar storm, solar flare, aurora, Carrington Event, space weather, Space Weather Prediction Center, global Hurricane

Katrina, geomagnetic disturbance, radiation storm, Easter Sunday Storm, Civil War Aurora.

~ *Search engines:* NASA (www.nasa.gov), National Academy of Science (www.nationalacademies.org), www.spaceweather.org, National Oceanic and Atmospheric Administration (www.noaa.gov), NASA's Student Observation Network (http://son.nasa.gov), Royal Observatory's Solar Stormwatch Project (www.solarstormwatch.com), Solar Dynamics Observatory (http://sdo.gsfc.nasa.gov).

~*App(lications):*
- Man vs. society: A science fiction story about the "truth" behind solar storms: They are a political ploy by a group of rebels orchestrating a planetary *coup d'etat.*
- Man vs. destiny: A futuristic story in which the prediction of a solar storm that threatens the existence of the human race leads a soldier to take dramatic action, ultimately saving the world—and ending his own life.
- Man vs. machine/technology: Historical fiction about how the Carrington Event's unexpected effect on machinery led to a spectacular showdown at the 1859 St. Louis Agricultural and Mechanical Fair.
- Man vs. machine: A nonfiction article with expert interviews on ways in which we can reduce the risk of potential catastrophe from a solar storm or other space events by altering our use of technology.
- Man vs. nature: Humorous survivor's guide on how to handle some of the problems that result from a major solar storm, like mixed-up cell phone service.

~ *Mashups:*
- Fiction: Combine real-life and fictional characters in a work of historical fiction about astronomer Richard Carrington, who discovered the impact of solar flares on the Earth, and his apprentice.
- Fiction: Weave real sun activity data into a fictional story about the last 24 hours before a solar storm is set to hit.

- Nonfiction: Combine maps, images, and primary source details as to how certain places or people have been affected by solar storms throughout history.
- Nonfiction: Compare and contrast the effects of a solar storm in historical times and the present or future.

~ *Virtual worlds:*
- A small group of tourists, led by a newbie space pilot on his first flight, embark on one of the first commercial space travel flights and are stranded when a solar storm strikes in mid-flight.
- Powerful electromagnetic fluctuations have the unexpected effect of producing superhuman powers in some people, leading to a power struggle within a remote community.
- A filmmaker and his estranged 13-year-old son set out across the country to document the effects of a devastating solar storm; the people they meet and their experiences have a surprisingly powerful impact on their relationship.
- The inventor of a powerful telescope looks out into space after a solar storm and makes a discovery that could change the world, but he is unsure of whom to trust or what to do with the information.

~ *User experiences:*
- Do you have personal recollections of a solar storm or another astronomical, meteorological, or geographic event? Use them as a background for a story or novel, or a personal experience article.
- Interview people who experienced a similar event; use their stories as the foundation for an article about the phenomenon.

~ *GPS data:* The immediate effects of a solar storm might be different depending on the setting. Consider what it might be like in the following places:
    - New York City
    - Petersburg, Alaska
    - A cruise ship in the Mediterranean or Indian Ocean

- An Antarctica research station
- Boston, MA, September 2, 1859, during the Carrington Event

~ *Tweets:*
- Develop dialogue based on a world in which forms of communication have changed or about to change dramatically.

 @StuartKTP: It's official. 24 hours til massive solar storm hits. Back to communication basics. Pass me notes via my new P.O. Box: 41° 40' 47.2434.

 @Makoshark: You know those coordinates are under a heavy rock in Bryce Canyon?

 @StuartKTP: Hey, I left paper and a pen. Let me know if you need a refresher course.

- Develop dialogue based on a world in which space travel is commonplace.

 @Melanie69: Ready for the field trip? Will meet you at Brookline space station in 5 minutes.

 @Sterling: Can't find my solar glasses! Don't let the space-bus leave without me!!

 @Melanie69: Mrs. D. has extra pair, I bet. We can't be late. The solar flare is happening in 2 hours and we'll have a front-row seat!

- Develop dialogue based on a world in which auroras are believed to have healing properties.

 @JayBird: Just got notification—Tina made the waiting list for the next Healing Lights trip! Hope we are on our way to Fairbanks in 2031!

 @KyleOConnor: Great news! I've heard of many miracles during Healing Lights. Why a waiting list?

 @JayBird: The health board decides. The health care rationing plan leaves us no choice.

~ *Tag clouds:* Develop the following imagery into a paragraph or the beginning of a story: auroras like the waves of a rainbow; the Sun's ripple effect on the Earth simmered and blazed like a Sun goddess mother-in-law feuding with her terrestrial daughter-in-law; flares so powerful it was like night turned into day; ghostly auroras; cyber cocoon.

~ *Blogmeme:* Based on the specific elements listed below (or any other combination of elements), flesh out the main characters of your fiction using the accompanying questions. For the nonfiction suggestions, determine your audience: Who would be your typical reader? What range of audience would you have?

Fiction: 2,000 passengers are on board a cruise ship in the Mediterranean, 24 hours before a massive solar storm is to occur.
- What is the one thing in the world your character would do anything to avoid?
- What is the one thing in the world your character would do anything to obtain?
- Define your character's greatest strength and biggest weakness.
- Who is the most important person in your character's life before the story starts?
- How does your main character believe others perceive him or her?

Nonfiction:
- Tell the story of the Carrington Event, the solar super-storm of 1858, from the point of view of a *New York Times* reporter gathering stories.
- Profile a modern-day scientist who tracks solar storms in his daily work.
- Discuss the impact of scientist Richard Carrington, his life and work.

- From the point of view of the chief engineer, tell the story of the 1989 Quebec power grid failure due to solar storms, and how the grid was improved as a result.

~ *Bits and bytes:*
Choose one of the following prompts to begin a story:
- Penny counted them, 16 trucks in all, as they rumbled down the dirt road in front of her house.
- He woke up in complete darkness.
- "Eighty-five Dollars Is All It Takes to Set Your Mind at Ease" read the sign in the store window. It was the first store to reopen in Jackson, but Hamp had a hard time figuring out exactly what it was selling.

Choose one of the following prompts to begin a nonfiction article. The first is a portion of an actual conversation in 1859 between telegraph operators in Boston and Portland, Maine, on the night of the Carrington Event. It was reported in the *Boston Traveler.* The second prompt is a quote from a contemporary expert.

Boston operator: Please cut off your battery entirely for 15 minutes.
Portland operator: Will do so. It is now disconnected.
Boston operator: Mine is disconnected, and we are working with the auroral current. How do you receive my writing?
Portland operator: Better than with our batteries on. Current comes and goes gradually.
Boston operator: My current is very strong at times, and we can work better without the batteries, as the aurora seems to neutralize and augment our batteries alternately, making current too strong at times for our relay magnets. Suppose we work without batteries while we are affected by this trouble.
Portland operator: Very well. Shall I go ahead with business?
Boston operator: Yes. Go ahead.

- "If a Carrington Event happened now, it would be like a Hurricane Katrina, but 10 times worse," says Paul Kintner, a plasma physicist at Cornell University.

~ *Links:*
- "Space Tourism May Mean One Giant Leap for Researchers," by Kenneth Chang, *New York Times,* February 20, 2011 (www.nytimes.com/2011/03/01/science/space/01orbit.html?pagewanted=allNYTimes.com)
- "Alien Solar System Is Like Ours, But Weirder," by Tariq Malik. MSNBC, August 24, 2010 (www.msnbc.msn.com/id/38833299/ns/technology_and_science-space/t/alien-solar-system-ours-weirder)

Headline 2: "Hunt for the Cat Killer After 12 Pets Are Slaughtered or Killed in Quiet Cul-de-Sac"

U.K. Daily Mail, May 16, 2011 (www.dailymail.co.uk/news/article-1387579/Hunt-cat-killer-12-pets-slaughtered-kidnapped-Norfolk-cul-sac.html)

Neighborhood residents in Harleston, Norfolk, in the U.K. suffered a string of mysterious cat deaths since 2007. Nine cats died of antifreeze poisoning; one from injuries after a "brutal kick"; and two others went missing, indicating foul play. The presence of an apparent cat killer has the neighborhood on edge, with some moving away and others putting up posters of the deceased cats. The Royal Society for the Prevention of Cruelty to Animals conducted an investigation.

~*Keywords:* ethylene glycol, Animal Welfare Act, hunter, animal hoarding, cat lovers, puppy mills.

~ *Search engines:* Royal Society for the Prevention of Cruelty to Animals (www.rspca.org.uk); American Society for the Prevention of Cruelty to Animals (www.aspca.org); People for the Ethical Treatment of Animals (www.peta.org); The Cat Fanciers Association (www.cfa.org/Client/home.aspx).

App(lications):

- Cat vs. society: A nonfiction article featuring interviews with a folklore, history, or sociological expert, about the association of cats with witchcraft, or cat superstitions around the world.

- Cat vs. man: An article on the domestication of cats, based on the discovery of a cat buried with a human 8,000 years ago in Cyprus.

- Cat vs. man: Profile the cat social relationships and their special attachment to women. (See http://news.discovery.com/animals/cats-humans-pets-relationships-110224.html)

- Man vs. society: Tell the fictional story of a serial killer backwards, from the time of his arrest to the perpetration of crimes against animals in his youth, one of the signs of antisocial behavior included in the Macdonald Triad.

- Man vs. nature: Describe some of mass animal deaths in the past and their possible natural explanations.

Mashups:

- Fiction: Tell the story of a blind cat that is adopted by a deaf protagonist.

- Fiction: News reports, maps, and the journals of a neighborhood cat-killer converge in a mystery that leaves the identity of the killer unknown until the end.

- Nonfiction: Tell the story of the death of the last known animal in an endangered species and the explorer who tracked it.

Virtual worlds:

- Families around the world whose cats have mysteriously disappeared are surprised to find that, several days later, the cats return yet seem slightly different. Panic sets in as the cats are perceived to have higher-order thinking processes and special powers.

- The mysterious deaths of several neighbors have one thing in common: each person was seen with the same cat on the day before their death.

- An American woman newly immigrated to Egypt finds it difficult to connect with her peers until she adopts a stray cat, which alters the course of her future relationships.

~ *User experiences:*
- Do you have personal recollections about a missing or dying pet of any kind? Write an essay about the experience and convey a universal truth.
- Interview personnel at animal cruelty agencies and write an informational article about how readers can help prevent crimes against animals.

~ *GPS data:* Animal deaths or extinction would prompt different reactions depending on the setting. Consider what it might be like if the following situations occurrred.
- Bat deaths in caves throughout Asia or South America
- Widespread dog illness in shelters throughout New England
- Bird deaths from the sky over Africa
- Cow deaths in Montana

~ *Tweets:*
- Develop dialogue based on a world in which cats are a rare and endangered species.

> *@NewsmanABC:* Can you tell us what you saw, ma'am?
> *@WendySee:* What looked like a brown cat with gold, glinty eyes just ran through my backyard!
> *@NewsmanABC:* How do you know? Have you ever seen a cat personally?
> *@WendySee:* No, but I've seen pictures! I'm sure it was a cat . . . or maybe it was a fox.

- Develop dialogue based on the premise that cat scratches are lethal.

> *@HusbandMine9:* I could really use some help up here— cats are climbing the outside walls!

@DarlingWife: Get to the cellar, fast. Sounds like things are being ripped apart up there!

@HusbandMine9: So you won't come up here and help?

@DarlingWife: We may not enjoy living together, but dying together isn't going to solve anything.

~ *Tag clouds:* Develop a descriptive paragraph or story using the feline imagery suggested by these literary figures.

- "I love cats because I enjoy my home; and little by little, they become its visible soul." Jean Cocteau
- "Cats, like butterflies, need no excuse." Robert A. Heinlein
- "Cats, no less liquid than their shadows, offer no angles to the wind. They slip, diminished, neat, through loopholes less than themselves." A. S. J. Tessimond
- "Minnaloushe creeps through the grass/Alone, important and wise/And lifts to the changing moon/His changing eyes." W. B. Yeats, "The Cat and the Moon."

~ *Blogmeme:* Flesh out the characters using the accompanying elements and questions, or for nonfiction, determine your typical reader or broader audience.

Fiction: When a government orders villagers to kill off all of their dogs and cats in response to a rabies attack, one villager holds out—and comes up with a plan.

- What is the one thing in the world your character would do anything to avoid?
- What is the one thing in the world your character would do anything to obtain?
- Define your character's greatest strength and biggest weakness.
- Who is the most important person in your character's life before the story starts?

- How does your main character believe others perceive him or her?

Nonfiction:
- Investigate why federal wildlife services sometimes do predator control, and argue for or against it.
- Interview an animal pathologist who solves cases to save wildlife.
- Outline an article on crime-fighting animals.

~ *Bits and bytes:*
Choose one of the following prompts to begin a story.
- "That cat's been right about every patient so far," the nurse said. "Call the family. It's time to say goodbye."
- There are cat-lovers and cat-haters. Mark was definitely one of the latter.
- Arching its back, the cat sprinted the last few feet into the forest circle, counting 10 other felines already gathered around the hollowed-out tree trunk.

Choose one of the following prompts to begin a nonfiction article.
- "I do see both sides, but I'm not sure hunting cats is the answer," said cat owner Lisa Hanson of Brown County. (http://abcnews.go.com/US/LegalCenter/story?id=662272&page=2
- Cats vs. rats: How did what they eat affect human history and society?

~ *Links:*
- "San Diego's Frozen Zoo," CBS News. www.cbsnews.com/stories/2002/10/14/tech/main525521.shtml
- "'No One Knows Where They'll Hit Next': Washington State Warned of Bloodthirsty Roving Wild Dog Pack After They Kill 100 Animals" (www.dailymail.co.uk/news/article-2001982/No-knows-ll-hit--Washington-state-warned-bloodthirsty-roving-wild-dog-pack-

kill-100-animals-including-350lb-llama.html

- "Cat Steals From Everyone in San Mateo Neighborhood" (www.sfgate.com/cgi-bin/article.cgi?f=/c/a/2011/06/19/ BAIN1JVID8.DTL&tsp=1)

Headline 3: Day the Earth Moved: How the Earthquake Tilted the World's Axis by 25 cm (And Could Even Cost Us a Millisecond a Day)

U.K. Daily Mail, March 14, 2011 (www.dailymail.co.uk/sciencetech/ article-1365821/Japan-earthquake-tsunami-Earths-day-length-shortened-axis-tilted-25cm.html?ito=feeds-newsxml)

The 2011 earthquake in Japan was so powerful that it altered the Earth's axis, shifted parts of Japan's coastline, and opened up enormous ruptures in the sea floor. Such changes could cause subtle differences in the length of the day and in the seasons.

~ *Keywords:* seismology, tectonic plates, Japan Trench, tsunami, tremors, epicenter, aftershocks, Richter Scale, Moment Magnitude Scale, seismic trends, megathrust earthquake, geophysicists, scenario earthquakes, ShakeMaps

~ *Search engines:* National Institute of Geophysics and Volcanology in Italy (www.bo.ingv.it); U.S. Geological Survey (www.usgs.gov); Earthquake Research Institute, University of Tokyo (www.eri.u-tokyo. ac.jp/eng); National Earthquake Information Center (http://earth-quake.usgs.gov/regional/neic/); World Data Center (www.ngdc. noaa.gov/wdc/wdcmain.html).

~ *App(lications):*
- Man vs. god: Scientists on the brink of discovering a way to predict earthquakes have no idea of the real source of devastation: a squabble between Greek gods Hephaestus and Cybele.
- Man vs. man, man vs. nature: Two teams of explorers race to find the "lost continent," which supposedly disappeared completely after a massive earthquake in 1906.

- Man vs. supernatural: A crew of oceanographers set up temporary quarters near the newly formed rupture along the Japan Trench and are tormented by strange occurrences and psychological tricks.

~ *Mashups:*
- Fiction: Connect the stories of several fictional characters across a geographical area that has just had an earthquake, with their corresponding locations on a ShakeMap (http://earthquake.usgs.gov/earthquakes/shakemap).
- Nonfiction: Compare historical structures with contemporary structures and the comparative earthquake data to determine how buildings held up during an event.
- Nonfiction: Compare earthquake and soil data to examine the role that soil plays in the destruction caused by earthquakes.

~ *Virtual worlds:*
- A down-on-his-luck businessman who becomes stranded in a small town in Missouri after a major earthquake adopts a local business after the owner's sudden death, unexpectedly inspiring a town transformation that turns his own life around in the process.
- Far into the future, a series of severe earthquakes causes unprecedented continental shifts, resulting in a fusion of Japan with the western U.S. coast. A fictional story illustrates the social implications of such an event by focusing on how it plays out in a newly integrated middle-school classroom.
- A national security analyst uncovers what he believes to be coded communications that forewarn of earthquakes, but his findings are dismissed as laughable—until he discovers that the earthquakes are being produced by something other than natural forces.
- A newlywed husband and wife visiting Yellowstone on their honeymoon experience an earthquake that takes them into the future—and into their future children's lives.

~ *User experiences:*
- Have you personally experienced an earthquake, flood, tornado, or other natural disaster? Write a personal experience essay about what you learned as a result of the experience.
- Interview people who have survived natural disasters and use their tips and advice to write a survivor's guide.

~ *GPS Data:* The effects of an earthquake differ depending on the setting. Consider what it might be like for people experiencing an earthquake in the following places.
- A sky-rise office building
- On a fishing vessel
- In a classroom
- In an amusement park
- On a lake

~ *Tweets:*
Develop dialogue based on a world in which earthquakes can be predicted like the weather.

> *@Abilitis*: QuakeCast says a quake is likely Tuesday—is it real this time?
> *@MintyAB:* Better safe than sorry. Get out now!
> *@Abilitis:* I've packed 6 times in the last 2 months. I'm waiting til my cat says it's real.
> *@MintyAB:* Man vs. beast? Let's bet.

Develop dialogue based on a world in which Southern California becomes the least populated area of the country, due to its high frequency of earthquakes.

> *@MacyC:* My map lists San Francisco as a ghost town, but there are still a few people living here. Where's the real ghost town?
> *@Alfa:* L.A. is better. The SoCal Preservation Alliance has been there and preserved everything related to its history.

@Majong: Yeah, "preserved" is the right word; now it's a tourist trap of a different kind. San Diego wins hands down. Population: less than 100.

⤳ *Tag clouds:* Earthquakes and other natural disasters have given rise to myths and imagery throughout history. They are not a small part of the Old Testament and *Revelation*, for example. Take inspiration from the following passages and develop the imagery to describe challenging events or experiences, whether physical, psychological, or spiritual.

- "In that day the Lord with his hard and great and strong sword will punish Leviathan the fleeing serpent, Leviathan the twisting serpent, and he will slay the dragon that is in the sea." (Isaiah 27:1-3)

-"Every valley shall be lifted up, and every mountain and hill be made low; the uneven ground shall become level, and the rough places a plain." (Isaiah 40:4)

- The word of the Lord came to me a second time, saying, "What do you see?" And I said, "I see a boiling pot, facing away from the north." Then the Lord said to me, "Out of the north disaster shall be let loose upon all the inhabitants of the land." (Jeremiah 1:13–14)

⤳ *Blogmeme:* Flesh out the characters using the accompanying elements and questions, or for nonfiction, determine your typical reader or broader audience.

Fiction: A young man who has committed a terrible crime survives an earthquake only to discover that time has begun moving in reverse.

- What is the one thing in the world your character would do anything to avoid?

- What is the one thing in the world your character would do anything to obtain?

- Define your character's greatest strength and biggest weakness.
- Who is the most important person in your character's life before the story starts?
- How does your main character believe others perceive him or her?

Nonfiction:
- Using primary sources, write about the Arkansas earthquake of 1811 and how it affected people living there.
- Tell about the various citizen-science projects related to earthquakes and how they are helping to increase understanding and awareness. (See Science for Citizens, for example, at http://scienceforcitizens.net).
- Write about the 1811-1812 New Madrid, Missouri, Earthquake Bicentennial events.

~ *Bits and bytes:*
Choose one of the following prompts to begin a story:
- Everyone's eyes widened in terror as the news was delivered on the radio. An earthquake in China, another in Turkey, another in Iran, and another in Indonesia. All at exactly the same time.
- "It was just like he'd predicted," she thought. "9:35 A.M. Tuesday, February 6."

Choose one of the following prompts to begin a nonfiction article.
- In the days leading up to the 2003 earthquake, cell phones were reported as not working in north China's Inner Mongolia region.
- What will the world's landmass look like 250 million years from now?

- *Links:*
    - "Can Animals Sense Earthquakes?" (http://news.nation-algeographic.com/news/2003/11/1111_031111_earth-quakeanimals.html)
    - "Heat: The 'Most Dangerous Natural Disaster,'" by Joel Rose, NPR, July 23, 2011 (www.npr.org/2011/07/23/138626251/heat-the-most-dangerous-natural-disaster)

Headline 4: "Maccas, JK Rowling, Lesbian Bloggers: Hoaxers Take Over the World Wide Web"

Sydney Morning Herald, June 14, 2011 (www.smh.com.au/technology/technology-news/maccas-jk-rowling-lesbian-bloggers-hoaxers-take-over-the-world-wide-web-20110614-1g127.html)

An increasing number of Internet hoaxes are being uncovered, from claims that McDonalds charges African American customers extra to J. K. Rowling buying a house in Tasmania to two American white males impersonating lesbians bloggers. Hoaxes can be damaging to a company's brand, or have the potential to cause physical harm. People who believed that one of the lesbians—supposedly a Middle-Eastern woman named Amina—was real went to some lengths to campaign for her release upon reading that she had been kidnapped.

- *Keywords:* urban legend, social media, hoax, fraud, swindle, scam, scare tactics, myth, conspiracy, rumor

- *Search engines:* Snopes.com, Scambusters.org, UrbanLegends.about.com.

- *App(lications):*
    - Man vs. self: Write a fictional story about a partying 21-year-old with the same name as a prominent historic figure who finds out that he has been left a fortune by his namesake—who lived more than 100 years ago. After he goes to great lengths to secure the fortune, he discovers that it was all a hoax.

- Man vs. destiny: Write an informational article exploring the 2012 end-of-the-world hoax, and the truth behind the significance of the date in Mayan history.

- Man vs. man: Write a creative nonfiction article about a little-known historical hoax that had unintended consequences.

~ *Mashups:*

- Nonfiction: Compare and contrast historical hoaxes with today's technology-based hoaxes.

- Fiction: Write a mystery about a group of homeless kids who are recruited to participate in what they are told is a time-travel experiment but is actually a cover-up for murder.

- Nonfiction: Tell the real-life story of so-called spirit photographer William H. Mumler.

~ *Virtual worlds:*

- A financially struggling man whose severely autistic brother claims to be in regular contact with aliens makes a fortune when he decides to promote his small town as the "welcoming pad for extraterrestrials."

- *Crowdsourcing* begins in earnest when a museum introduces a popular online computer game to enlist the public's help in digitizing its collection—until a college student notices her bank account waning in correlation with how often she plays the game. More than $50,000 is stolen from individuals before the gaming hoax is uncovered.

- When a man returns to his village for the first time in 30 years and finds out that residents are still feuding over an age-old debacle, he secretly dismantles the only bridge that connects two sides of the village. Townspeople invent all kinds of explanations as to what might have happened to it; they eventually must figure out a way to work together to rebuild the bridge.

- In an effort to save his career, a social psychologist stages a hoax on the Titanic Anniversary Cruise by starting a rumor that the ship has hit an uncharted rock.

⮑ *User experiences:*

- Have you ever been taken in by a hoax, or felt the effects of one? Or maybe you have even perpetrated one yourself. Write about your experiences and what you learned from them.

- Interview an expert about how to track down the truth when it comes to uncovering a hoax.

- Everyone has received chain letters in some form or another. They have multiplied exponentially with the Internet. Research and write on this phenomenon and why people fall for them.

⮑ *GPS data:* Consider the potential effects of the following hoaxes, related to time and place.

- A worldwide hoax convincing people that it is a different date than it really is.

- A hoax perpetrated inside a hospital about the outbreak and origin of an infectious disease.

- A scam perpetrated by food manufacturer claims that people who ingest a particular brand of food are in fact being implanted with a GPS device inside their body.

⮑ *Tweets:*

Develop dialogue based on the real email hoax purportedly from a hit man who threatened the recipients with murder.

> *@Patbull:* Someone you know has paid me to kill you. You have 2 days to stop assignment with $50,000. If you inform police, you will die.
> *@BetsyB:* Is it Roger? I *knew* he was mad! That little snake.
> *@Patbull:* Huh?

Develop dialogue based on the real discovery of a mysterious round object in the Gulf of Bothnia.

> *@R2D3:* Headlines today: "New Stonehenge" found at the bottom of the Baltic Sea! Could be a UFO!
> *@Stardate:* When is it a UFO and when is it just a rock?

@Misty: Could be a WWII battleship!

@Stardate: Yeah, and I bet there's a treasure trove on board.

@R2D3: So, Stardate, we can count you out on the recovery mission, I'm guessing?

@Stardate: The only thing that needs to be recovered here is some sanity.

~ *Tag clouds:* Generate images—metaphors, similes, and so on—from these related words: hoax, humbug, cozen, dupe, befool, prank, trickster, delude, chicanery, sting, gull.

~ *Blogmeme:* Flesh out the characters using the accompanying elements and questions, or for nonfiction, determine your typical reader or broader audience.

Fiction: A teenager in a well-to-do family dies of sickness at an early age but leaves a secret will granting his identity to his best friend, who struggles with his abusive, unemployed father.
- What is the one thing in the world your character would do anything to avoid?
- What is the one thing in the world your character would do anything to obtain?
- Define your character's greatest strength and biggest weakness.
- Who is the most important person in your character's life before the story starts?
- How does your main character believe others perceive him or her?

Nonfiction:
- Describe how the Hitler Diaries were discovered to be a hoax.
- Write about some of the most famous sports hoaxes.

~ *Bits and bytes:*
Choose one of the following prompts to begin a story:
- A bank robbery for $1. It was ingenious.
- He came to the library every day to read a different book. He claimed he was looking for something that someone had told him was hidden here.

Choose one of the following prompts to begin a nonfiction article:
- Debunking myths in the classroom? Investigating hoaxes and hunting for the facts may be one of the best ways to educate students.
- How did they get caught? Balloon Boy's family? Crop circle creators? The Amityville Horror hoax?

~ *Links:*
- "Top 10 April Fool's Day Hoaxes 2011," *Telegraph*, April 1, 2011. (www.telegraph.co.uk/news/newstopics/howaboutthat/8421249/Top-10-April-Fools-Day-hoaxes-2011.html)
- "Madeleine Pulver Bomb Hoax Crime a Real-Life Thriller," The Telegraph, August 5, 2011 (www.dailytelegraph.com.au/news/sydney-nsw/ill-detonate-bomb-threat-to-maddie/story-e6freuzi-1226108265266)
- The Museum of Hoaxes (www.museumofhoaxes.com)

Headline 5: "Why Chinese Mothers Are Superior"
Wall Street Journal, January 8, 2011 (http://online.wsj.com/article/SB10001424052748704111504576059713528698754.html)
Amy Chua, a Chinese mother living in Connecticut, explains how Chinese parents raise "such stereotypically successful kids." She compares the strict and sometimes harsh Chinese method of raising children to the Western method, which she says is too concerned with children's self-esteem and gives too much leeway to kids when it comes to doing and getting what they want.

~ *Keywords:* tiger mom, cultural differences, behavioral control, self-esteem, authoritarian parenting, helicopter parents, curling parents, extreme parenting, lawnmower parents.

~ *Search engines:* Battle Hymn of the Tiger Mother, New Tiger in Town (http://tigersophia.blogspot.com/); Parenting.com (www.parenting.com/article/sites-we-love-21391644); American Academy of Pediatrics (www.aap.org).

~ *App(lications):*
- Man vs. self: A tiger mom who has become nationally known and even revered by some for her strict parenting techniques finds it hard to comply with her own principles as she struggles to raise a child with ADHD.
- Man vs. destiny: A nonfiction piece that explores how stifling tiger-mom tactics could conflict with the person a child is meant to become.
- Man vs. man: A nonfiction piece about what to do when parenting styles conflict among a child's immediate caregivers, i.e., between mother/father, parent/nanny, parent/grandparent.
- Man vs. nature: A nonfiction piece that explores how the differing natures of siblings may challenge certain parenting strategies.
- Man vs. machine: Science fiction about robots who replace faulty parents.

~ *Mashups:*
- Fiction: Compare and contrast parenting styles in a fictional story about two young girls or boys and their mothers, told entirely in journal entries.
- Fiction: Write an "unauthorized" fictional biography of Albert Einstein had he grown up with a tiger mom.
- Nonfiction: Analyze the intersection of the "tiger mom" effect when applied to stepchildren.

~ *Virtual worlds:*

- When a young Chinese mother dies in a car accident, her husband puts the burden of raising their 8-year-old daughter on the girl's older sister, who is only 15.

- Two sets of grandparents who care for their grandchildren during the day duke it out in a competition to see whose babysitting tactics are superior, while the children unite and conspire against them.

- Headlines are made when a twentysomething drug user sues his parents over their permissive parenting style, which he claims prevented him from reaching his full potential as an adult.

- In a future world where babies are built rather than born, the competitive parent-selection process leads to oppressive brainwashing and societal outcasts.

~ *User experiences:*

- Compare and contrast your parenting style with that of your parents and grandparents.

- Interview people with offbeat parenting styles or in unique parenting situations and convey their insights.

~ *GPS data:* Parenting styles vary among families and locales. Consider what parenting might be like in the following places or situations:

- Commune
- Orphanage
- African village
- A Western family living in China

~ *Tweets:*

Develop dialogue based on a world in which parents are graded by the government on their parenting skills.

@Barbie: Help! Failed my Parent Code Board test today!

@HD21: So sorry, Barb. What now?

@Barbie: They say cameras will be installed at home. Six weeks of monitoring then another evaluation. What if I fail again?

@HD21: Don't even think about it! I'll vouch for you if need be.

Develop dialogue based on a world in which parents must obey their children.

@Dsimone: Katie threatened to leave if I wouldn't stop cleaning her room.

@Oodeo: We had the same problem. Mark got violent when he thought we weren't listening to him.

@Dsimone: If she leaves home I'll never forgive myself!

@Oodeo: I know. Those KidHavens are the worst idea ever. Giving them a place away from us isn't going to solve anything.

~ *Tag clouds:* Phrases used in relation to Amy Chua's book: tiger mother's cubs are being raised to rule the world, wild kingdom of tiger moms, maternal lair, a "Sputnik moment," national identity crises, prizeless slackers.

Take inspiration from the images penned by two literary women:
- "Mama exhorted her children at every opportunity to 'jump at de sun.' We might not land on the sun, but at least we would get off the ground." Zora Neale Hurston
- "And so our mothers and grandmothers have, more often than not anonymously, handed on the creative spark, the seed of the flower they themselves never hoped to see—or like a sealed letter they could not plainly read." Alice Walker

~ *Blogmeme:* Flesh out the characters using the accompanying elements and questions, or for nonfiction, determine your typical reader or broader audience.

Fiction: A young mother forfeits her own life for the sake of raising an uber-child.

- What is the one thing in the world your character would do anything to avoid?
- What is the one thing in the world your character would do anything to obtain?
- Define your character's greatest strength and biggest weakness.
- Who is the most important person in your character's life before the story starts?
- How does your main character believe others perceive him or her?

Nonfiction:

- Tell the story of a single dad with a tiger-mom mindset.
- Compare parenting in the U.S. by different cultures and in different communities.

~ *Bits and bytes:*

Choose one of the following prompts to begin a story:

- Everyone said she was the best in the business, that her tactics could turn anybody's life around—until today, that is.
- She looked me straight in the eye. "Of course I love you. If I didn't love you, I wouldn't be so terribly disappointed in how you turned out."

Choose one of the following prompts to begin a nonfiction article:

- Sophia Chua-Rubenfeld says, "I'm way more scared of my dad than my tiger mom."
- More than 100,000 Americans live in China.

~ *Links:*

- "The Tiger Nanny: The Missing Link in the Parenting Debate," *Time*, January 21, 2011 (http://healthland.time.com/2011/01/21/

the-tiger-nanny-the-missing-link-in-the-parenting-debate/)

- "Good Dads and Not-So-Good Dads in the Animal Kingdom,"
Scientific American, June 19, 2011. (www.scientificamerican.com/
blog/post.cfm?id=good-dads-and-not-so-good-dads-in-t-2011-06-19)

Headline 6: "Epidemiology: Study of a Lifetime"

Nature News, March 1, 2011 (www.nature.com/news/2011/
110301/full/471020a.html)

Medical researchers for the U.K.'s National Survey of Health and
Development began collecting health information on more than
5,000 newborns in 1946. The 3,000 now living turned 65 and have a
lifetime of personal information in files marked with their names,
making them some of the best-studied people on the planet. It is the
longest running *birth-cohort study* in the world.

~ *Keywords:* human subjects research, epidemiology, evidence-
based medicine, public health research, biostatistics, causal relationships, medical technologists.

~ *Search engines:* National Survey of Health and Development
www.nshd.mrc.ac.uk/); Medical Research Council (www.mrc.ac.uk/
index.htm); National Institutes of Health (www.nih.gov); Healthy
Ageing Across the Life Course (www.halcyon.ac.uk); Centers for
Disease Control and Prevention (www.cdc.gov).

~ *App(lications):*
- Man vs. self: A lifelong birth-cohort study participant who keenly
feels the effects of someone "watching him" battles his own feelings
of worthlessness and anxiety.
- Man vs. supernatural: A young researcher taking over on a lifelong individual case study discovers that the study subject has faked
his identity as a person from the past to cover up his true identity: an
alien being who has quietly been assimilating humans into his own
race.

- Man vs. destiny: Tell the story of how epidemiology played a role in dramatically altering the course of events in history (i.e., how it helped researchers to track down the cause of a virus, or changed people's perceptions about something)

~ *Mashups:*
- Fiction: Tell the story of a study participant's mental state during her engagement and marriage preparation, from two differing (and often humorous) points of view: the researcher and the bride-to-be.
- Nonfiction: Record an interview with one or more study participants and write an article for the Web, incorporating audio excerpts.
- Nonfiction: Examine how epidemiology study data has been used in court cases.

~ *Virtual worlds:*
- When data related to two of the study members is accidentally swapped, one man is told that he has a life-threatening disease while the other mistakenly gets a clean bill of health, dramatically altering the way they live their lives.
- A researcher in a lifelong study becomes obsessed with her subject, who reveals criminal tendencies at an early age. The researcher continually and secretly helps cover up his wrongdoings, until she becomes the target herself.
- After a bored middle-aged man who is part of a lifelong study steals a look at his file and finds that his only distinguishing characteristic is his "outstanding normality," he plans the adventure of a lifetime to compensate.
- A college student conducting research into online dating sets up a dating site to gather information, then falls for one of the participants and sabotages his potential romances.

~ *User experiences:*
- Have you ever participated in a study of any kind, or do you know someone who has? Write about the experience.

- Use primary sources to tell the true story of a human case study gone awry.

~ *GPS data:* Studies on humans vary dramatically according to their intent, location, and time. Consider what studies might take place, or what could go wrong, in the following settings:
- Third-world country
- Boarding school
- Psychiatric ward
- Affluent home versus a financially struggling home

~ *Tweets:*

Develop dialogue based on a world in which participating in a scientific study is a mandatory civic duty, like jury duty.

> *@Dsimone:* Just got called to participate in a study on weight gain. Help! How do I get out of it?
>
> *@Marky:* Ouch! I just got one about exercise and the brain.
>
> *@Dsimone:* Sounds pretty good compared to eating fast food for four months.
>
> *@Marky:* Fast food? Better than too much exercise. Maybe we can switch.

Develop dialogue based on a world in which it is not required to notify study subjects that they are being studied:

> *@Flipbean:* I've been watching her for two years. She eats trash and doesn't take care of herself. I predict she'll die early.
>
> *@Voomia:* Maybe you should give her a copy of your data. It might make her change her ways.
>
> *@Flipbean:* That's exactly the point. I can't let her know I'm watching, or she'll act differently. The data will be wasted.
>
> *@Voomia:* Maybe you're lucky. My subject is likely to live forever! What a health nut.

~ *Tag clouds:* noisy data, life as a guinea pig, living life under the microscope, scandalous science, control experiment, "seeding the idea that disease evolves as a result of events throughout life."

~ *Blogmeme:* Flesh out the characters using the accompanying elements and questions, or for nonfiction, determine your typical reader or broader audience.

Fiction: A participant tries to withdraw from a lifelong study after finding it intrusive but discovers that there is no way out.
- What is the one thing in the world your character would do anything to avoid?
- What is the one thing in the world your character would do anything to obtain?
- Define your character's greatest strength and biggest weakness.
- Who is the most important person in your character's life before the story starts?
- How does your main character believe others perceive him or her?

Nonfiction:
- The power of surveys and studies: Are they truthful, misleading, or creating a new reality?
- Discuss the kinds of errors researchers might make in conducting a long-term study.
- Look at the differences in understanding about and use of genetics between 1946 and today.

~ *Bits and bytes:*
Choose one of the following prompts to begin a story:
- I had to get them to trust me first.
- Every year, there it was, the first one to arrive: the dreaded birthday card from the NIH.

Choose one of the following prompts to begin a nonfiction article:
   - "I'm fascinated by the idea of an alternative biography; the scientists have a completely different story about me, backed up by facts and figures from throughout my life, from the one I carry about in my head," said David Ward, a member of the NSHD study.
   - "I suppose when I first learnt it was a survey I felt quite proud, that I was selected to be Mr. Average in a way," said a participant in the NSHD study.

~ Links:
   - "How the Case Against the MMR Vaccine Was Fixed," *BMJ*, January 5, 2011 (www.bmj.com/content/342/bmj.c5347.full)
   - "Iowa to Pay Subjects $925K for Stuttering Study, 1930s Experiment Tried to Cause Speech Issues by Baiting, Belittling Orphan, " MSNBC, August 17, 2007 (www.msnbc.msn.com/id/20327467/ns/health-health_care/t/iowa-pay-subjects-k-stuttering-study)

Headline 7: "Tourists Mimic Polar Pioneers, Except with Planes and Blogs"
   New York Times, January 15, 2011 (www.nytimes.com/2011/01/16/world/16pole.html?_r=1)
   On December 14, 1911, Norwegian Roald Amundsen and his team of explorers were the first to reach the South Pole. Thousands of people planned extensively to mark the hundredth anniversary, and the January 17, 1912, anniversary of British explorer Robert Falcon Scott's expedition, by flying to the Antarctic and skiing in, driving in, racing in, or simply reenacting Amundsen's original journey.

~ *Keywords:* glaciology, Robert Falcon Scott, Roald Amundsen, katabatic winds, Amundsen-Scott Research Station, Sir Ernest Shackleton, *Endurance,* Douglas Mawson.

~ *Search engines:* Norweigan Polar Institute (www.npolar.no/en); Polar Research Journal (www.polarresearch.net/index.php/polar);

Polar Explorers (www.polarexploreres.com); Extreme World Races (www.extremeworldraces.com); Antarctic Ice Marathon (www.ice-marathon.com); North Pole Marathon (www.npmarathon.com).

~ *App(lications):*
- Man vs. self: Tell the story of a person with a disability overcoming an extreme challenge.
- Man vs. man: A virtual version of *Around the World in Eighty Days* pits international teams against one another as they use geo-immersion to follow a global trail of clues from their own homes, using only computers and teamwork.
- Man vs. destiny: Consider what might have happened if Robert Falcon Scott had not died as a result of his Antarctic expedition.

~ *Mashups:*
- Fiction: Tell the story of a global race in the future to stake out land in the last frontier, the Antarctic as the polar ice caps melt; intersperse periodic team GPS locations and diary entries.
- Nonfiction: Map the routes of all the early polar explorers and highlight their accomplishments.
- Nonfiction: Tell the intertwined memoirs of an early polar explorer and a real-life, modern-day Antarctic racer.

~ *Virtual worlds:*
- When a group of South Pole tourists accidentally wanders off the beaten path, they discover what could potentially be a the remants of an earlier civilization in an unexplored area of Antarctica and vie against one another for possession.
- An 80-year-old man dying of cancer makes an unusual last request of his teenage nephew: Team up to participate in a rickshaw run across the Rajasthan desert.
- Descendants of Amundsen and Scott are encouraged by a scheming reporter to face off in what turns into a comedic modern-day Antarctic competition.

- In a future world where prisons are obsolete, criminals are left in the planet's harshest environments to fend for themselves, or die.

~ *User experiences:*
- Have you or someone you know ever participated in an extreme race? Tell your story and what you learned by the experience.
- Interview a polar geologist about his or her job or little-known aspects of the polar ecosystem.

~ *GPS data:* Consider what extreme sports and resulting stories might take place in the following settings:
- Chile's Atacama desert
- Australia's Kimberley Outback
- Bouvet Island in the Antarctic
- Outer space

~ *Tweets:*
Develop dialogue based on a world in which the Earth's dwindling population is forced to migrate to the Antarctic, one of the only habitable places left on Earth.

@*Climtoe:* Finished Day 1 of Happy Camper Survival School today. Think I'm going to die out in the cold!

@*Majestic18:* What happened?

@*Climtoe:* Couldn't repair my snowmobile and fell into a crevasse.

@*Majestic18:* What if you don't pass?

@*Climtoe:* If I don't get at least a C it'll mean desk duty in the research station. I'll never see the light of day again!

Develop dialogue between two travel enthusiasts who met online and plan to meet in person for the first time at a remote destination:

@*Browser:* Romania it is. Bran Castle?

@*Aivee:* No idea how to get there, but fine with me. When do you plan to leave?

@Browser: Leaving Monday. First one to arrive buys dinner.
@Aivee: How will I recognize you?
@Browser: Look for the American flag.
@Aivee: Or you, for the Canadian flag.

⌐ *Tag clouds:* risk recreation, expressed intolerance of boredom, sensation-seeking, thrills, perilous. Sketch stories that might reflect the following quotes:

- "Adventure is just bad planning." Roald Amundsen
- "An adventure is only an inconvenience rightly considered. An inconvenience is an adventure wrongly considered." G. K. Chesterton
- Life is either a daring adventure or nothing. Security does not exist in nature, nor do the children of men as a whole experience it. Avoiding danger is no safer in the long run than exposure." Helen Keller

⌐ *Blogmeme:* Flesh out the characters using the accompanying elements and questions, or for nonfiction, determine your typical reader or broader audience.

Fiction: Thrillseekers in the 1800s find a unique way to save their dying mining town: by turning the local mine train into one of the first roller coasters.

- What is the one thing in the world your character would do anything to avoid?
- What is the one thing in the world your character would do anything to obtain?
- Define your character's greatest strength and biggest weakness.
- Who is the most important person in your character's life before the story starts?
- How does your main character believe others perceive him or her?

Nonfiction:
   - Discuss the important scientific discoveries that came about as a result of the first explorers' Antarctic expeditions.
   - Tell the story of the first 18 men who lived through a winter in the Antarctic in 1957.
   - Investigate the discovery of other famous places such as Machu Picchu, or places yet to explore, such as deep ocean.

~ *Bits and bytes:*
Choose one of the following prompts to begin a story:
   - He waited patiently for me to sign the waiver, the one that ended with the sobering sentence: "I may die." He had to know why I was having trouble picking up the pen. Or, who knows, maybe he didn't.
   - You name it, I've done it: skydiving, mountain climbing, BASE jumping, paragliding . . . I could go on, but you get the idea. Everyone thinks I have a death wish, but I think it's something else.

Choose one of the following prompts to begin a nonfiction article:
   - "It is an incredible legacy from the friendship of two men on the ice," said polar historian David Wilson.
   - "Great God! This is an awful place." Robert Falcon Scott

~ *Links:*
   - "The Race to the Bottom of the Ocean," *The Guardian*, August 8, 2011 (www.guardian.co.uk/environment/2011/aug/08/richard-branson-james-cameron-bottom-ocean)
   - "Explorers-in-Residence Program," National Geographic Society (www.nationalgeographic.com/field/grants-pro-grams/explorers-in-residence)

Headline 8: "Remembering the Civil War"

Salamanca Press, July 13, 2011 (www.salamancapress.com/ news/article_83b5180a-ad7e-11e0-8f1a-001cc4c03286.html)

In Salamanca, New York, a group of men and women meet for conversations about and remembrances of the Civil War. All are descendants of members of the 154th New York Infantry, and their families have met annually for 150 years.

~ *Keywords:* genealogy, molecular genealogy, DNA, family tree, genetic genealogy, ancestral journey, forensic genealogy.

~ *Search engines:* Sorenson Molecular Genealogy Foundation (www.smgf.org); Chronicling America (http://chroniclingamerica. loc.gov); National Archives (www.archives.gov); *Family Tree* (www.familytreemagazine.com); Council for the Advancement of Forensic Genealogy (www.forensicgenealogists.org); *Civil War History* (http://muse.jhu.edu/journals/civil_war_history)

~ *App(lications):*
- Man vs. self: During the American Civil War, an adopted woman battles her personal demons when a biological uncle reveals a mother who does not want to be found, and introduces her to a long-lost brother with whom she begins to forge a relationship.
- Man vs. man: A college student who fabricates a family connection to a famous pirate for a class essay suddenly finds himself being followed by a trio of strangely dressed men.
- Man vs. destiny: With the help of his grandfather, a middle-schooler creates a real-life family memory game based on his own family, but finds that the cards have unusual powers to change history when placed in different positions.

~ *Mashups:*
- Fiction: The wife of a U.S. soldier in Afghanistan begins doing genealogical research after finding an old photograph in her attic,

only to discover that the man in the photo is her husband's ancestor —and a soldier during the Civil War. Weave stories of the two soldiers and the universal experiences of war and family.

- Nonfiction: Incorporate primary sources and travel itineraries into the true stories of one or more people involved in genealogical research.

- Nonfiction: Combine the brief written memoirs of you and your spouse, sibling, parent, or child with audio clips to tell the complete story of a particular event.

~ *Virtual worlds:*

- Eleven-year-old Christy begins to have doubts about what family means after one of her classmates comments that Christy's new baby brother is only her half-brother and her father just a step-father.

- A historian and reality show host who travels the country examining Civil War gravestones and exploring the history connected to them is stunned to discover the gravestone of a relative she did not know she had, and the extraordinary secret her ancestor carried to the grave.

- In a futuristic society, genealogy *scans* are done for everyone at the age of 21, at which point the newly adult population is divided into one of 10 quadrants, depending on who your ancestors were.

~ *User experiences:*

- Interview a relative about your family history.
- Interview a Civil War re-enactor about this unusual hobby.

~ *GPS data:* Consider what a reunion might look like for ancestors of people in the following places, people, or times:
  - Immigrants on Australian convict ships
  - Eighteenth-century French monarchy
  - Jewish Cohanim line dating back to 1396 BCE
  - Passengers of the Titanic
  - Rat Pack in the 1960s

~ *Tweets:*
Develop dialogue between two game show contestants who are distantly related but do not know all the details yet. Each must choose which one of their fellow contestants is their relative.

> *@Demixer:* I've always thought that I must be a distant relative of Ghengis Khan rather than Ghandi. What about you?

> *@Jaxcast:* Hmmm, more like Caesar, I think. Fair, but still in charge.

> *@Demixer:* Do you prefer dogs or cats?

> *@Jaxcast:* Actually, I'm more of a ferret person myself.

Develop dialogue between a doctor and a patient who wants to alter her DNA to distance herself from an unsavory relative, and join a more prominent family tree.

> *@Coginti:* I'll just need you to sign this contract stating that you'll never disclose the fact that you had this operation or any mention of who performed it.

> *@Jumpvine:* Trust me, I want to keep this a secret even more than you do.

> *@Coginti:* If you don't mind my asking, who is it you're trying to avoid?

> *@Jumpvine:* Let's just say there's a killer out there—and not a famous, intriguing one, mind you--that I'd like to have in someone else's family tree. I'm trying to marry up, you know.

~ *Tag clouds:* Update and enliven these clichéd images of connection: like two peas in a pod, adding branches to your family tree, ancestral roots, blood is thicker than water, thick as thieves.

~ *Blogmeme:* Flesh out the characters using the accompanying elements and questions, or for nonfiction, determine your typical reader or broader audience.

Fiction: A quiet librarian assisting a client with a genealogy search becomes obsessed with the client's unusual background, and with the client herself.

- What is the one thing in the world your character would do anything to avoid?
- What is the one thing in the world your character would do anything to obtain?
- Define your character's greatest strength and biggest weakness.
- Who is the most important person in your character's life before the story starts?
- How does your main character believe others perceive him or her?

Nonfiction:
- Write an article about the ways in which old photographs can provide valuable clues in the genealogical research process.
- Write an article about how to get uninterested family members involved (or at least intrigued) in your family research.

~ *Bits and bytes:*
Choose one of the following prompts to begin a story.
- This was it. The last cemetery in Montana on her list. There were neat checkmarks next to each one, showing no signs of her building frustration over not finding what she came for.
- This was some kind of family reunion, she thought, taking in the strange scene unfolding in front of her. Most of these people she didn't even know, and the ones she did, well, she probably didn't know them half as well as she thought she did.

Choose one of the following prompts to begin a nonfiction article.
- According to some experts, everyone's family tree would eventually merge, when traced back far enough. Your next door neighbor could also be your fortieth cousin.

- Four swabs. One cheek. Your genetic journey of a lifetime is about to begin.

~ *Links:*
- "Technology Brings Digital Memories to Grave Sites," by Bellamy Pailthorp, NPR, May 30, 2011 (www.npr.org/2011/05/30/ 136676964/technology-brings-digital-memories-to-grave-sites)
- "Finding Roots Tough for African Americans," by Maggie Fox, MSNBC.com, October 12, 2006 (www.msnbc.msn.com/id/ 15240873/ns/technology_and_science-science/t/finding-roots-tough-african-americans)
- "Teaching Civil War History 2.0," by Kevin M. Levin, *New York Times,* January 21, 2011 (http://opinionator.blogs.nytimes.com/ 2011/01/21/teaching-civil-war-history-2-0/
- Best of History Websites, Civil War (http://besthistorysites.net/ index.php/american-history/1800/civil-war)

Headline 9: "What's the World's Favorite Number?"

NPR, July 22, 2011 (www.npr.org/blogs/krulwich/2011/07/22/ 138493147/what-s-your-favorite-number-world-wide-survey-v1)

Writer and math enthusiast Alex Bellos is on a hunt to determine the world's favorite number. He set up a website for people to log their favorites, and as of the date of the July date this piece was published, he had more than 13,000 submissions. He expects to produce a report sometime in 2012. There is no real determination yet, as to what makes a number someone's favorite, but some of the musings have been comical, and even insightful.

~ *Keywords:* numerology, gematria, number mysticism, astrology, master numbers.

~ *Search engines:* Favorite Number (www.favoritenumber.net); American Mathematical Society (www.ams.org); the MacTutor History of Mathematics Archive (www-history.mcs.st-and.ac.uk/history);

Math in Daily Life (www.learner.org/interactives/dailymath/ resources.html); Society for Industrial and Applied Mathematics (www.siam.org/careers/matters.php).

~ *App(lications):*
- Man vs. self: Using a documentary style, tell the story of a woman with OCD who has a fixation with a particular series of numbers, or a fear of certain numbers.
- Man vs. machine: A man who buys an antique camera from a tag sale quickly starts to realize that the camera has a mind of its own. It displays a numerical command for items in focus, with mysterious and sometimes dangerous consequences.
- Man vs. society: A new brand of superhero is born when a visitor from outer space arrives on Earth and unwittingly begins fighting crime by relying on his superior math skills.

~ *Mashups:*
- Fiction: Explore the use of numbers and math in solving crimes, or a mystery involving numbers and an art theft involving the work of an artist inspired by math, such as M. C. Escher.
- Nonfiction: Explore the mathematical imagination through short profiles of famous mathematicians.
- Nonfiction: Compare Pythagoras's number representations with modern-day studies of people's feelings about particular numbers.

~ *Virtual worlds:*
- A mathematician obsessed with the number 10 feels compelled to follow his obsession wherever it takes him when he receives the news that something dramatic will happen on October 10, 2020.
- The story behind the Codex Gigas (the thirteenth-century so-called *Devil's Bible*) takes an even more mysterious turn when a group of forensic document experts uncovers what they believe to be a numbers-based code buried within the text.
- After the violent death of her parents, a 13-year-old girl in the

1830s reluctantly joins the traveling circus. With no particular skills, the girl is made an apprentice to the fortune teller, who teaches her to use a number system to concoct outlandish fortunes for her clients.

~ *User experiences:*
- Conduct your own interviews about your family and friends' favorite numbers, and the reasons why, or explore their experiences with math, good or bad.

~ *GPS data:* Consider the following places and times and the stories that might evolve from a focus on numbers.
- Ancient Egypt
- Massachusetts in the 1600s
- Florence, Italy in the fifteenth century
- A fantasy world of your own creation

~ *Tweets:*
Develop dialogue between the owner of a mathematics/logic-based dating service and a potential client:

@Martini303: Good news! You and Anya are a perfect match according to the "What Animal Would You Most Want To Be" test and the "Knowledge of Greek Gods and Goddesses" test.

@SimonDirk: Great! When can I meet her?

@Martini303: According to our personality charts and your numerology readings, the optimal time for you to meet would be June 12, 2017.

@SimonDirk: What?! That's five years from now!

@Martini303: The good news is, she's guaranteed to be single. Her scores were abysmal on cuddlability and most disturbing on the "Are You a Sociopath?" test.

~ *Tag clouds:* anthropomorphized fantasies, numerical coincidences, number sense, Triskaidekaphobia. Use math concepts, and the math used by artists, to create rhetorical images: golden ratio, Fibonacci, calculus, math in Gothic architechture, Escher, Möbius, Bach, musical scales.

~ *Blogmeme:* Flesh out the characters using the accompanying elements and questions, or for nonfiction, determine your typical reader or broader audience.

Fiction: A young cancer patient and his sidekick stumble onto the shortwave messages from a numbers station—shortwave radio locations of unknown origin—and realize that they've gotten too close to decoding the messages when strange things start happening to them.
- What is the one thing in the world your character would do anything to avoid?
- What is the one thing in the world your character would do anything to obtain?
- Define your character's greatest strength and biggest weakness.
- Who is the most important person in your character's life before the story starts?
- How does your main character believe others perceive him or her?

Nonfiction:
- Explain Hebrew numerology and its significance.
- Explore the history of mathematics, including the various number systems around the world and ways in which they have become interconnected.
- Explain the development of mathematics throughout history and how it is connected with religion, mythology, daily life, and science.

~ *Bits and bytes:*

Choose one of the following prompts to begin a story.

- There were 30 people at the party, 20 chairs placed strategically around the room (too many chairs inhibits mingling), 10 types of hors d'oeuvre displayed tastefully, and exactly 0—she glanced around again just to make sure—ex-boyfriends present. So far things were off to a good start.

- "I never remember anything else from my dreams, except that— the number 11."

Choose one of the following prompts to begin a nonfiction article.

- "One is lonely and 2 is much nicer. It means company." Are there warm and fuzzy numbers? Cold and calculating ones?

- Can numbers sometiems do a better job of communicating than words?

~ *Links:*

- "The Art of Mathematics," by Kelly Crowe, *Wall Street Journal,* July 16, 2011 (http://online.wsj.com/article/SB10001424052702303-678704576440300881356530.html). Dorothea Rockburne expresses math theories in art.

- "Happy Square-Prime Sandwich Day," by Carl Bialik, July 15, 2011 (http://blogs.wsj.com/numbersguy/happy-square-prime-sand-wich-day-1072)

- "The Mathematics of Terrorism," by Andrew Curry, *Discover,* December 1, 2010 (http://discovermagazine.com/2010/jul-aug/07-the-mathematics-of-terrorism)

- "Get Better at Math by Disrupting Your Brain," by Alvaro Pascuel-Leone, *Scientific American,* December 2, 2010 (www.scientifi-camerican.com/article.cfm?id=get-better-at-math-by-disrupting-brain

Headline 10: "Robot Shows the Way for Blind Student"

CNN.com, K12Lab, February 9, 2011 (www.k12lab.com/inspiration/robot-guides-blind-student-to-classes)

Several middle-schoolers at San Jacinto Junior High in Texas build a robot to help friend and fellow classmate Dante Hall, who went blind as the result of an asthma attack. Hall, who also lost feeling in his fingertips, is having difficulty learning braille, and finds his way around school using a cane. A group of enterprising seventh graders banded together to help him, determined to build a robot that could guide him through school to each of his classes.

~ *Keywords:* robotics, humanoid, ROBOTC, mechatronics, telepresence, artificial intelligence, robot ethics, android, RoboCup, robopsychology.

~ *Search engines:* Personal Robots Group, MIT (http://robotic.media.mit.edu/); Playtime Computing System (http://robotic.media.mit.edu); The Tech Museum (www.thetech.org); IEEE Spectrum (http://spectrum.ieee.org/robotics); Robotics Trends (www.roboticstrends.com); Robot Hall of Fame (www.robothalloffame.org).

~ *App(lications):*
- Man vs. society: A group of individuals with bionic body parts emerge as elite citizens in the aftermath of a nuclear war.
- Man vs. destiny: A nonfiction essay about how teaching robots about human behavior can teach us something about ourselves.
- Man vs. machine/technology: In a world slowly being taken over by robots, humans are forced to implant tiny robots into their brains to encourage desired thought and action.
- Man vs. machine: The robot-sharing information network, RoboEarth, must be destroyed if humans are to regain control over the planet.
- Man vs. nature: A team of researchers studying cyberflora is surprised to discover that the mechanical flowers have infiltrated

their natural surroundings and are slowing turning natural plants and flowers into mechanisms with a mission.

~ *Mashups:*
- Fiction: Place a character based on author Isaac Asimov in a "back to the future"-type adventure that has him facing the very robots and the laws that he created.
- Fiction: Incorporate GPS data into a futuristic action-thriller that pits man against humanoid. While the humanoids can be tracked using GPS data, they are almost impossible to identify in the midst of humans.
- Fiction: Create a robot's computer journal entries to depict a robot's life from its point of view.
- Nonfiction: Combine how-to instructions on making robots with informational text and expert interviews.
- Nonfiction: Combine art and robotics with a piece on robotic art.

~ *Virtual worlds:*
- After 100 years in cryogenics, three people wake up to a world filled with robots, realizing that they are the last three humans on Earth.
- An American spy goes undercover as a robot in China to steal technology secrets, leading to comedic adventures and an unexpected friendship between the "robot" and a Chinese employee.
- Seventh-graders band together to prove their humanoid teacher's innocence and save her from destruction after a classroom incident that ended in the accidental wounding of a student.
- One firehouse's robo-dog, invented by the fire chief's daughter, helps bring together a neighborhood that is threatened by wildfires.

~ *User experiences:*
- How might you react to having a robot in the house, or working with robots? Or, if you have personal experience interacting with robots, write a fiction or nonfiction piece based on your experiences.

- Interview researchers who are working on some aspect of robotics—self-driving cars, social robots, etc.—or people involved in something related to robots, i.e. kids' programs, contests, robot laws, etc. and write a nonfiction article about it.

~ *GPS data:* The implications of using robots would be different depending on the scenario. Consider what it might be like if robots were placed in the following settings.
- Part of an underwater scientific research team
- Medical research centers
- U.S. military base in the Middle East
- Farm in Iowa
- The site of an international disaster

~ *Tweets:*
Develop dialogue based on a world that is run by robots.
@HD86: The prototype of the robot super-race is complete and ready for release.
@C318: How soon can you get it here?
@HD86: Uncertain. It has already formed an emotional attachment to the bedsheets and will need to be weaned.

Develop dialogue based on a scenario that has the first robot running for president.
@Jilly6: ARTIE for president!
@Manhand: How can you support that bot to run the country? Are you crazy?
@Jilly6: He's smarter than you! He's programmed to prevent history from repeating itself, and he's an expert in economics!
@Jilly6: Plus, he's cute. :)

~ *Tag clouds:* robocalypse, robots that can touch your heart, more human than humans, flesh-and-blood robots.

Develop a paragraph or story with imagery (metaphors, symbols, and so on) inspired by the following quotes about technology.

- "Technology is a way of organizing the universe so that man doesn't have to experience it." Max Frisch

- "Any sufficiently advanced technology is indistinguishable from magic." Arthur C. Clarke

- "Technology adds nothing to art. Two thousand years ago, I could tell you a story, and at any point during the story I could stop, and ask, Now do you want the hero to be kidnapped, or not? But that would, of course, have ruined the story. Part of the experience of being entertained is sitting back and plugging into someone else's vision." Penn Jillette

~ *Blogmeme:* Flesh out the characters using the accompanying elements and questions, or for nonfiction, determine your typical reader or broader audience.

Fiction: A plane full of passengers is held hostage by robots.

- What is the one thing in the world your character would do anything to avoid?

- What is the one thing in the world your character would do anything to obtain?

- Define your character's greatest strength and biggest weakness.

- Who is the most important person in your character's life before the story starts?

- How does your main character believe others perceive him or her?

Nonfiction:

- Discuss some of the more unusual developments in the robotics industry, and their use in different capacities, such as herding, farming, medicine, military, rescues.

- Will there be a need for law enforcement specifically for robots?

- In what way might robots of the future provide emotional connection; for instance, in nursing homes and with the learning-disabled?

~ *Bits and bytes:*
Choose one of the following prompts to begin a story.
- The young girl sang and skipped down the sidewalk, completely unaware that a silent, miniature drone floated behind her just a few dozen feet away.
- The robot's decision-making process took only a second. Three seconds later, to the surprise of the partygoers, a man lay dead on the kitchen floor.
- She just couldn't bring herself to give it a human face.

Use the following prompt to begin a nonfiction article.
- "You have to think about robots having intelligence that could surpass our own," says Stephen S. Wu, a partner at Cooke Kobrick & Wu in Los Altos, California. "And then we could say if the robots are more intelligent than we are, maybe they should have intellectual property rights." From "Robot Rules," by Richard Acello, *ABA Journal,* May 1, 2010 (www.abajournal.com/mobile/comments/robot_rules)

~ *Links:*
- "Robo-Ethicists Want to Revamp Asimov's 3 Laws," by Priya Ganapati, *Wired,* July 22, 2009 (http://www.wired.com/gadget-lab/2009/07/robo-ethics)
- "One Robot, One Vote?" by Neil Reynolds, *The Globe and Mail,* May 7, 2010 (www.theglobeandmail.com/news/opinions/one-robot-one-vote/article1560761/)
- "Robot Wars Prepare Kids for Manufacturing Jobs" by Chris Arnold, NPR, May 31, 2011 (www.npr.org/2011/05/31/136716245/robot-gladiators-prepare-kids-for-manufacturing-jobs)
- "The Trouble with Humanoid Droids," by Brenda I. Koerner, *Wired*, March 29, 2011 (www.wired.com/magazine/2011/03/st_essay_ugly_robots)

Contests

CONFERENCES

CONFERENCES

Conferences

CONTESTS

Contests & Awards for Adult & Children's Writers

Abilene Writers Guild Annual Contest

P.O. Box 2562, Abilene, TX 79604

www.abilenewritersguild.org/contests.cfm

This annual competition is open to all writers and awards prizes in ten categories, including children's stories, novels, poetry, flash fiction, memoir/nostalgia, and general interest articles. Guidelines vary for each category. Visit the website to download the annual contest guidelines. Entry fee, $10 for short pieces; $15 for novel entries. *Deadline:* Submissions are accepted from October 1 to November 30. *Award:* First place in each category, $100; $65, second place; $35, third place.

Jane Addams Children's Book Award

Marianne I. Baker, Chair MSC 6909, 7210B Memorial Hall, James Madison University, 800 S. Main St., Harrisonburg, VA 22807

www.janeaddamspeace.org

Honoring authors and illustrators of children's literature who reach standards of excellence while promoting the themes of peace, social justice, equality of the sexes, and a unified world, this award competition is held annually. Books of fiction, nonfiction, or poetry targeting children ages 2 through 12 that were published in the year preceding the contest are eligible. *Deadline:* December 31. *Award:* Honorary certificate and a cash award.

Alligator Juniper's National Writing Contest

Prescott College, 220 Grove Ave., Prescott, AZ 86301

http://www.prescott.edu/experience/publications/alligatorjuniper

Alligator Juniper is published annually by Prescott College, and features the winners in national contests. This contest accepts original, unpublished entries in the categories of fiction, creative nonfiction, and poetry. Fiction and nonfiction entries should not exceed 30 pages. Poetry, limit 5 poems per entry. Entry fee, $15. *Deadline:* October 1. *Award:* First prize in each category, $1,000 and publication in *Alligator Juniper*.

American Book Awards

Before Columbus Foundation, The Raymond House, 655 13th Street, Suite 302, Oakland, CA 94612

www.beforecolumbusfoundation.com/submission.html

These awards are sponsored by the Before Columbus Foundation, a nonprofit educational and service group that promotes multicultural literature and widens the audience for cultural and ethnic diversity in American writing. The awards are given for excellence and an outstanding contribution to American literature. Two copies of a book may be submitted by anyone—author, publisher, agent—for consideration in the next year. All genres are eligibile, including adult books, children's books, anthologies, and multimedia. No fees or forms are requested. *Deadline:* December 31. *Award:* Given in a ceremony at the University of California, Berkeley.

Sherwood Anderson Fiction Award

Mid-American Review, Dept. of English, Box W, Bowling Green State
   University, Bowling Green, OH 43403
www.bgsu.edu/studentlife/organizations/midamericanreview

Sponsored by *Mid-American Review,* the literary journal of Bowling
Green State University, this competition is open to all writers and
accepts short story entries of high literary merit. Entries may be in
any genre of fiction, but must be original, unpublished material.
Entry fee, $10. *Deadline:* October 1. *Award:* First place, $1,000 and
publication in *Mid-American Review.* Four finalists are also considered
for publication.

Arizona Authors Association Literary Contest

Contest Coordinator, 6145 W. Echo Lane, Glendale, AZ 85302
www.azauthors.com/contest_index.html

This annual contest sponsored by the Arizona Authors Association
and Five Star Publications and is open to all writers in English. It
accepts unpublished and published works in categories including
short stories, poetry, essays, articles, true stories, and novels. In
2011, two special categories included short stories from Arizona residents, set in the state or with Arizonans as characters; and an essay
with an Arizona theme, setting, or narrator. Each category is divided
into three groups: elementary school; junior high and high school;
and college and adults. Entry fee, $20. *Deadline:* July 1. *Award:*
Category winners, $100 and publication in *Arizona Literary Magazine.*

Atlantic Writing Competition

Writers' Federation of Nova Scotia, 1113 Marginal Road, Halifax NS
   B3H 4P7 Canada
www.writers.ns.ca/awc.html

Open to writers living in Atlantic Canada, this annual competition
accepts entries of adult novels, YA novels, short stories, poetry, writing
for children, plays, and magazine articles or essays. Previously

unpublished material only. Entry fees: novel categories, $35; all other categories, $25. WFNS members receive a $5 discount on entry fees. Published authors may not enter the competition in the genre that they have been published. Limit one entry per category. *Deadline:* November or December. *Award:* First- through third-place winners in each category receive awards ranging from $200 to $50.

Autumn House Poetry, Fiction, and Nonfiction Contests

P.O. Box 60100, Pittsburgh, PA 15211
www.autumnhouse.org/contest-submissions

Autumn House Press sponsors this annual contest that accepts collections of fiction, poetry, and for the first time, nonfiction. All fiction genres are welcome. Poetry collections, 50 to 80 pages. Fiction, 200–300 pages. Nonfiction, 200-300 pages on any subject; forms include personal essays, memoir, travel, historical narratives, nature or science writing. Entry fee, $30. *Deadline:* June 30. *Award:* Winning entry is published by Autumn House Press, and awarded $2,500. All entries are considered for publication.

AWP Award Series

George Mason University, MS 1E3, Fairfax, VA 22030-4444
www.awpwriter.org/contests/series.htm

The nonprofit Association of Writers & Writing Programs holds this annual award series for fiction, creative nonfiction, and poetry. The competition is open to all writers; guidelines are available at the website. *Deadline:* Entries must be postmarked between January 1 and February 29. *Award:* Poetry and short fiction winners, $5,500 and publication; novel and nonfiction winners, $2,500 and publication.

Marilyn Baillie Picture Book Award

Canadian Children's Book Centre (CCBC), 40 Orchard View Blvd.,
    Suite 101, Toronto ON M4R 1B9 Canada
www.bookcentre.ca

Fiction, nonfiction, or poetry in picture book form, for readers ages three to eight, is eligible for this award. It is given to "outstanding" books "in which the author and illustrator achieve artistic and literary unity." Titles published in the year preceding the contest are eligible for entry. Winners are chosen by a jury appointed by the CCBC. *Deadline:* December. *Award:* $20,000 and a certificate.

Doris Bakwin Award for Writing

Carolina Wren Press, 120 Morris St., Durham, NC 27701
http://carolinawrenpress.org/submissions/contests

This biennial contest, held in odd-numbered years, seeks collections of shorts stories, novels, and memoirs written by women. It encourages submissions from new and established writers and accepts unpublished material only. Guidelines are posted on the website in late summer. Entry fee, $20. *Deadline:* Janurary to March. *Award:* From $150 to $600. The publisher also runs the Carolina Wren Press Poetry Series, a contest held in even-numbered years.

Baltimore Review Competition

www.baltimorereview.org

The newly relaunched online *Baltimore Review* is continuing to hold an annual competition for original, unpublished poetry, fiction, or creative nonfiction. Entry fee, $10. Submit via the website. *Deadline:* August to November. *Award:* First place, $300 and publication in *Baltimore Review*; second place, $200; third place, $100.

Pura Belpré Medal

American Library Association, 50 East Huron, Chicago, IL 60611
http://www.ala.org/alsc/awardsgrants/bookmedia/belpremedal

This annual award is named in honor of Pura Belpré, the first Latina librarian at the New York Public Library. Medals are presented to a Latino/Latina writer and to an illustrator in recognition of literature that best portrays and celebrates the Latino cultural experience for young readers. Authors and illustrators must be residents or citizens of U.S. or Puerto Rico; submissions must be published in the U.S. or Puerto Rico in the contest year. Fiction and nonfiction published in Spanish, English, or bilingual format are eligible. *Deadline:* December 31. *Award:* Winners are presented with medals at a June celebration.

Geoffrey Bilson Award for Historical Fiction for Young People

Canadian Children's Book Centre (CCBC), 40 Orchard View Blvd., Suite 101, Toronto ON M4R 1B9 Canada
www.bookcentre.ca

Books of historical fiction for young people by Canadian authors are celebrated by this annual contest. Books published in the year preceding the contest are eligible for entry. Winners are chosen by a jury appointed by the CCBC. Picture books, short story collections by more than one author, and plots involving time travel are not eligible. *Deadline:* December. *Award:* $5,000 and a certificate.

Waldo M. and Grace C. Bonderman Youth Theatre Playwriting Competition

140 West Washington St., Indianapolis, IN 46204
www.irtlive.com/artists_information/playwrights

This competition is open to writers who participate in the Bonderman Workshop, held every other year in Indianapolis. The competition accepts unpublished plays for children. Plays for children in grades three through five should be approximately 30 to 45 minutes in length; plays for students in grades six and above should have a minimum performance length of 45 minutes. Submissions must include a synopsis and a cast list. No musicals. *Deadline:* June 30. *Award:* The top four winners receive $1,000 and a staged reading of their plays.

The *Boston Globe-Horn Book* Awards

The Horn Book, 56 Roland St., Suite 200, Boston, MA 02129

www.hbook.com/bghb

These prestigious awards celebrate excellence in literature for children and young adults. A committee of three judges evaluates books submitted by U.S. publishers and selects a winner and up to two Honor Books in the categories of picture book, fiction and poetry, and nonfiction. No entry fee. *Deadline:* May 15. *Award:* Winners receive $500 and an engraved silver bowl. Honor recipients receive an engraved plate.

Boulevard Short Fiction Contest for Emerging Writers

6614 Clayton Road, PMB 325, Richmond Heights, MO 63117

www.boulevardmagazine.org/partners.html

Writers who have not yet published a book of fiction, creative nonfiction, or poetry with a nationally distributed press are eligible to compete in this annual contest. Entries must be original, unpublished work, to 8,000 words. Entry fee, $15. *Deadline:* December 31. *Award:* $1,500 and publication in *Boulevard*.

Briar Cliff Review Writing Competition

3303 Rebecca St., Sioux City, IA 51104-2100

www.briarcliff.edu/bcreview

This annual contest accepts unpublished entries of fiction, creative nonfiction, and poetry. Fiction and creative nonfiction should not exceed 6,000 words. Poetry entries may include up to three poems. Entry fee, $20. *Deadline:* November 1. *Award:* First prize in each category is $1,000 and publication in *Briar Cliff Review*.

Marilyn Brown Novel Award

Jen Wahlquist, English Literature Dept., Mail Stop 153, Utah Valley University, 800 West University Pkwy., Orem, UT 84058

www.uvu.edu/english/marilyn_brown_novel/index.html

Under the stewardship of Utah Valley University's English Department, this award is given annually for the best unpublished literary mainstream novel focusing on realistic cultural experiences of the Utah Region, or Latter-day Saints experiences. No science fiction or fantasy; mainstream literature only. Minimum of 200 pages; no maximum. No entry fee. Limit one entry per competition. *Deadline:* October 1. *Award:* $1,000.

Randolph Caldecott Medal

American Library Association (ALA), 50 E. Huron, Chicago, IL 60611
www.ala.org/alsc/caldecott.html

Named in honor of the English illustrator, Randolph Caldecott, this award is presented to the artist of the most distinguished American picture book for children published in the preceding year. It is open to all U.S. citizens. Honor books are also recognized. *Deadline:* December 31. *Award:* The winner is announced at the ALA Midwinter Meeting and is presented with the Caldecott Medal at an awards banquet.

California Book Awards

595 Market St., San Francisco, CA 94105
www.commonwealthclub.org/bookawards

This contest was established to find the best California writers and spotlight the high-quality literature produced in the state. The competition awards California authors with gold and silver medals in recognition of outstanding literary works. Awards are presented in the categories of fiction, nonfiction, poetry, first work of fiction, Californiana, YA literature, juvenile literature, and notable contribution to publishing. Submit six copies of entry. No entry fee. *Deadline:* December 16. *Award:* Consists of 6 to 8 gold medals and up to 6 silver medals.

Canadian Library Association's Book of the Year for Children

10 Abilene Dr., Toronto, ON M9A 2M8 Canada

www.cla.ca

Recognizing Canadian works of children's literature for ages 12 and under, this award is presented annually to works of creative writing (fiction, poetry, narrative, nonfiction, and retellings) by Canadian citizens. All titles submitted for this award must be published in the year preceding the contest. *Deadline:* December 31. *Award:* Winner receives a leather-bound copy of their book.

Canadian Writer's Journal Short Fiction Contest

Box 1178, New Liskeard ON P0J 1P0 Canada

www.cwj.ca/04-00fiction.htm

This contest, sponsored by *Canadian Writer's Journal*, accepts unpublished work by Canadians in any genre, to 2,500 words. Awards are presented in March and September. Each entry must be accompanied by a brief author biography. Entry fee, $5. *Deadline:* April 30. *Award:* First place, $150; second and third place, $100 and $50, respectively. Winning entries are published in *CWJ*.

CAPA Competition

Connecticut Authors and Publishers Association, c/o Daniel Uitti, 223 Buckingham Street, Oakville, CT 06779

http://aboutcapa.com/writing_contest.htm

This annual contest accepts entries of short stories (to 2,000 words), children's stories (to 2,000 words), personal essays (to 1,500 words), and poetry (to 30 lines). The competition is open to all writers and accepts multiple entries, provided each entry is accompanied by an official entry form. Submit four copies of entry. Entry fee, $10 per story/personal essay or up to three poems. *Deadline:* December 23. *Award:* First place, $100; second place, $50. Winning entries are published in CAPA's newsletter.

Children's Writer Contests

95 Long Ridge Road, West Redding, CT 06896
www.thechildrenswriter.com/ad028

Every year *Children's Writer* newsletter sponsors two contests, each with a specific theme and requirements. Upcoming themes vary, as do the age ranges of the intended audience of children— from preschool to high school. Recent contests have included poetry and middle-grade mysteries. No entry fee for subscribers; $13 entry fee includes an eight-month subscription. Multiple entries are accepted. *Deadline:* February and October. *Award:* Cash prizes vary, with first place as much as $500. Winning entries are published in *Children's Writer*.

Christopher Awards

5 Hanover Square, 11th Floor, New York, NY 10004
www.christophers.org

These annual awards are sponsored by the Christophers, a Catholic organization with a ministry of communications. The awards recognize artistic work in publishing, film and television that creates a positive change in society and promotes self-worth. Profiles of courage, stories of determination, and chronicles of constructive action and empowerment are accepted. All entries must be published in the year preceding the contest. *Deadline:* November. *Award:* Winners are presented with bronze medallions at a ceremony in New York City.

Crossquarter Short Science Fiction Contest

P.O. Box 23749, Santa Fe, NM 87502
www.crossquarter.com/contest.html

Short story entries of science fiction, fantasy, and urban fantasy are accepted in this annual competition. The contest is sponsored by Crossquarter Publishing and looks for entries that portray the best of the human spirit. Entries should not exceed 7,500 words.

Submissions must be electronic. Reading fee, $15. *Deadline:* March 15. *Award:* First place, $250; second- to fourth-place, from $125 to $50; fifth- through fifteenth-place, honorable mention. All winners will receive publication by Crossquarter Publishing.

Sheldon Currie Fiction Prize

The Antigonish Review, P.O. Box 5000, St. Francis Xavier
   University, Antigonish NS B2G 2W5 Canada
http://antigonishreview.com

The Sheldon Currie Fiction Prize is held each year. It is open to well-written, unpublished short stories on any subject matter. Entries should not exceed 20 pages. Entry fee, $30 from the U.S. and $25 from Canada; $40 from outside North America. *Deadline:* May 31. *Award:* First place, $600; second place, $400; third place, $200. The three winning entries are published in the *Antigonish Review.*

Delacorte Press Contest for a First Young Adult Novel

1745 Broadway, 9th Floor, New York, NY 10019
www.randomhouse.com/kids/writingcontests

This annual contest encourages young adult contemporary fiction. It is open to writers living in the U.S. and Canada who have not yet published a YA novel. Manuscripts should be between 100 and 224 typed pages. Limit two entries per competition. All entries must feature a contemporary setting and plot suitable for readers ages 12 to 18. *Deadline:* Submissions must be postmarked between October 3 and December 31. *Award:* Book contract with Random House, advance on royalties of $7,500, and $1,500 cash.

Jack Dyer Fiction Prize

Dept. of English, Faner Hall 2380, Mail Code 4503, Southern
   Illinois University–Carbondale, 1000 Faner Dr., Carbondale,
   IL 62901
http://craborchardreview.siuc.edu/dyer.html

Open to U.S. residents, this annual competition is sponsored by *Crab Orchard Review,* the literary journal of Southern Illinois University–Carbondale. It is open to submissions of unpublished fiction, to 6,000 words. Entry fee, $20 per entry. Limit 3 entries per competition. *Deadline:* Postmarked between March 1 and May 2. *Award:* Publication in the winter/spring *Crab Orchard Review* and a minimum payment of $200.

Margaret A. Edwards Award

50 East Huron St., Chicago, IL 60611
www.ala.org/ala/mgrps/divs/yalsa/booklistsawards/bookawards/
margaretaedwards/margaretedwards.cfm

This award was established by the American Library Association's Young Adult Services Association and honors a living author for a body of work and special contribution to YA literature. The winner's writing will have been popular over a period of time and is generally recognized as helping teens to become better aware of who they are and their role in society. Nominations are accepted from librarians and teens. *Deadline:* June 1. *Award:* $1,000.

Arthur Ellis Awards

3007 Kingston Road, Box 113, Toronto ON M1M 1P1 Canada
www.crimewriterscanada.com

The Arthur Ellis Awards were established to honor excellence in Canadian mystery and crime writing. The contest is open to writers living in Canada or Canadian writers living elsewhere in the world. It accepts published entries in several categories, including best short story, best nonfiction, best first novel, best juvenile novel, best novel, best crime writing in French, as well as the best unpublished crime novel. Processing fee, $35 for books, $15 for short stories. *Deadline:* January 31. *Award:* Winners receive a wooden statue at the annual awards dinner.

William Faulkner–William Wisdom Creative Writing Competition

624 Pirate's Alley, New Orleans, LA 70116-3254

www.wordsandmusic.org/competition.html

This annual competition was set up to preserve the storytelling heritage of New Orleans and the Deep South by Pirate's Alley Faulkner Society. Unpublished entries are accepted in seven categories: novel, novella, novel-in-progress, short story, essay, poetry, and short story by a high school student. Entry fees range from $10 to $40 depending on category. Visit the website for complete guidelines. *Deadline:* Entries must be received between January 1 and May 15. *Award:* Publication in the Faulkner Society's annual literary journal, *The Double Dealer.* Ranges from $250 to $7,500.

Shubert Fendrich Memorial Playwriting Contest

P.O. Box 4267, Englewood, CO 80155-4267

www.pioneerdrama.com/playwrights/contest.asp

This competition encourages the development of quality theatrical material for educational and community theaters. It is open to playwrights who have not been published by Pioneer Drama Service. Manuscripts must have a running time between 20 and 90 minutes. *Deadline:* Ongoing. *Award:* Publishing contract and advance against royalties of $1,000.

Fineline Competition for Prose Poems, Short Shorts

Mid-American Review, Dept. of English, Box W, Bowling Green State University, Bowling Green, OH 43403

www.bgsu.edu/studentlife/organizations/midamericanreview

The literary journal of Bowling Green State University, *Mid-American Review,* sponsors this competition for literary quality prose poems and short, short stories. Entries must be original and unpublished material. Length, no longer than 500 words. Submit a set of three prose poems or stories. Verse will be automatically disqualified.

Entry fee, $10. *Deadline:* July 1. *Award:* First place, $1,000 and publication in *Mid-American Review.*

H. E. Francis Award

Dept. of English, University of Alabama, Huntsville, AL 35899
www.uah.edu/hefranciscontest

This annual award is sponsored by the Ruth Hindman Foundation and the UAH English Department. It accepts original, unpublished short stories that are judged by a nationally known panel of editors. Manuscripts must not exceed 5,000 words. Entry fee, $15. *Deadline:* December 31. *Award:* $1,000.

Don Freeman Memorial Grant-in-Aid

3646 Wood Lake Road, Bellingham, WA 98226
www.scbwi.org/Pages.aspx/Don-Freeman-Grant

Members of the Society of Children's Book Writers and Illustrators who intend to make picture books their primary contribution to children's literature are eligible for this grant, which is underwritten by Amazon.com. The grant is presented annually to help artists further their understanding, training, and work in the picture book genre. *Deadline:* Entries must be postmarked between January 2 and February 2. *Award:* Winner, $2,000; runner-up, $500.

John Gardner Memorial Prize for Fiction

Harpur Palate, English Dept., Binghamton University, Box 6000, Binghamton, NY 13902-6000
http://harpurpalate.blogspot.com/p/contests.html

This contest was established to honor John Gardner's dedication to the creative writing program at Binghamton University. It is open to all writers and accepts previously unpublished short story entries. Entries should not exceed 8,000 words. Entry fee, $15 (includes a one-year subscription to *Harpur Palate*). *Deadline:* February 1 to April 15. *Award:* $500 and publication in the summer issue of *Harpur Palate.*

Glimmer Train Contests
1211 NW Glisan St., Suite 207, Portland, OR 97209
www.glimmertrain.com/writguid1.html

Glimmer Train sponsors a contests each month of the year, including Family Matters, Fiction Open, Short Story Award for New Writers, and Very Short Fiction. Lengths vary. Electronic submissions are preferred. *Deadlines:* Vary. *Award:* First place award ranges from $1,200 to $2,000 and includes publication in *Glimmer Train*, and 20 copies of the issue with the winning story.

The Golden Kite Awards
8271 Beverly Blvd., Los Angeles, CA 90048-4515
www.scbwi.org/Pages.aspx/Golden-Kite-Award

Presented annually by the Society of Children's Book Writers & Illustrators, the Golden Kites recognize excellence in children's fiction, nonfiction, picture book text, and picture book illustration. SCBWI members whose work has been published in the year preceding the contest are eligible. *Deadline:* June 1 to December 16. *Award:* $2,500 and an expense-paid trip to the award ceremony at the Golden Kite luncheon during SCBWI's summer conference in August. Four honor book recipients also receive recognition.

John Guyon Literary Nonfiction Prize
Dept. of English, Faner Hall 2380, Mail Code 4503, Southern Illinois
University–Carbondale, 1000 Faner Dr., Carbondale, IL 62901
http://craborchardreview.siuc.edu

Sponsored by *Crab Orchard Review*, the literary journal of Southern Illinois University–Carbondale, this competition awards excellence in original, previously unpublished literary nonfiction. The contest is open to U.S. residents. Entries should not exceed 6,500 words. Entry fee, $20 per entry (maximum 3 entries). *Deadline:* Postmarked between March 1 and May 2. *Award:* $2,000 and publication in the winter/spring *Crab Orchard Review*.

Lorian Hemingway Short Story Competition
P.O. Box 993, Key West, FL 33041
www.shortstorycompetition.com

Writers of short fiction whose work has not been published in a nationally distributed publication with a circulation of 5,000 or more are eligible to enter this competition, which receives submissions from around the world. It accepts original, unpublished short stories of up to 3,500 words. There are no restrictions on theme. Entry fee, $15 for entries postmarked by May 1; $20 for those postmarked by May 15. Online submissions accepted, with the same deadlines. *Deadline:* May 15. *Award:* First place, $1,500 and publication in *Cutthroat: A Journal of the Arts*; second and third place, $500.

***Highlights for Children* Fiction Contest**
803 Church St., Honesdale, PA 18431
www.highlights.com/highlights-fiction-contest

This annual contest sponsored by *Highlights for Children* is open to both published and unpublished writers over the age of 16. A funny story inspired by an unusual newspaper headline is this year's theme, and stories may be any length up to 750 words. Stories for beginning readers should not exceed 475 words. Clearly mark Fiction Contest on the manuscript. No entry fee. *Deadline:* Submissions must be postmarked between January 1 and January 31. *Award:* Three prizes of $1,000 (or tuition for the Highlights Foundation Writers Workshop at Chautauqua) and publication in *Highlights for Children*.

Monica Hughes Award for Science Fiction and Fantasy
Canadian Children's Book Centre (CCBC), 40 Orchard View Blvd.,
    Suite 217, Toronto ON M4R 1B9 Canada
www.bookcentre.ca

To be awarded first in 2012 by the Canadian Children's Book Centre, this award honors excellence in children's and young teen science fiction and fantasy. Books must be originally published between January 1 and December 31 of the previous year. Entries must be written by a Canadian. Acceptable subgenres or subjects include time travel, alternate or re-imagined histories, dystopian, utopian, aliens, steampunk, space operas, urban fantasies, the paranormal, domestic magic, faeries, talking animals, among others. Submit four copies of each title with a submissions form found on the website. *Deadline:* December 9. *Award:* $5,000 and a certificate.

Barbara Karlin Grant
8271 Beverly Blvd., Los Angeles, CA 90048
www.scbwi.org/Pages.aspx/Barbara-Karlin-Grant

The Barbara Karlin grant was set up by SCBWI to recognize and encourage aspiring picture book writers. It is presented to a full or associate SCBWI member who has not yet published a picture book. Works of fiction, nonfiction, retellings of fairy tales, folktales, or legends are eligible for consideration. Manuscripts should not exceed eight pages. No entry fee. New applications and procedures are posted on the website each year. *Deadline:* Submissions must be postmarked no earlier than March 15 and received no later than March 15. *Award:* $2,000; runner-up, $500.

Iowa Short Fiction Award
Iowa Writers' Workshop, 507 North Clinton St., 102 Dey House,
    Iowa City, IA 52242-1000
www.uiowapress.org/authors/iowa-short-fiction.htm

This annual competition of the Iowa Writers' Workshop at the University of Iowa calls for collections of short stories. It is open to writers living in the U.S. and abroad who have not previously published a volume of prose fiction. Manuscripts should be at least 150 double-spaced pages. No entry fee. *Deadline:* Entries should be postmarked between August 1 and September 30. *Award:* Award-winning manuscripts are published by the University of Iowa Press.

Coretta Scott King Book Awards

50 East Huron St., Chicago, IL 60611-2795

www.ala.org/ala/mgrps/rts/emiert/cskbookawards/index.cfm

Honoring Martin Luther King Jr. and his wife, Coretta Scott King, for their courage and determination, this award promotes the artistic expression of the African American experience through literature and graphic arts. Sponsored by the American Library Association, the awards are given to African American authors and illustrators for inspirational and educational contributions to children's and YA literature. Submit via online submissions form. *Deadline:* December 1. *Award:* A plaque, up to $1,500, and a set of *Encyclopaedia Britannica* or *World Book Encyclopedia.*

E. M. Koeppel Short Fiction Award

P.O. Box 140310, Gainesville, FL 32614

www.writecorner.com

Unpublished fiction in any genre is the focus of this annual competition open to all writers. Submissions should not exceed 3,000 words. Entry fee, $15; $10 for each additional entry. *Deadline:* Entries are accepted beginning October 1 and must be postmarked by April 30. *Award:* $1,100; editors' choice awards, $100 each.

Long Story Contest, International

White Eagle Coffee Store Press, P.O. Box 383, Fox River Grove, IL
60021

http://whiteeaglecoffeestorepress.com/page4.html

This worldwide competition was established to select a long literary story for publication. Unpublished single stories, multi-part stories, and self-contained novel segments are eligible. The judges place no restrictions on style, method, or subject matter. Entries should be 8,000–14,000 words. Entry fee, $15. *Deadline:* December 15. *Award:* $1,000 and 25 copies, plus 10 press kits to news source of choice.

Magazine Merit Award

8271 Beverly Blvd., Los Angeles, CA 90048

www.scbwi.org/Pages.aspx/Magazine-Merit-Award

The Society of Children's Book Writers & Illustrators sponsors this annual award in recognition of outstanding original magazine work written for young people. It accepts published entries in the categories of fiction, nonfiction, illustration, and poetry. SCBWI members only. No entry fee. Submit four copies of each entry, with proof of publication date. *Deadline:* December 15. *Award:* Winners in each category receive a plaque.

Memoirs Ink Writing Contest

10866 Washington Blvd., Suite 518, Culver City, CA 90232

www.memoirsink.com/contests

Held twice each year, this contest accepts original personal essays, memoirs, or stories based on autobiographical experiences. Entries must be previously unpublished and written in the first person. The contest is open to all writers, but accepts submissions in English only. Entries may be up to 1,500 words for the February contest; and to 3,000 words for the August contest. Entry fee, $15; $2 discount for previous entrants. Multiple submissions are accepted. *Deadline:* February 15 and August 15. *Award:* First place, $1,000; second place, $500; third place, $250.

Micro Award

Alan Presley, PSC 817, Box 23, FPO, AE 09622-0023

www.microaward.org

The Micro Award recognizes fiction under 1,000 words, otherwise known as flash fiction or nanofiction. Submissions must be prose fiction published either in print or electronically in the year preceding the award. Self-published fiction is eligible. Authors may submit one story; editors may submit two stories from their publications. *Deadline:* October 1 to December 31 *Award:* $500.

Milkweed Prize for Children's Literature

Milkweed Editions, 1011 Washington Ave. South, Suite 300,
   Minneapolis, MN 55415

www.milkweed.org/content/view/23/72

Fiction for readers ages 8 to 13 is the focus of this annual competition sponsored by Milkweed Editions. The prize was established to encourage authors to write for this important age group. Submissions with high literary merit that embody humane values and contribute to cultural understanding. No entry fee. *Deadline:* Ongoing. *Award:* $10,000 cash prize and publication by Milkweed Editions.

Minotaur Books/MWA Competition

175 Fifth Ave., New York, NY 10010

www.mysterywriters.org/?q=Contests-Writers

Open to all writers who have not yet published a novel, this competition is sponsored by Minotaur Books in conjunction with the Mystery Writers of America. It accepts original, book-length manuscripts in which murder or another serious crime is central to the plot. Do not mail manuscripts directly to Minotaur Books; email MB-MWAFirstCrimeNovelCompetition@StMartins.com for entry packet. *Deadline:* Request entry form by November 15; entries must be postmarked by November 30. *Award:* Publishing contract from St. Martin's Press/Minotaur Books and $10,000 cash advance against royalties.

Mythopoeic Society Fantasy Awards for Children's and Adult Literature

306 Edmon Low Library, Oklahoma State University, Stillwater, OK
   74078

www.mythsoc.org/awards

Honoring outstanding fantasy books for young readers that are written in the tradition of J. R. R. Tolkien and C. S. Lewis, this award is presented to picture books through YA novels, adult fantasy, and scholarly books. Entries are nominated by members of the Mythopoeic Society. Books and collections by a single author are eligible for two years after publication. *Deadline:* February 28. *Award:* A statuette.

National Book Awards

National Book Foundation, 95 Madison Ave., Suite 709, New York, NY 10016

www.nationalbook.org

The National Book Award recognizes outstanding literature for young people and adults. Awards are given for fiction, nonfiction, poetry, and YA literture. Full-length books, collections of stories, and collections of essays or poems are eligible. All entries must be published in the U.S. during the year preceding the contest. This competition is open to U.S. citizens only; books published or scheduled to be published in the previous year only. Entry fee, $125. Entries must be submitted by publishers. *Deadline:* Entry forms must be postmarked by June 15; books, bound galleys, or bound manuscripts due by August 15. *Award:* Category winners, $10,000; 16 finalists, $1,000.

National Children's Theatre Medal

280 Miracle Mile, Coral Gables, FL 33134

www.actorsplayhouse.org

Held yearly, this competition is sponsored by the Actors Playhouse at Miracle Theatre. It welcomes submission of unpublished musicals that are appropriate for children ages 5 to 12. Submissions should feature a cast with no more than 8 adults, who may play multiple roles. Works that received limited production exposure, workshops, or staged readings are encouraged, as are musicals with simple settings that appeal to both children and adults. Running time, 45 to 60 minutes. Entry fee, $10. Include sheet music and the submission form found at the website. *Deadline:* Entries must be postmarked by April 1. *Award:* $500 and a full production of the play at the National Children's Theatre Festival in May.

The John Newbery Medal
American Library Association, 50 East Huron St., Chicago, IL 60611
www.ala.org/alsc/awardsgrants/bookmedia

This prestigious medal is presented by the Association for Library Service to Children to honor the year's most distinguished contribution to American literature for children up to the age of 14. Titles eligible for consideration must have been written by a U.S. author and published in the year preceding the contest. Books are judged on literary quality and overall presentation for children. Nominations are accepted from ALSC members only. *Deadline:* December 31. *Award:* The Newbery Medal is presented to the winning author at the ALA midwinter banquet.

New Millennium Writings Award
P.O. Box 2463, Room M2, Knoxville, TN 37901
www.newmillenniumwritings.com/awards.php

This annual contest is sponsored by *New Millennium Writings,* a literary journal. It accepts entries in the categories of short-short fiction, fiction, nonfiction, and poetry. It accepts previously unpublished material, and material that has been published online or in a print publication with a circulation of under 5,000. Short-short fiction, to 1,000 words. Fiction and nonfiction, to 6,000 words. Poetry, to three poems, five pages total. Entry fee, $17 per submission. Submit online or via mail. *Deadline:* November 17. *Award:* $1,000.

New Voices Award
Lee & Low Books, 95 Madison Ave., New York, NY 10016
www.leeandlow.com/p/new_voices_award.mhtml

Encouraging writers of color who have not published a children's picture book, this annual award is sponsored by Lee & Low Books. It welcomes original material that addresses the needs of children of color, ages 5 to 12. Works of fiction, nonfiction, and poetry are accepted, but folklore and stories about animals are not. Entries should not exceed 1,500 words and must be accompanied by a cover letter with the author's contact information and relevant cultural/ethnic information. Limit two submissions per entrant. No entry fee. *Deadline:* Submissions will be accepted between May 1 and September 30. *Award:* $1,000 and publishing contract with Lee & Low Books; Honor Award winner, $500.

Ohio State University Prize in Short Fiction

Ohio State University Press, 180 Pressey Hall, 1070 Carmack Road,
    Columbus, OH 43210-1002
www.ohiostatepress.org

This annual award recognizes and awards excellence in a collection of short stories or novellas, or a combination, published or unpublished. Manuscripts must be between 150 and 300 typed pages; individual stories or novellas in the collection may not exceed 125 pages. Entry fee: $20. *Deadline:* Submissions must be postmarked in January. *Award:* Winning author receives publication, with a $1,500 advance against royalties.

Orbis Pictus Award for Outstanding Nonfiction
for Children

Kim Ford, 6617 Westminster Road, Memphis, TN 38120-3446
www.ncte.org/awards/orbispictus

This award for excellence in children's nonfiction recognizes books used in kindergarten to eighth-grade classrooms characterized by outstanding accuracy, organization, design, and style. Eligible titles must be published in the year preceding the contest. Nominations may come from National Council of Teachers of English (NCTE) members, or the education community. Textbooks, historical fiction, folklore, and poetry are not eligible. To nominate a book, write to the committee chair with the author's name, title of book, publisher, copyright date, and a brief explanation of why you liked the book. *Deadline:* December 31. *Award:* A plaque at the NCTE Convention.

Pacific Northwest Writers Association Literary Contest

PMB 2717, 1420 NW Goldman Blvd, Ste. 2, Issaquah, WA 98027

www.pnwa.org/displaycommon.cfm?an=6

Sponsored by the Pacific Northwest Writers Association, this annual contest accepts unpublished entries in 12 categories that include: young adult novel, screen writing, mainstream, adult short topics, poetry, children's picture book/chapter book, historical, and romance. Each entrant receives two critiques of their work. Entry fee, $35 for members; $50 for nonmembers. Limit one entry per category. *Deadline:* February 17. *Award:* First place, $700 and the Zola Award; second place, $300.

PEN Center USA Literary Awards

269 South Beverly Dr., #1163, Beverly Hills, CA 90212

http://penusa.org/awards

Writers living west of the Mississippi River are honored for their literary achievements through this annual awards program. Entries that have been published in the year preceding the contest are accepted for nomination in the categories of including children's literature, graphic literature, fiction, creative nonfiction, journalism, drama, teleplay, research nonfiction, poetry, translation, and screenplay. Entry fee, $35 per entry. *Deadline:* Book category submissions, December 31; non-book category submissions, January 31. *Award:* Category winners, $1,000 and a free PEN membership.

PEN/Phyllis Naylor Working Writer Fellowship

588 Broadway, Suite 303, New York, NY 10012

www.pen.org/page.php/prmID/281

This fellowship provides support for promising authors in the field of children's or YA fiction. Eligible authors must have published at least two novels. Books must be published by a U.S. publisher. Likely candidates are those whose books have been well-reviewed but have not achieved high sales volume. Nominations are accepted from editors and fellow writers and should include a detailed letter of support; a list of the nominated author's published work and reviews; and a description of the nominee's financial resources. Three copies of the outline of a work in progress and 50 to 75 pages of the text must also be submitted. *Deadline:* Letters of nomination must be postmarked between October 1 and February 1. *Award:* $5,000 fellowship.

Phoebe Winter Fiction Contest

Phoebe 2C5, George Mason University, 4400 University Dr., Fairfax,
  VA 22030
www.phoebejournal.com/?page_id=8

This annual contest is sponsored by *Phoebe,* the literary journal of George Mason University. It accepts unpublished short fiction. Entries should not exceed 7,500 words. Entry fee, $15 per submission. *Deadline:* December 1. *Award:* $1,000 and publication in *Phoebe.*

Pikes Peak Writers Fiction Contest

Pikes Peak Writers, P.O. Box 64273, Colorado Springs, CO 80962
www.ppwc.net/html/paul_gillette_awards.html

Open to writers who have not yet published book-length fiction or short stories, this contest accepts entries in the categories of children's books, YA, romance, mainstream, historical fiction, mystery/suspense, and science fiction/fantasy. Entry fee, $30. Critiques are available for $20. For book submissions, include a synopsis (to 1,250 words) and sample pages of the manuscript (beginning with chapter one or the prologue, to 4,000 words); short stories to 5,000 words. Describe the target market. Submissions must be sent electronically. *Deadline:* November 15. *Award:* The Paul Gillete Award, First place, $100 or a refund of the Pikes Peak Conference fee; second place, $50; third place, $30.

Edgar Allan Poe Awards

Mystery Writers of America, 1140 Broadway, Suite 1507, New York, NY 10001

www.mysterywriters.org/?q=AwardsPrograms

The Mystery Writers of America sponsors these annual awards, which are considered among the most prestigious for writers. They are presented for work published in the year preceding the contest in several categories that include best fact crime, best YA mystery, best juvenile mystery, best first novel by an American author, and best play. Books must be submitted by publisher. No entry fee. *Deadline:* Varies. *Award:* An Edgar Award is presented to each winner at a banquet; cash award.

Prairie Fire Press Contests

423-100 Arthur St., Winnipeg MB R3B 1H3 Canada

www.prairiefire.ca/contests.html

Two annual competitions honor works of creative nonfiction and short fiction. Creative fiction entries should not exceed 5,000 words and must be unpublished. Short fiction, to 10,000 words. Entry fee, $32. *Deadline:* November 30. *Award:* First prize, $1,250; second prize, $500; third prize, $250. Winning entries are published in *Prairie Fire* magazine.

Michael L. Printz Award for Excellence in Young Adult Literature

50 East Huron St., Chicago, IL 60611

www.ala.org/yalsa/printz

This award, from the Young Adult Library Services Association and *Booklist*, recognizes excellence in YA literature. Anthologies and works of fiction, nonfiction, and poetry that target ages 12 to 18 and were published in the preceding year are eligible. ALA committee members may nominate titles. Entries are judged on overall literary merit, taking into consideration theme, voice, setting, style, and design. Controversial topics are not discouraged. *Deadline:* December 1. *Award:* An award seal, presented at the ALA midwinter conference.

Prism international **Literary Nonfiction Contest**
Creative Writing Program, University of British Columbia, Buchanan
E462, 1866 Main Mall, Vancouver BC V6T 1Z1 Canada
http://prismmagazine.ca/contests

This annual contest honors excellence in literary nonfiction. Entries of creative nonfiction may be on any subject, and should not exceed 25 double-spaced pages. Entry fee, $28 for one story and $7 for each additional story (includes a one-year subscription to *Prism international*). *Deadline:* November 30. *Award:* Grand prize, $1,500 and publication in *Prism international*.

Prism international **Short Fiction Contest**
Creative Writing Program, University of British Columbia, Buchanan
E462, 1866 Main Mall, Vancouver BC V6T 1Z1 Canada
http://prismmagazine.ca/contests

This competition is open to all writers, with the exception of those currently enrolled in the creative arts program at the University of British Columbia. It looks for original, unpublished short stories to 25 double-spaced pages. Entry fee, $28 for one story and $7 for each additional story (includes a one-year subscription to *Prism international*). *Deadline:* January 29. *Award:* Grand prize, $2,000 and publication in *Prism international*. Three runner-up prizes of $200 are also awarded.

Roanoke Review **Fiction Contest**
221 College Lane, Salem, VA 24153
http://roanokereview.wordpress.com/

This annual contest is sponsored by the literary journal of Roanoke College and looks to encourage the writing of short fiction. It is open to all writers. Entries should not exceed 5,000 words. Entry fee, $15. All entrants receive a copy of the journal. Enter online or via maill. *Deadline:* December 1. *Award:* First place, $1,000; second place, $500. Winning entries are published in the *Roanoke Review.*

San Antonio Writers Guild Writing Contest

P.O. Box 34775, San Antonio, TX 78265
www.sawritersguild.com/Contests_and_Events

This competition accepts entries in the categories of novel, short story, flash fiction, essay/memoir, and poetry. It accepts previously unpublished submissions only. Word limits vary. Visit the website for complete information. Entry fee, $10 for members; $20 for nonmembers. *Deadline:* First Thursday in October. *Award:* First place, $100; second place, $50; third place $25.

David B. Saunders Creative Nonfiction Prize

Cream City Review, Dept. of English, University of Wisconsin-
    Milwaukee, P.O. Box 413, Milwaukee, WI 53201
www.creamcityreview.org/submit/#contests

Original, unpublished entries of creative nonfiction are accepted for this annual competition. Entries should not exceed 30 pages. Entry fee, $15. *Deadline:* December 31. *Award:* $1,000 and publication in *Cream City Review.*

The A. David Schwartz Fiction Prize

Cream City Review, Dept. of English, University of Wisconsin-
    Milwaukee, P.O. Box 413, Milwaukee, WI 53201
www.creamcityreview.org/submit/#contests

Sponsored by the literary journal of the University of Wisconsin, *Cream City Review,* and Karry W. Schwartz Bookshops, this prize is offered annually. The competition accepts previously unpublished works of fiction. Entries should not exceed 30 pages. Entry fee, $15. *Deadline:* December 31. *Award:* $1,000 and publication in *Cream City Review.*

Seven Hills Literary Contest

P.O. Box 3428, Tallahassee, FL 32315

www.twaonline.org/pgs/contst/svn_hlls/12svn_hlls.html

Sponsored by the Tallahassee Writers' Association, this annual contest offers prizes in the categories of best short story, creative nonfiction, flash fiction, and children's chapter books/stories (for children 4–8). The competition is open to all writers and accepts unpublished, original entries only. Entries should not exceed 2,500 words (500 words for flash fiction). Entry fee, $12 for members; $17 for nonmembers. *Deadline:* November 31. *Award:* First place, $100; second place, $75; third place, $50. Winners are published in *Seven Hills* literary journal.

Mary Shelley Award for Imaginative Fiction

Rosebud Magazine, N3310 Asje Road, Cambridge, WI 53523

www.rsbd.net/NEW

Established to promote all forms of speculative and imaginative fiction in a literary context, this contest accepts original, unpublished works of fantasy, fiction, horror, and mystery, as well as entries that stretch beyond the boundaries of these genres. Entries should be between 1,000 and 3,500 words. Entry fee, $10. *Deadline:* September 1. *Award:* First place winner receives $1,000 and publication in *Rosebud.* Four runners-up receive $100 and publication.

Kay Snow Writing Contest

2108 Buck St., West Linn, OR 97068

www.willamettewriters.com/1/kaysnow.php

This annual competition, sponsored by the Willamette Writers, encourages writers to reach their personal goals. It accepts original, unpublished entries in the categories of adult fiction, adult nonfiction, juvenile short story or article, poetry, screenwriting, and student writing. Entry fee, $10 for members; $15 for nonmembers. Word lengths vary for each category. Visit the website for complete guidelines. *Deadline:* April 23. *Award:* First prize, $300; second prize, $150; third prize, $50. Student writers are awarded in three grade divisions: first place, $50; second place, $20; third place, $10.

Society of Midland Authors Awards

P.O. Box 10419, Chicago, IL 60610

www.midlandauthors.com/contest_about.html

Authors and poets who reside in, were born in, or have strong ties to any of the 12 Midwestern states are eligible to enter this annual contest. Awards are presented for adult fiction and nonfiction, biography, poetry, and children's fiction and nonfiction. Entries must have been published in the year preceding the contest. No entry fee. *Deadline:* February 15. *Award:* Cash award and a recognition plaque.

So to Speak Contests

George Mason University, MSN 2C5, 4400 University Dr., Fairfax, VA 22030

http://sotospeakjournal.org/contests/

So to Speak, a feminist literary journal, sponsors this contest for fiction, nonfiction, and poetry. Entries may also be personal essays, memoirs, and profiles. Fiction and nonfiction, to 4,500 words. Poetry, to five poems per submission, not to exceed 10 pages. Entry fee, $15. *Deadline:* Nonfiction and poetry deadline, October 15. Fiction deadline, March 15. *Award:* First prize in each category is $500 and publication in *So to Speak.*

John Spray Mystery Award

Canadian Children's Book Centre (CCBC), 40 Orchard View Blvd., Suite 217, Toronto ON M4R 1B9 Canada

www.bookcentre.ca

This award, established in 2011 by the Canadian Children's Book Centre, honors outstanding mysteries for readers 8 to 16. Entries may be thrillers, crime novels, or whodunits, and must be written by a Canadian. Titles published in the year preceding the contest are eligible for entry. No fantasy, science fiction, or graphic novels. *Deadline:* December 9. *Award:* $5,000 and a certificate.

SouthWest Writers Annual Contest
3721 Morris NE, Albuquerque, NM 87110
www.southwestwriters.com/contestAnnual.php

This annual contest is sponsored by SouthWest Writers and honors distinguished unpublished work in a variety of categories including: novel, short story, short nonfiction, personal essay, book-length non-fiction, children's book, screenplay, and poetry. Entry fees range from $10 to $35 (additional fee to receive a critique). Manuscript critiques are available for an additional fee. *Deadline:* May 1. *Award:* Cash prizes ranging from $50 to $150 are awarded to the top three entries in each of 14 categories. First-place winners compete for a $1,000 Storyteller Award.

Stanley Drama Award
Wagner College, One Campus Road, Staten Island, NY 10301
www.wagner.edu/stanley_drama

The Stanley Drama Award was set up to encourage and reward aspiring playwrights. The competition is open to original, full-length plays or musicals, or a series of two or three related one-act plays that have not been professionally produced or published as trade books. Musical entries must be accompanied by an audiocassette or CD. Entry fee, $30. *Deadline:* October 31. *Award:* $2,000.

Sydney Taylor Manuscript Competition
Aileen Grossberg, 204 Park St., Montclair, NJ 07042-2903
www.jewishlibraries.org/ajlweb/awards/st_ms.htm

This annual competition is open to original fiction containing Jewish content targeting children ages 8 to 11. Entries should deepen a child's understanding of Judaism. Manuscripts should be between

64 and 200 pages. Short stories, plays, and poetry are not eligible. No entry fee. Limit one entry per competition. *Deadline:* December 15. *Award:* $1,000.

Utah Original Writing Competition

617 East South Temple, Salt Lake City, UT 84102
http://arts.utah.gov/funding/competitions/writing.html

Since 1958, this annual competition has honored Utah's finest writers in several categories, including YA book, novel, personal essay, short story, poetry, and general nonfiction. The competition accepts unpublished entries from residents of Utah only. Writers entering works in the categories of novel, general nonfiction, book-length collection of poems, and juvenile book may not have a book published or accepted for publication in the category. Word lengths vary for each category. Check the website for complete information. No entry fee. *Deadline:* Entries are accepted beginning April 4 and must be postmarked by June 23. *Award:* $200 to $1,000.

Laura Ingalls Wilder Medal

American Library Association, 50 East Huron St., Chicago, IL 60611
www.ala.org/alsc/awardsgrants/bookmedia/wildermedal

Every other year this award is presented to honor an author or illustrator whose body of work has contributed substantially to children's literature. It is open to books that were published in the U.S. during the year preceding the contest. Nominations are made by Association for Library Services to Children members. The winner is chosen by a team of children's librarians. *Deadline:* December 31. *Award:* A bronze medal is presented to the winner.

Tennessee Williams Fiction Contest

938 Lafayette St., Suite 514, New Orleans, LA 70113
www.tennesseewilliams.net/index.php?topic=contests

This competition is open to writers who have not yet published a book of fiction. It accepts entries up to 7,000 words by hard copy or through the website. Entries are subject to blind judging. Author's name should not appear on manuscript itself. Include a cover letter with story title, name, and full contact information. Entry fee, $25. *Deadline:* Submissions are accepted between June 1 and November 15. *Award:* $1,500, airfare and accommodations at the Tennessee Williams Literary Festival, a reading at the festival, and publication in *Louisiana Literature.*

Tennessee Williams One-Act Play Competition
938 Lafayette St., Suite 514, New Orleans, LA 70113
www.tennesseewilliams.net/index.php?topic=contests

This annual contest recognizes and rewards excellence in one-act plays from writers around the world. The winning script should require minimal technical support and a small cast of characters. Multiple entries are accepted. Entry fee, $25 per entry. Plays should run no longer than one hour and must not have been previously produced or published. *Deadline:* November 1. *Award:* $1,500 and a full production of the play at the Tennessee Williams New Orleans Festival.

Paul A. Witty Short Story Award
International Reading Association, P.O. Box 8139, Newark, DE 19714
www.reading.org/Resources/AwardsandGrants/childrens_witty.aspx

The International Reading Association presents this annual award to a short story that was published in a magazine for children during the year of the contest. Submissions should be of the highest literary merit. No entry fee. *Deadline:* November 15. *Award:* $1,000.

Work-in-Progress Grants
8271 Beverly Blvd., Los Angeles, CA 90048
www.scbwi.org/Pages.aspx/WIP-Grant(1)

Each year, the Society of Children's Book Writers & Illustrators offers several grants to children's writers to complete projects that are not currently under contract. Grants are available to full and associate members of SCBWI in the categories of general work-in-progress; contemporary novel for young people; nonfiction research; and previously unpublished author. All applications should include a 750-word synopsis and a writing sample of no more than 2,500 words. *Deadline:* Submissions must be postmarked no earlier than February 15 and received no later than March 15. *Award:* Seven winners receive $2,000; seven runners-up receive $500.

WOW! Women on Writing Flash Fiction Contests
www.wow-womenonwriting.com/contest.php

This ezine presents quarterly flash fiction contests to inspire creativity and communication and provide recognition to its winners. All styles of writing are welcome. Entries should be from 250 to 750 words. Accepts entries through the website only. Entry fee, $10. *Deadline:* February 28; May 31; August 31; and November 30. *Award:* First place, $350; second place, $250; third place, $150; seven runners up; 10 honorable mentions. Winners also receive publication on the *WOW!* website.

Writers at Work Fiction Writing Competition
P.O. Box 540370, North Salt Lake, UT 84054-0370
www.writersatwork.org

Writers at Work, a nonprofit literary arts organization, sponsors this annual contest that recognizes emerging writers of fiction. Writers not yet published in the category of their entry are eligible to submit original work. Manuscripts must not exceed 7,500 words. Only online submissions are accepted. Entry fee, $20. *Deadline:* September 15. *Award:* First prize, $1,000 and publication in *Quarterly West;* second prize, $350; third prize, $150.

Writer's Digest Annual Writing Competition
4700 East Galbraith Road, Cincinnati, OH 45236
www.writersdigest.com/competitions

This annual competition calls for entries in 10 different categories including children's/YA fiction, short stories, screenplays, magazine article, and plays. It accepts previously unpublished work only. Multiple entries are accepted. Word counts vary. Entry fee, $15 for the first poem and $10 for each additional poem; all other entries, $25 for the first manuscript and $15 for each additional manuscript submitted in the same online session. *Deadline:* See website. *Award:* Grand prize, $3,000. Other prizes are also awarded.

Writers-Editors Network Annual International Writing Competition
P.O. Box A, North Stratford, NH 03590
www.writers-editors.com

Open to all writers, this contest honors authors of fiction, nonfiction, children's literature, and poetry. Entries of children's literature must be previously unpublished or self-published only. Poetry may be traditional or verse. Specific category guidelines are available at the website. Entry fees vary for each category. *Deadline:* March 15. *Award:* First-through third-place awards are $100, $75, and $50.

Writing for Children Competition
Writers' Union of Canada, 90 Richmond St. East, Suite 200, Toronto
ON M5C 1P1 Canada
www.writersunion.ca

Canadian writers who have not yet published a book are eligible to enter this competition from the Writers' Union of Canada. It was established to encourage new Canadian talent in the field of children's literature. Entries should not exceed 1,500 words. Entry fee, $15. Multiple entries are accepted. *Deadline:* April 24. *Award:* $1,500.

Zoetrope: All-Story Short Fiction Contest

916 Kearny Street, San Francisco, CA 94133
www.all-story.com/contests.cgi

Sponsored by *Zoetrope: All-Story*, a magazine founded by Francis Ford Coppola, this annual contest seeks to encourage talented writers and to introduce those writers to leading literary agencies. Unpublished literary fiction of all genres are accepted. Submissions should be 5,000 words or less. Entries from outside the U.S. are welcome. Entry fee, $15 per story. *Deadline:* Entries are accepted between July 1 and October 3. *Award:* First prize, $1,000; second prize, $500; third prize, $250. The three prizewinners and seven honorable mentions are considered for representation by several prominent literary agencies.

Conferences for Adult & Children's Writers

American Independent Writers Annual Conference

1001 Connecticut Ave. NW, Suite 701, Washington, DC 20036

www.amerindywriters.org

American Independent Writers (AIW) was founded in 1975 and includes writers in all genres in its membership. The organization supports and advocates for the community of writers, encouraging both craft and business. It holds an annual one-day conference of workshops and panels with editors, agents, and writers. *Date:* June. *Location:* Washington, DC area. *Cost:* $99 for AIW members, and $129 for nonmembers in advance; higher at the door.

American Society of Journalists and Authors Annual Writers Conference

1501 Broadway, Suite 302, New York, NY 10036

www.asja.org/wc

Held each spring since 1971, this conference offers concurrent morning and afternoon panels, which are ranked to help beginning to advanced writers choose appropriately. More than 100 editors, authors, agents, and publicists take part in this weekend event, which allows time for keynote speeches and networking. *Date:* April 26–28. *Location:* New York, New York. *Cost:* $375 for members (early registration, $335); $385 for nonmembers (early registration, $345). One-day rates are also available.

Ann Arbor Book Festival Writer's Conference
1118 Granger Ave., Ann Arbor, MI 4810
www.aabookfestival.org

Coinciding with the Ann Arbor Book Festival, this annual conference is a full Saturday event. Attendees can sign up for three small-group sessions focused on writing skills and one large-group session on publishing, all of which are led by a noted group of authors and instructors. *Date:* June. *Location:* Ann Arbor, Michigan. *Cost:* $100.

Annual Writers Conference at Penn
University of Pennsylvania, College of General Studies, 3440 Market
   St., #100, Philadelphia, PA 19104
www.pennwriters.org

Sponsored by Pennwriters, a multi-genre writer's organization, this annual event joins writers of all levels and genres with agents, editors, and fellow authors for three days of workshops, critiques, pitch sessions, and networking. The option of a one-day conference is available. *Date:* May. *Location:* Lancaster, Pennsylvania. *Cost:* $275 for three-day conference, including meals; $194 for one day.

Antioch Writers' Workshop
c/o Antioch University Midwest 900 Dayton St., Yellow Springs, OH
   45387
www.antiochwritersworkshop.com

This weeklong conference features morning lectures and afternoon intensives, with evenings reserved for readings, panel discussions, and workshops. Programs focus on fiction, nonfiction, screenwriting, playwriting, poetry, and the business of publishing. *Date:* July. *Location:* Yellow Springs, Ohio. *Cost:* $610 ($550 for past registrants and local residents), plus $125 non-refundable registration fee. *A la carte* tuition, $250–$325. Manuscript critique, $75.

Appalachian Heritage Writers Symposium

Southwest Virginia Community College

P.O. Box SVCC, Richlands, VA 24641

http://appheritagewritersym.wordpress.com

Fiction, memoir, poetry, and children's writing workshops, as well as panel discussions, are offered during this two-day symposium. *Date:* June. *Location:* Richlands, Virginia. *Cost:* $50; includes continental breakfast and awards luncheon. College credit, optional.

Arizona State University Writers Conference

P.O. Box 875002, Tempe, AZ 85287

www.asu.edu/pipercwcenter/conference

Intimate master classes, panel discussions on publishing and the writing life, readings, and conversations with faculty are the main components of this four-day conference. Its emphasis is on developing fiction, nonfiction, and poetry in a true community of writers. *Date:* February. *Location:* Tempe, Arizona. *Cost:* $375 (early registration, $335). Master class tuition (registration required), $125. Discounts are available.

Aspen Summer Words

Doerr-Hosier Center at the Aspen Meadows, 845 Meadows Road,
    Aspen, CO 81611

www.aspenwritersfoundation.org

Aspen Summer Words is a six-day festival and retreat for writers in all their guises, from novelists and poets to filmmakers, songwriters, and comedians. The writing retreat includes workshops in fiction, memoir, poetry, young writers, and digital storytelling. Online applications are accepted through April 15. *Date:* June. *Location:* Aspen, Colorado. *Cost:* Application processing fee, $25. Five-day juried workshop, $665; $415, beginning fiction; two-day readers retreat, $233; other fees vary. Some scholarships are available.

Bay to Ocean Writer's Conference

P.O. Box 544, St. Michael's, MD 21663

www.baytoocean.com

The Eastern Shore Writers' Association sponsors this one-day conference of workshops, speeches, and panels on topics pertaining to the craft of writing and the business of publishing. Presenters include authors, editors, publishers, journalists, freelance writers, and literary agents. Manuscript reviews are offered. *Date:* February. *Location:* Chesapeake College, Wye Mills, Maryland. *Cost:* Contact for cost information.

Erma Bombeck Writers' Workshop

University of Dayton, 300 College Park, Dayton, OH 45469

www.humorwriters.org

"The workshop for humor writing, human interest writing, networking, and getting published," this event is held every other year. The next conference is scheduled for 2012. Past sessions covered such topics as writing a humor column for a national newspaper and creating humorous children's books. The faculty is made up of experienced and entertaining writers and publishing professionals. *Date:* April. *Location:* Dayton, Ohio. *Cost:* $375.

Canadian Authors Association CanWrite! Conference

74 Mississaga Street East, Orillia ON L3V 1V5 Canada

www.canauthors.org/conference.html

"Applying Technology to Your Writing" is the theme of the 2010 CanWrite! Conference. Attendees will learn computer tips for making their writing life easier, and how to create PowerPoint presentations to enhance book launches. Other workshops will explore the world of ebooks and explain electronic rights for writers. Fiction, nonfiction, poetry, public speaking, and writing for young adults are some of the other sessions planned. *Date:* May/June. *Location:* Location of the next conference is yet to be confirmed. *Cost:* To be announced. One-day rates are also available.

Cape Cod Writers' Conference
Cape Cod Writers' Center
P.O. Box 408, Osterville, MA 02655
www.capecodwriterscenter.org

Over the course of five days, attendees take part in morning and afternoon courses and master classes on the craft of writing romance, mystery, poetry, screenwriting, journalism, memoir, and children's fiction, among others. Panels, faculty readings, and speeches are also scheduled during this annual conference. *Date:* August. *Location:* Hyannis, Massachusetts. *Cost:* $185 per course; $150 for mentoring; $150 for manuscript evaluation. Registration fee, $35 (waived for members). Shorter courses are offered at lower rates.

Carolinas Writers Conference
South Piedmont Community College
P.O. Box 126, Polkton, NC 28135
http://ansoncountywritersclub.org/

About 250 to 400 people attend this annual event, which focuses on the craft of writing and the promotion of reading. The program covers children's and YA writing; fiction, including the genres of romance, science fiction, fantasy, horror, and mystery; screenwriting; poetry; marketing; and publishing. *Date:* April. *Location:* Wadesboro, North Carolina. *Cost:* $30.

Cat Writers' Association Writers Conference

22841 Orchid Creek Lane, Lake Forest, CA 92630

www.catwriters.org

The business and technical aspects of a career that centers on writing about cats are explored at this three-day annual conference, which also offers panels and lecture sessions on various fiction genres, nonfiction, and writing for children and young adults. Private 15-minute appointments with editors/agents are available. *Date:* November. *Location:* Visit the website for location. *Cost:* $150 for members; $200 for nonmembers (early registration, $100 for members and $125 for nonmembers).

Chautauqua Institution Conferences

P.O. Box 28, Chautauqua, NY 14722

http://writers.ciweb.org

The Writers' Center at Chautauqua Institution sponsors weekly workshops during the summer months. Topics include business and technical writing, playwriting, autobiography/memoir, journalism, poetry, romance, mystery, and humor writing, among others. A four-day Writer's Festival is held as well, which features workshops, panel discussions, readings, and lectures. *Date:* Summer workshops, June, July, and August. Writers' Festival, June. *Location:* Chautauqua, New York. *Cost:* Summer workshops, $100/ week. Writers' Festival, $400 (10 percent discount for returnees.)

Colgate Writers' Conference

13 Oak Drive, Hamilton, NY 13346-1398

http://cwc.colgate.edu/home.aspx

Veteran and novice writers alike are welcome at this annual week-long conference. Mornings are devoted to craft talks and workshops, while afternoons are set aside for individual consultations with instructors. Panel discussions, readings, and informal conversations round out the program. *Date:* June. *Location:* Hamilton, New York.

Cost: $995 for residential attendees; $750 for day students; $1,245 for novel and memoir tutorial students. Discounts and fellowships are available.

DFW Writers' Conference
http://dfwwritersconference.org

Sponsored by the DFW (Dallas-Fort Worth) Writers' Workshop, this annual two-day conference offers writers at different levels of experience the opportunity to network with fellow writers and meet agents, published authors, and editors. Registration gives participants access to more than 40 classes on the art and business of writing, and includes agent appointments on a first-come, first-served basis. *Date:* May. *Location:* Hurst, Texas. *Cost:* $295.

East Texas Christian Writers Conference
East Texas Baptist University
One Tiger, Marshall, TX 75670
www.etbu.edu/news/cwc/workshops.htm

In addition to one-hour writing workshops scheduled for Saturday, this conference also holds pre-conference workshops on Friday afternoon. Workshops offer intense, personal, and practical application for those willing to get directly involved in the writing process. The conference gives aspiring writers the opportunity to have contact, conversation, and exchange of ideas with each other. *Date:* October. *Location:* Marshall, Texas. *Cost:* Individual, $80; student, $60. (Early registration, $75.) Fee covers the Friday evening banquet and attendance at five to six writing workshops on Saturday. Preconference workshops, $30 additional.

Green Mountain Writer's Conference
47 Hazel St., Rutland, VT 05701
www.vermontwriters.com

At this annual weeklong conference, developing writers

attend workshops run by professional authors who teach the craft of writing fiction, creative nonfiction, poetry, journalistic pieces, nature articles, essays, memoir, and biography. Working sessions and writing assignments are scheduled around readings and panel discussions. *Date:* August. *Location:* Tinmouth, Vermont. *Cost:* $525 (early registration, $500); includes snacks, lunches and readings.

Highlights Foundation Writers Workshop at Chautauqua

814 Court St., Honesdale, PA 18431

www.highlightsfoundation.org/chautauqua

Seminars, small group workshops, and intensive one-on-one sessions with prominent children's authors, illustrators, editors, critics, and publishers fill the days of this annual weeklong conference, while evenings are reserved for a variety of informal and cultural activities. This conference is designed for writers at all levels, from beginning to published, who are interested in writing or illustrating for young readers. *Date:* July. *Location:* Chautauqua, New York. *Cost:* $2,400 ($1,985 for first-time attendees registering early); includes all meals; additional cost for lodging.

Idaho Writers' League Annual Writers Conference

828 Callie St., Chubbuck, ID 83202-2945

www.idahowritersleague.coml

This two-day conference offers morning and afternoon workshops, luncheons, and a banquet. The theme for this year's conference is "Flights of Fancy." Check website for list of workshop topics and presenters. *Date:* September. *Location:* Pocatello, Idaho. *Cost:* $100 for members ($100, early registration); $120 for nonmembers (early registration, $135). One-day and half-day rates available.

Iowa Summer Writing Festival

C215 Seashore Hall, University of Iowa, Iowa City, IA 52242

www.continuetolearn.uiowa.edu/iswfest

Weeklong and weekend workshops are held over the course of six weeks and four weekends at this well-known annual event for serious writers. Some workshops are devoted to critiquing manuscripts that participants bring with them, others to generating new work through exercises and assignments. Writing for children and young adults, screenwriting, playwriting, poetry, travel writing, and nature writing are some of the many workshops offered. *Date:* June and July. *Location:* Iowa City, Iowa. *Cost:* $560 to $585 per week; includes special events, dinner on the Sunday evening of registration, and the Friday banquet. Weekend only, $280; includes Saturday breakfast.

Jackson Hole Writers Conference
P.O. Box 1974, Jackson, WY 83001
www.jacksonholewritersconference.com

In addition to workshops led by novelists, creative nonfiction writers, poets, agents, editors, and publishers, this conference offers three manuscript critiques. The 2010 conference offered classes on fiction, creative nonfiction, poetry, YA fiction, memoir, and magazine writing. This four-day event is held annually. *Date:* June. *Location:* Jackson Hole, Wyoming. *Cost:* $390; includes all conference events, the welcome cocktail party, and the barbecue. Manuscript critique, $30, or $110 for longer manuscripts.

James River Writers Conference
320 Hull St., #136, Richmond, VA 23224
www.jamesriverwriters.org

In addition to workshops, panel discussions, and speeches, this conference offers the opportunity for one-on-one meetings with literary agents or editors and first-page critique sessions. Last year's two-day conference featured workshops on pitching articles, stories, and books; using Facebook to maximize exposure; and one-on-one meetings with agents. *Date:* October. *Location:* Richmond, Virginia. *Cost:* $190; one-day only, $125. Pre-conference workshop, $40.

Jewish Authors Conference: Writing for Adult Readers

520 8th Avenue, 4th Floor, New York, NY 10018

http://jewishbookcouncil.org

The Jewish Book Council holds an annual day-long conference attended by authors, editors, agents, and publicists. The overall focus is publishing books on Jewish themes, Jewish publishing, and networking with others in the field. *Date:* December. *Location:* New York City, New York. *Cost:* $139; early registration, $119.

Jewish Children's Book Writers & Illustrators Conference

520 8th Avenue, 4th Floor, New York, NY 10018

http://jewishbookcouncil.org

Sponsored by the Jewish Book Council, which promotes public awareness of books that "reflect the rich variety of the Jewish experience," this day-long conference is held annually. It offers presentations from authors, literary agents, publishers, and editors designed to help new as well as published authors advance their careers. *Date:* November. *Location:* New York City, New York. *Cost:* $141; early registration, $121. Private consultations, $35, preregistration required.

Kentucky Women Writers Conference

232 East Maxwell St., Lexington, KY 40506

www.uky.edu/WWK

This two-day conference, held annually since its inception in 1979, attracts women at all stages of their writing careers. Workshops are limited to 12 members each. Pre-registration is required, and enrollment is done on a first-come, first-served basis. Fiction, nonfiction, poetry, and writing for young adults are among the workshops offered. *Date:* September. *Location:* Lexington, Kentucky. *Cost:* $90 for one day; $175 for two days (early registration, $80 for one day and $150 for two days).

Kenyon Review Writers Workshop
Kenyon College, Gambier, OH 43022
www.kenyonreview.org/workshops/writers

Generating and revising new writing are the focus of the *Kenyon Review* workshops in poetry, fiction, and literary nonfiction. The retreat is scheduled around morning workshops, private time for writing in the afternoon, and public readings in the evening by instructors, visiting writers, and participants. Applications are accepted January 1 to May 1. *Date:* June 16–23. *Location:* Kenyon College, *Cost:* $1,195; $200 discount for returning participants.

Manhattanville Summer Writers' Week
2900 Purchase St., Purchase, NY 10577
www.mville.edu/admissions/graduate-schools/graduate-business-writing-liberal-studies/summer-writers-week.html

Three-hour workshops are held each morning of this five-day conference. Participants choose from workshops offered in the categories of fiction, poetry, nonfiction, children's/YA, and alternative media Afternoons are devoted to special workshops, readings, sessions with editors and agents, and individual manuscript consultations. A major presenter is scheduled each year. *Date:* To be announced. *Location:* Purchase, New York. *Cost:* $725; two graduate credits available for an additional fee.

Mendocino Coast Writers Conference
College of the Redwoods
P.O. Box 2087, Fort Bragg, CA 95437
www.mcwc.org

This three-day conference, which is limited to 100 participants, features all-day genre intensives. Those who wish to attend one of these novel, short fiction, memoir, or poetry intensives are required to pre-submit a sample of their work, which will be critiqued in the small group sessions. Those attending only the afternoon lectures and discussions are not required to send work in advance; however, those who wish to take advantage of a 30-minute consultation with an author, editor, or agent must pre-submit 10 pages of a manuscript. *Date:* July. *Location:* Mendocino Campus of College of the Redwoods, California. *Cost:* $575; early registration, $525. $60 fee for private consultation with conference faculty.

Northern Colorado Writers Conference
108 East Monroe Drive, Fort Collins, CO 80525
http://northerncoloradowriters.com

Writers of all genres and levels attend this annual two-day conference for inspiration and information. Sponsored by Northern Colorado Writers, the event offers over 20 workshops on a variety of topics for both fiction and nonfiction. Last year's program included an editor's panel, editor pitch sessions, and read and critique sessions with authors and editors. *Date:* March. *Location:* Fort Collins, Colorado. *Cost:* Visit the website for cost information.

North Wildwood Beach Writers' Conference
www.nwbwc.com

Speakers, workshops, manuscript evaluations, contests, and a book bazaar are the components of this day-and-a-half event. Workshops cover writing for children and young adults; fiction writing, including romance; nonfiction writing, including journalism and memoir; screenwriting; and poetry. Other workshops cover marketing and the business of publishing. *Date:* June. *Location:* North Wildwood, New Jersey. *Cost:* See website for information.

Oklahoma Writers' Federation Writers Conference
Barbara Shepard, OWFI, P.O. Box 54302, Oklahoma City, OK 73154
www.owfi.org

This annual three-day conference has been held for more than 40 years. Workshops generally cover writing and marketing fiction (including science fiction and thrillers) and nonfiction for children, young adults, and adults. The theme for the 2011 conference is "Story Weavers." *Date:* May. *Location:* Oklahoma City, Oklahoma. *Cost:* $175 (includes 2 days of seminars, two banquets); early registration, $150. Single-day seminars, $70 each. Extra workshops, $15–$25.

Outdoor Writers Association of America Annual Conference
http://owaa.org

First held in 1927, this gathering attracts writers who specialize in informing the public about outdoor recreational activities and the responsible use of natural resources. This year's theme is "North to Alaska for New Frontiers in Journalism." Workshops and seminars focus on craft improvement as well as on issues of specific interest to those who write about the outdoors. Topics include the business and technical sides of writing, marketing, and publishing, photography, technology, and nature journalism. The three-day conference also devotes sessions to national and local news related to outdoor activities and conservation. *Date:* September. *Location:* Fairbanks, Alaska. *Cost:* Visit the website for cost information.

Pacific Northwest Children's Book Conference
Portland State University
1515 SW Fifth Avenue, Suite 102, Portland, OR 97201
www.ceed.pdx.edu/children

At this five-day conference, participants attend morning lectures on topics such as plotting, dialogue, and revision; afternoon intensive workshops; critique sessions; first-page analyses; and faculty readings. Speakers featured in previous years included Liz Bicknell, Editorial Director of Candlewick Press, and author Margaret Bechard. *Date:* July. *Location:* Portland, Oregon. *Cost:* Visit the website for cost information.

Pet Writing Conference

The Pet Socialite, Inc., 362 Broome St., #20, New York, NY 10013

www.petwritingconference.com

Animal-interest authors and journalists gather at this one-day event each year to attend seminars and workshops about the business side of pet writing, as well as for networking opportunities with veterinarians and representatives of animal organizations. One-on-one sessions with agents and book and magazine editors are also available. The timing of the conference coincides with the Westminster Kennel Club Dog Show, held nearby. *Date:* February. *Location:* New York, New York. *Cost:* Visit the website for registration information.

Pikes Peak Writers Conference

P.O. Box 64273, Colorado Springs, CO 809662

www.pikespeakwriters.com

This annual conference offers more than 30 workshops that focus on fiction writing for children and teens as well as for adults. In addition, agents and editors are available to attendees seeking to pitch their work. Manuscript evaluations and critique sessions round out the three-day program. *Date:* April. *Location:* Colorado Springs, Colorado. *Cost:* Visit the website for cost information.

St. David's Christian Writers' Conference

87 Pines Road East, Hadley, PA 16130

www.stdavidswriters.com

Four days of workshops led by nationally known authors and editors are the centerpiece of this Christian writing conference, which also offers one-on-one tutorials and professional critiques for additional fees. Keynote addresses and literary readings, evening meditations, and after-hours social events are other components of the conference. The theme for this year's conference is "Writers Under Construction." *Date:* June 19–23. *Location:* Grove City, Pennsylvania.

Cost: Rates vary depending on whether participants are commuting or staying on campus. Visit website for this year's tuition costs.

San Francisco Writers Conference
1029 Jones St., San Francisco, CA 94109
www.sfwriters.org

San Francisco Writers sponsors this President's Day Weekend conference, which features more than 50 workshops, panels, social events, and one-on-one networking with presenters. In addition, editors from major publishing houses participate in Ask-A-Pro sessions. Speed Dating for Agents is an optional add-on event. *Date:* February. *Location:* San Francisco, California. *Cost:* $595 (early registration, $495). $645 including Speed Dating for Agents.

Sewanee Writers' Conference
University of the South, 119 Gailor Hall, Stamler Center, 735 University Ave., Sewanee, TN 37383-1000
http://sewaneewriters.org

With a focus on fiction, playwriting, and poetry, the Sewanee Writers' Conference offers workshops that meet for five two-hour sessions on alternating days. Over the course of the 12-day program, participants attend daily readings, lectures on craft, panel discussions, and Q&A sessions with distinguished faculty members. *Date:* July/August. *Location:* Sewanee, Tennessee. *Cost:* Visit the website for cost information.

Society of Children's Book Writers & Illustrators (SCBWI) Annual International Conferences
8271 Beverly Boulevard, Los Angeles, CA 90048
www.scbwi.org

The annual summer conference, which is celebrating its forty-first year, was joined 13 years ago by a winter conference. Both conferences offer workshops, master classes, manuscript and portfolio consultations, panel discussions, and a variety of keynote speeches over the course of their three-day programs. The faculty consists of more than 50 authors, illustrators, editors, and agents. *Date:* January and August. *Location:* Winter conference, New York, New York. Summer conference, Los Angeles, California. *Cost:* Visit the website for cost information.

SCBWI Big Sky Fall Conference

www.scbwi.org/Regional-Chapters.aspx?R=4&sec=Conf

The Montana chapter of SCBWI hosts this weekend gathering for attendees to "learn, write, and share" with fellow children's authors and illustrators. Opportunities for both critiques and intensives followed by roundtable discussions are offered. The conference features writing and illustrating workshops led by authors, editors, and agents centering around story, craft, and character. *Date:* September. *Location:* Visit the website for location. *Cost:* Visit the website for cost information.

SCBWI Carolinas Fall Conference

P.O. Box 1216, Conover, NC 28613

www.scbwi.org/Regional-Chapters.aspx?R=12&sec=Events&g=1334

The fall conference of the Carolinas SCBWI has been held for 18 years. The theme of the 2011 conference was "Filling the Blank Page." Sessions and workshops covered writing for the middle-grade reader, picture book creation, and making an impression on the first page. Manuscript critiques are available for an additional fee. *Date:* November. *Location:* North Carolina. *Cost:* Visit website for registration information.

SCBWI Florida Regional Conference

http://scbwiflorida.com

"Wizarding World of Writing" is the theme for this year's three-day conference. Scheduled throughout the weekend are workshops, first-page critiques, and writing and illustrating intensives. Time is also reserved for informal critique groups and keynote speeches on a variety of topics related to children's writing. The theme this year is "Mad About Children's Publishing." *Date:* January. *Location:* Miami, Florida. *Cost:* $285. $190 for Saturday only.

SCBWI Kansas Fall Conference

P.O. Box 3987, Olathe, KS 66063
www.kansas-scbwi.org

Writers at all stages of their careers gather at this two-day conference to attend workshops led by editors, agents, authors, illustrators, and other prominent professionals from the world of children's and young adult publishing. Panel discussions, keynote speeches, and manuscript critiques round out the event. Topics at the 2011 conference featured Newberry winning author Clare Vanderpool, and one-on-one consultation "auditions" with five agents. *Date:* September/October. *Location:* Overland Park, Kansas. *Cost:* Costs vary depending on days attending, and sessions or critiques desired.

SCBWI MD/DE/WV Summer Conference

www.scbwi.org/Regional-Chapters.aspx?R=22

This regional conference offers writers and illustrators a hands-on, craft-centered literary weekend for writers of books for children and young adults, fiction and nonfiction. Indivually focused break-out sessions are also available. *Date:* July. *Location:* Knoxville, Maryland. *Cost:* Visit website for registration information.

SCBWI Michigan Spring & Fall Conferences

www.kidsbooklink.org

The workshops at this weekend conference are led by award-winning authors and illustrators; literary agents; and art directors and editors from major publishing houses. Although the conference is open to members and nonmembers, only SCBWI members are eligible to enter the lottery for a paid manuscript or portfolio critique. *Date:* May, October. *Location:* Spring conference, Grand Rapids, Michigan. Fall conference, to be announced. *Cost:* Varies.

SCBWI Mid-Hudson Valley Conference
http://scbwi-easternny.org

The Mid-Hudson Valley SCBWI holds two conferences a year, in June and November. The spring conference is a single day, and the Falling Leaves Master Class takes place over a weekend. Break-out sessions, hands-on workshops, panel discussions round out the day, and manuscript critiques are available. *Date:* November. *Location:* Silver Bay, New York. *Cost:* Members, $225; nonmembers, $250.

SCBWI Midsouth Fall Conference
P.O. Box 396, Cordova, TN 38088
www.scbwi-midsouth.org

Editors and art directors from prominent publishing houses and bestselling authors are among the presenters at this weekend conference. Attendees may enter a fiction manuscript contest or illustrator contest. An art director/editor session on picture books, a talk about book packagers, and critiques for query letters were three new offerings at the 2010 conference. Individual paid manuscript and portfolio critiques are available. *Date:* September. *Location:* Nashville, Tennessee. *Cost:* Visit the website for cost information.

SCBWI Nevada Tahoe Writers' Retreat
P.O. Box 19084, Reno, NV 89511
www.nevadascbwi.org

The Nevada chapter of the Society of Children's Book Writers and Illustrators offers this hands-on, intensive weekend of group and one-on-one critiques with guest authors and literary agents, as well as workshops. *Date:* October or November. *Location:* Lake Tahoe, Nevada. *Cost:* $425 for members; $475 for nonmembers.

SCBWI New England Annual Conference

www.nescbwi.org

The 2012 conference embraces the theme is Keeping It Real: Reality and World-building in Fiction, Nonfiction, and Illustration. Paid editor critiques, peer critiques, a query session with agents, keynote speeches, book signings, and book sales are scheduled around the workshops and writing intensives presented at this weekend conference. *Date:* April. *Location:* Springfield, MA. *Cost:* Visit the website for cost information.

SCBWI New Mexico Handsprings Conference

P.O. Box 1084, Socorro, NM 87801

www.scbwi-nm.org

The New Mexico SCBWI holds this annual conference with presentations by successful authors and literary agents, in addtion to critiques, illustrator portfolio displays, mini book launches, and workshops. *Date:* October. *Location:* University of New Mexico, Albuquerque, New Mexico. *Cost:* Visit the website for cost information.

SCBWI Oregon Spring Conference

P.O. Box 336, Noti, OR 97461

www.scbwior.com

This annual conference brings together an esteemed team of professional authors, illustrators, editors, art directors, and agents. Features of the two-day event include first page sessions, intensives for illustrators, keynote presentations, master craft workshops, and individual manuscript and portfolio consultations. Continuing education credits are available. *Date:* May. *Location:* Portland, Oregon. *Cost:* Visit website for registration information.

SCBWI Rocky Mountain Conference
www.rmcscbwi.org

The Rocky Mountain chapter of SCBWI holds a fall conference each year. In addition to workshops presented by editors from some of the best-known New York City-based publishing houses, this conference offers manuscript critiques with editors, agents, and published authors; one-on-one portfolio reviews; and first-page critiques. A weekend conference, it attracts writers and illustrators from Colorado and Wyoming. *Dates:* September. *Location:* Lakewood, CO. *Cost:* Visit website for registration information.

SCBWI San Francisco North/East Bay Fall Conference
www.scbwinorthca.org

This one-day conference for children's writers and illustrators at all stages of their careers offers a program full of inspiration, craft development and mastery, marketing tips, and more. One of the two all-day sessions focuses on picture books. *Date:* October. *Location:* Oakland, California. *Cost:* Visit the website for cost information.

SCBWI Southern Breeze Fall Conference
P.O. Box 26282, Birmingham, AL 35260
http://www.scbwi.org/Regional-Chapters.aspx?R=42&sec=Conf

Four sessions comprised of approximately 30 workshops are offered at this two-day event where attendees can tailor the day to fit their specific interests. The faculty includes authors, illustrators, agents, art directors, editors, and other publishing professionals. Both private and group critiques are also available. *Date:* October. *Location:* Birmingham, Alabama. *Cost:* Visit website for registration information.

SCBWI Spring Spirit Conference

P.O. Box 487, Placerville, CA 95667

www.scbwi.org/Regional-Chapters.aspx?R=5

The California North/Central regional chapter of SCBWI hosts this one-day conference, which offers a diversity of workshop options for attending writers and illustrators. The event closes with a question-and-answer panel. Written manuscript and art sample critiques are available for an additional fee. *Date:* April 21. *Location:* Rocklin, California. *Cost:* To be announced; check website updates.

SCBWI Texas: Austin Regional Conference

201 University Oaks Blvd., Suite 1285 #170, Round Rock, TX 78665

www.austinscbwi.com

"Something for Everybody" is the name of this year's regional conference for people who write, illustrate, or share the passions for children's literature. Hour-long general assembly sessions are held throughout the course of this three-day gathering. In addition to small-group intensives, consultations with literary agents, editors, and accomplished authors and illustrators are available for an additional fee. Personal social media evaluations and portfolio reviews are also offered. *Date:* February. *Location:* Austin, Texas. *Cost:* $150 for members (early registration, $135); $165 for nonmembers (early registration, $150).

SCBWI Texas: Houston Annual Conference

www.scbwi-houston.org

This conference offers a full-day of networking with other writers and learning about the world of publishing through talks by impressive guest presenters. Author/editor critiques are available for an additional fee. *Date:* March 31. *Location:* Katy, Texas. *Cost:* $125 members; $150 nonmembers. Early registration, $110 members, $135 nonmembers.

SCBWI Ventura–Santa Barbara Writers' Day
www.scbwisocal.org

Spotlight presentations by authors and illustrators, an editors' panel, and speeches by representatives from major publishing houses are the featured activities at this annual event. Limited space is available for manuscript or portfolio critiques. *Date:* October. *Location:* Thousand Oaks, California. *Cost:* Visit website for registration information.

South Carolina Writers Workshop Conference
P.O. Box 7104, Columbia, SC 29202
www.myscww.org

This weekend conference begins on Friday morning with optional intensive workshops. Saturday and Sunday are filled with sessions on various career topics. In previous years, conferences have featured interactive *slush fest* sessions with agents and editors. One-on-one pitch sessions and critique appointments with conference faculty members are available for an additional fee. *Date:* October. *Location:* Myrtle Beach, South Carolina. *Cost:* Visit website for this year's registration information.

Southern California Writers' Conference
1010 University Ave., #54, San Diego, CA 92103
www.writersconference.com

Interactive workshops, panels, special events, and one-on-one consultations are scheduled during this three-day conference. Planned workshops cover fiction, non-fiction, "read and critique," and business and marketing. Screenwriters, authors representing a variety of genres, agents, and editors are among the faculty members. *Date:* February. *Location:* San Diego, California. *Cost:* $425; Saturday/Sunday only, $350. Early registration discounts. Additional fees for critique sessions and one-on-one consultations.

Space Coast Writers' Guild Annual Conference
P.O. Box 262, Melbourne, FL 32902-0262
www.scwg.org

The goal of this two-day conference is to provide inspiration, entertainment, and encouragement for writers of all genres. The Guild brings together area authors with publishers, agents, and editors from around the country, and occasionally from around the world. A self-publishing workshop is among the presentations and workshops scheduled for this year's event. Others cover plays, YA novels, first chapters, breaking into publishing, memoirs, settings, and more. *Date:* January 27–28. *Location:* Cocoa Beach, Florida. *Cost:* $165 for members; $195 for nonmembers. Half-day and single-day rates are available.

Tin House Summer Writers Workshop
P.O. Box 10500, Portland, OR 97296
www.tinhouse.com/writers-workshop/

Held on the campus of Reed College, this weeklong program consists of morning workshops limited to 12 participants. Craft seminars and career panels are scheduled in the afternoons, with author readings held in the evenings. Workshops are led by the editors of *Tin House* and Tin House Books. For an additional fee, mentorships are available to participants who have completed a collection of stories or poems, a memoir, or a novel. *Date:* July. Applications are accepted beginning January 1 through March 15. *Location:* Portland, Oregon. *Cost:* Visit the website for cost information. Scholarships are available.

Wesleyan Writers Conference
294 High Street, Room 207, Middletown, CT 06459
www.wesleyan.edu/writing/conference

This conference, now in its fifty-sixth year, welcomes all writers, from beginners to veterans. The five-day program consists of seminars, readings, panels, lectures, and optional manuscript consultations. Each seminar typically includes a lecture, a discussion, and optional writing exercises. Seminar topics include novel, short story, fiction techniques, narrative in fiction and nonfiction, poetry, literary journalism, short and long-form nonfiction, memoir, and multimedia and online work. Private manuscript consultations are available with faculty members or teaching fellows. Attendees also have the opportunity to meet with editors and agents who are looking for new writers. *Date:* June 14–17; one-day program available June 16. *Location:* Middletown, Connecticut. *Cost:* Day students, tuition, $975; with meals, $1,250. Boarding rate, $1,425. One-day, $225. Scholarships and fellowships are available.

Western Writers of America Convention
www.westernwriters.org

Workshops, panels, discussions with editors and authors, and book signings are all part of this five-day convention. Workshops focus on writing fiction and nonfiction—including writing for children and young adults—and all are geared toward preserving the rich history of the American West. The business side of publishing is also examined, as is marketing. *Date:* June 12–16. *Location:* Albuquerque, New Mexico. *Cost:* Visit the website for updates.

Willamette Writers Conference
9045 SW Barbur Boulevard, Suite 5A, Portland, OR 97219-4027
www.willamettewriters.com

Participants have almost 100 workshops to choose from at this weekend conference. Topics include historical fiction, self-help books, children's books, screenplays, mysteries, romance, and science fiction, among many others. Literary agents, Hollywood agents and producers, and editors are among the workshop leaders. Only those attending the conference for the full three days may submit up to two manuscripts for advanced critiques for an additional fee.

Date: August 3–5. *Location:* Portland, Oregon. *Cost:* Visit the website for cost information.

Winnipeg International Writers Festival

624-100 Arthur St., Winnipeg MB R3B 1H3 Canada

www.thinairwinnipeg.ca

Workshops, lectures, interviews, keynote speeches, and readings fill the days of this weeklong festival, which has been held annually since 1997. More than 50 representatives from the publishing world offer presentations on playwriting, poetry, children's and young adult writing, journalism, mystery, horror, and other topics. Programs target children as well as adults, and are presented in both English and French. *Date:* September. *Location:* Winnipeg, Manitoba. *Cost:* Visit the website for updates.

Write on the Sound Writers' Conference

700 Main St., Edmonds, WA 98020

www.ci.edmonds.wa.us/artscommission/wots.stm

Sponsored by the City of Edmonds Art Commission, this conference is a highly anticipated regional event that fills up early. With more than 30 workshops to choose from, it draws noted authors and other publishing professionals as faculty. The program begins on Friday afternoon with pre-conference workshops, and continues with two full days of workshops and other events on Saturday and Sunday. Manuscript critique appointments are available for an additional fee. *Date:* October. *Location:* Edmonds, Washington. *Cost:* Visit the website for cost information. The conference brochure will be available in July.

Writers in Paradise

4200 54th Ave. South, St. Petersburg, FL 33711

www.writersinparadise.com

This eight-day program from Eckerd College offers workshops on short story, novel, nonfiction, and YA writing. Lectures, panels, roundtable discussions, readings, and book signings fill out the rest of the schedule at this annual convention. Individual manuscript consultations are offered for an additional fee. *Date:* January 14–22. *Location:* St. Petersburg, Florida. *Cost:* $700; optional manuscript consultation, $200. Scholarships available.

The Write Stuff
Greater Lehigh Valley Writers Group
3650 Nazareth Pike, PMB #136, Bethlehem, PA 18020-1115
www.glvwg.org

This weekend conference has been held annually since 1993. In addition to writers' workshops, it offers sessions on the business of writing, panel discussions, manuscript critiques, opportunities to meet with agents and editors, and a book fair. *Date:* March 16–17. *Location:* Allentown, Pennsylvania. *Cost:* Visit the website for cost information.